# The Beginnings of Writing

## Charles A. Temple
UNIVERSITY OF HOUSTON

## Ruth G. Nathan
OAKLAND UNIVERSITY

## Nancy A. Burris
UNIVERSITY OF HOUSTON

ALLYN AND BACON, INC.
Boston • London • Sydney • Toronto

*For Edmund Henderson*

**Acknowledgments:**

Figure 1 – 1 on p. 2 is reprinted by permission from *Word,* Vol. 27 (1971).

Figure 11 – 3 on p. 190 is reprinted by permission of Donald Murray.

Quotation on p. 209 is from POP CORN & MA GOODNESS by Edna Mitchell Preston. Copyright © 1969 by Edna Mitchell Preston. Reprinted by permission of Viking Penguin Inc.

Quotation on p. 209 is a text excerpt from pages 30 – 31 of WILLIAM'S DOLL by Charlotte Zolotow. Text Copyright © 1972 by Charlotte Zolotow. By permission of Harper & Row, Publishers, Inc.

Quotation on p. 211 is a text excerpt from HOLD MY HAND by Charlotte Zolotow. Text Copyright © 1972 by Charlotte Zolotow. By permission of Harper & Row, Publishers, Inc.

Quotation on p. 216 is from Sheb Wooley, "The Purple People Eater." By permission of Channel Music Company.

**Series Editor:** Margaret Quinlin

Copyright © 1982 by Allyn and Bacon, Inc.
470 Atlantic Avenue, Boston, Massachusetts 02210

**Library of Congress Cataloging in Publication Data**

Temple, Charles, 1947 –
  The beginnings of writing.

  Bibliography: p.
  Includes index.
  1.   English language — Composition and exercises.
2. Children — Writing.   I. Nathan, Ruth.   II. Burris,
Nancy.   III.   Title.
LB1576.T44        372.6        81 – 15001
ISBN 0 – 205 – 07679 – 3        AACR2
ISBN 0 – 205 – 07699 – 8 (pbk.)


10 9 8 7 6 5 4 3 2 1   87 86 85 84 83 82

Printed in the United States of America.

# Contents

*Preface*     vii

**1**   **A Child Discovers How to Write**     1

How Children Learn to Talk     3

How Writing Systems Are Organized     10

Activities     15

References     16

**Part One**   **The Beginnings of Writing**     **17**

**2**   **The Precursors of Writing**     18

Early Writing and a Theory of Perception     19

How Children Perceive Writing     21

Conclusion     25

References     26

**3**   **Features of Children's Early Writing**     27

The Recurring Principle     28

The Generative Principle     29

The Sign Concept     31

The Flexibility Principle     33

Linear Principles and Principles of Page Arrangement     36

Spaces between Words     40

Conclusion     41

References     42

iii

**4  What Children Do with Early Graphics**                         43
Children Write on Their Own                                          43
Strategies for Early Writing                                        47
Parents and Teachers Encourage Early Exploration of Print           50
Conclusion                                                          54
References                                                          54

*Exercises for Part One*                                            55

**Part Two    The Beginnings of Spelling**                          **57**

**5  Invented Spelling**                                            59
The Disappointments of English Spelling                             59
Letter-Name Spelling                                                60
How We Make Speech Sounds: A Long but Necessary
    Digression                                                      65
How Vowels Are Produced                                             73
The Developmental Dimension of Invented Spelling                    78
Early Phonemic Spelling                                             81
Conclusion                                                          81
References                                                          82

**6  Learning Standard Spelling**                                   84
How English Got Its Strange Spelling                                85
Some Learnable Patterns of Modern English Spelling                  87
Conclusion                                                          102
References                                                          102

**7  Making Progress in Spelling**                                  103
The Stages of Spelling Development                                  104
Assessing Children's Spelling Development                           109
Helping Children Make Progress in Spelling                          111
Conclusion                                                          120
References                                                          120

*Exercises for Part Two*                                            122

**Part Three    The Beginnings of Composition**                     **125**

**8  The Functions and Emerging Forms in Children's
    Composition**                                                   126
Reviewing What Children Know                                        126
Composition: What Is It?                                            130
The Purpose and Function of Children's Writing: Some Useful
    Categories                                                      131
Conclusion                                                          144
References                                                          145

**9 Writing in the Poetic Voice** 146
Assignments and What They Are For 148
Between the Expressive and the Poetic: Writing in the
Transitional Voice 153
Writing in the Poetic Voice: Teaching Implications 163
Conclusion 166 —
References 166

**10 Approaching the Transactional Voice** 167
Assignments for Expository Writing 169
Conclusion 185

**11 Writing: The Children and the Teacher** 186
The Process of Writing 186
The Forces at Work during the Writing Process 188
Atmosphere, Assignment, and Response: The Teacher's Role in
the Writing Process 191
Conclusion 204
References 205

*Exercises for Part Three* 206

**Epilogue Playing with Literature and Language: Amy's Story** 209

*References* 216
*Suggested Further Reading* 217
*Translations* 219
*Index* 227

# Preface

This is a book about young children's writing. It is focused on children between the ages of four and eight, and illustrates what they themselves do to discover how to communicate with others via the printed medium. Thus, we lay out two eyebrow-raising contentions early: first, that children as young as four begin to write; and second, that learning to write is something that children do in large measure by discovery.

In *The Beginnings of Writing* we present in detail the early scribbling behaviors of children which are important precursors of writing. We analyze thoroughly the phenomenon of "invented spelling," and follow children's development as spellers from the stage in which they arrange letters randomly on the page to the stage in which most words are spelled correctly. The beginnings of composition are treated as well. We follow children from their early unstructured and self-centered composing up to the point where their concern for their topic and for their audience both take hold, and their writing acquires a more easily recognizable form as either narrative, expository, persuasive, and so on.

In order to understand the role of discovery in children's writing, the reader must first have a notion of what there is to be discovered. Quite a few pages in this book are devoted to the description of our written language — because we adults are so familiar with it that we tend to overlook the peculiar thing written language is to children. We treat the visual characteristics of writing, the sound-symbol relationship, spelling and its history, and the forms of composition in what we hope is sufficient detail to enable the reader to see the more important features children grapple with as they learn to write.

Though the main emphasis in this book is on the children's role in learning to write, we include both general guidelines and specific procedures for teachers of beginning writers and for parents. Both have important work to do, if children are to become fluent writers. The best teaching, however, responds to what the child is trying to do. To make that statement more than an empty cliché, our aim in this book is to make it possible to see what a beginning writer is trying to do.

**The Plan of the Book**

The book is divided into four parts. An introductory chapter sets the focus on children's writing development, highlights the process of learning to talk as a parallel phenomenon to learning to write, and describes our writing system in comparison to some other systems that exist around the world.

Then follows Part One, "The Beginnings of Writing," in which we study children's early efforts to make scribbles and squiggles that *look like* writing. This section begins with a discussion of the psychological act of perception, so that we can understand in what sense children's early scribbles might be attempts to gain control over *distinctive features* of adult writing. A later chapter outlines principles of standard writing that can be seen emerging in children's pseudowriting, and the final one in this section describes ways teachers and parents can help children progress through this early phase of writing happily and smoothly.

Part Two, "The Beginnings of Spelling," draws on recent research in the phenomenon of invented spelling. We describe children's development as spellers in five stages and present a brief background on the history and present structure of our English spelling system to give the reader a clearer idea why children make the inventions they do. Part Two concludes with a chapter that explains how to assess a child's development through the stages of spelling, and how teachers and parents can help children along in this important aspect of writing.

Part Three, "The Beginnings of Composition," summarizes recent psychological and linguistic studies of children's self-expression through writing, and places them against the background of a description of the standard forms of composition. Particular attention is paid to the way writing assignments succeed or fail to encourage children to move outside of themselves and adopt particular modes of composition; or more specifically, to write stories, wage written arguments, make written instructions, and write descriptions. The section closes with a chapter devoted to the teaching of composition, a chapter which covers the nature of the composing process, along with the contributions made by the intellectual atmosphere of the classroom, by assignments, revising and editing, peer review, and publishing of classroom material.

Early reviewers of this manuscript suggested that we put the last section first, since expression and communication are of primary importance in any act of writing. Their concern was correct. Surely the force that motivates children's intense efforts to discover how to make letter forms and to spell words with them is the urge to express something to someone. This is evident if you study the samples of children's writing that are found in the sections of the book devoted respectively to the discovery of letter forms and of spelling patterns. Everything the children wrote was intended as an expression or a message.

We put letter forms first because the phenomena we describe there can be observed in young children before their compositional strategies can be discerned. Spelling was placed next because forming letters leads naturally to the question of how they can be arranged into words. When children spell they have long been composing; nevertheless, we held off the discussion of composition until after the subject of spelling had been dealt with in order to make our presentation clearer.

In the interest of an uncluttered presentation we have also rather arbitrarily held off to the Epilogue our discussion of the importance of children's experiences with literature to their development as writers. This discussion contains a detailed account of what one child read and wrote during the early years in which she was becoming a writer.

The entire book is profusely illustrated with children's work. The samples were collected either by or for the authors in Michigan and Texas. They represent quite a cross section of children: not only North and South, but public school and private school; gifted and talented and Title I classes; boys and girls; black, white, and Mexican-American are included in the mix.

Because of the invented spelling, many of the samples are difficult to read. Rewritten versions of most are included in an appendix at the end of the book.

A list of the sources the authors used in preparing the material is included at the end of each chapter. A list of suggested readings is included at the end of the book. At the end of each section the reader will find suggested learning activities. The reader who wants more than a general understanding of the topic will be well advised to sample one or two of these activities before leaving one section for another. The college instructor who is using this book as a text may want to assign some of these to her students.

Throughout Part Two, which deals with spelling, we have found it necessary to refer sometimes to *sounds,* sometimes to *letters,* sometimes to individual words, and sometimes to children's *invented spelling for words.* In order to avoid confusion, we have settled on the following system. *Sounds are represented by lower-case letters in italics.* Vowel sounds are marked "long" with a straight bar over the letter, and "short" with a curved one: *ā* and *ă. Letters of the alphabet are represented by capital letters:* T, N, and W. *Words are put in quotation marks:* For example, we spell "cat" CAT. *Invented spellings are all in capitals.* For example, Hilda wrote KIT for "cat."

We the authors recognize that we would have little to say in these pages without the work of more than a hundred children; or the cooperation of their teachers, who not only allowed us into their classrooms but also gathered writing samples for us themselves. The children are too numerous to mention. Among the teachers are Sheila Carlip, Marian Carter, Myrtlene Houck, Pat Marek, Aline Spinks, and Marilyn Pope. Others helped too, and we are grateful to all. Many thanks. Thanks, too, are due the parents who kindly granted permission to have their children's work reproduced in these pages, and also to Mrs. Post and Mrs. Hansen, two school secretaries who helped us reach many of the parents. Frances Temple prepared all of the writing samples for publication and made many valuable suggestions throughout (including the suggestion that we write this book).

We also owe a debt to the several scholars who originated the insights we have relayed in these pages. We especially appreciate the generosity of the following in allowing us to quote from their writings: Marie Clay (and her editor at Heinemann Educational Books, Phillippa Stratton), Linda Lavine, and Carol Chomsky. Though Edmund Henderson most directly influenced the section on spelling, the ideas of Charles Read, Jim Beers, Jean Gillet, Shane Templeton, Tom Gill, Charlene Gill, Elizabeth Sulzby, Jane Kita, Richard Gentry, Darrell Morris, and Jerry Zutell are strongly in evidence in what we have written. We are grateful to all of them.

The section on composition had three main mentors: James Britton, Donald Murray, and the team of researchers at the University of New Hampshire's Writing Study Project. We are especially grateful to Lucy Calkins for sharing her ideas with us.

At the University of Houston Victoria Campus, Chancellor Robert Maxson not only gave us the support of his office but also shared with us his considerable talent as an author. He is chiefly responsible for the fact that we got through all of this in good spirits. Christian Buys, Vice Chancellor at UHVC, encouraged us and critiqued the manuscript at an important stage. Stanley Wills and Diane Prince shared the resources of the Division of Education with us, removed worries, and made our work on the book a lot easier than it might have been.

Secretaries who typed parts of the manuscript were Helen Collier, Janis Edwards, Sharon Meier, Lynn Silkey, and Mary Skovira. And colleagues who lent a hand at the last minute were Kathy Lentz and Lamoine Lane.

At Allyn and Bacon, the education editor, Margaret Quinlin believed in our work from the first. She is an artist; her sessions with us were as fascinating as they were helpful. Sue Canavan, editorial assistant, was a good friend and effective problem-solver.

# 1

# A Child Discovers How to Write

At a preschool in Cambridge, Massachusetts, a four-year-old girl had just completed a drawing of a person fishing. At her side was a language researcher who was studying the beginnings of writing in young children. The researcher wondered what would happen if she asked the little girl to write about her picture. The little girl looked at her quizzically for a moment and then began to write these letters:

YUTS A LADE YET FEHEG AD HE KOT FLEPR

She wrote laboriously, talking to herself as she wrote the letters one at a time. The researcher was elated, and she read the words immediately: "Once a lady went fishing and she caught Flipper."[1] (See Figure 1–1.)

There are at least two mysteries in that story: How was the girl able to write those words? She was too young to have been taught to write, and anyway, nobody would have taught her to write like that. And how was the lady able to read her words? This second question we can answer quickly. The researcher could read what the girl wrote because the made-up "system" of spelling she used to write her words was exactly like the invented spelling of many other children that researcher had observed, and therefore the researcher knew what to expect. The first question, how the girl was able to write this way, will take us much of the rest of this book to answer.

Children can discover how to write if adults stimulate and encourage them to do so. Writing, the act of expressing thoughts by means of written symbols, is a mysterious process. No one understands exactly how we learn to do it, but it appears that we learn to write at least as much by

1

**FIGURE 1–1**
*No Name*
*Age 4*
*From Carol*
*Chomsky (used*
*by permission)*

KUTZ A LADE YET FEH
EG AD HE KOT     FLEPR

discovering how as by being taught. Learning to write is largely an act of discovery. This book is about that act. It is also about another act of discovery, as parents and teachers see revealed in children's early productions outlines of the nature of the writing process, the nature of our written language, and the nature of the process by means of which children learn to write.

If every child went about discovering how to write in his or her unique way, this book could not have been written, for there would have to be as many books on young children's writing as there were young children. But research and the experience of teaching and parenting have shown us a remarkable thing: Even when they are not taught about writing, most children make essentially the same discoveries about it, in essentially the same order. This is truly mysterious, for our writing system and the using of it is a vast and complex matter. That most children should follow the same path in coming to understand it is remarkable, and it is not the result of mere coincidence. Children, it seems, have a unique biological endowment that disposes them to learn to talk.[2] Given the proper circumstances, it is likely that this language-learning facility extends to the learning of written language as well. Children learn to talk by following a very narrow path, too. Moreover, they learn to talk by exerting an intellectual effort that appears natural yet has tremendous force.

Learning to talk has been more thoroughly scrutinized and is better understood than learning to write, and the dynamics involved are somewhat clearer and closer to general recognition. Therefore, it is in order to pause for a brief sketch of how it is children learn to talk. In many ways, this discussion should continue to inform us through the rest of the book.

Have you ever wondered how children learn to talk? Many people, when asked that question, respond that they do it by imitating. This is at least partially true: Without imitation, we couldn't account for the fact that children in Texas usually learn Texan English, children in Paris usually learn Parisian French, and not vice versa. But imitation as an answer doesn't take us very far. For one thing, children routinely say things they've never heard: "Mommy, come quick — Waldo swallowed a frog!" That is a novel statement for a novel situation. When you think about it, it is inconceivable that children could learn in advance by imitation all of the sentences they will ever have to say.

**How Children Learn to Talk**

At this point some observers would amend their position to say that children don't imitate others sentence by sentence. Instead, they imitate the nouns and verbs and sentence structures of others around them; they can fit their own words into these imitated structures to create novel sentences. But the facts of children's speech do not fit this explanation either. Children produce many sorts of grammatical constructions that they have not heard before. A two year old says, "Allgone milk" and "Daddy bye bye," and for a time, rarely utters sentences with more than two words in them. A three year old says, "I seed two gooses" and "I have small foots" — two particular plural forms that nobody else in the family uses.

At any given point in development, a child's speech more closely resembles the speech of other children at the same stage of development than it does the speech of adults in the child's environment — even if there are no other children around. Any explanation of children's speech that depends on strict imitation cannot stand up to these facts.

What *do* children do as they learn to talk? Children seek from their early days to make sense of the communication around them. As their minds and muscles mature, they attempt — through a sort of gradual trial and error process — to construct a system of *rules* that will allow them to produce sentences like those they hear others use. "Rules" is used here in a loose sense. They are not consciously saying to themselves: "Hmm . . . whenever I mean more than one, I must put an S on the end of the noun." Yet some sort of unspoken assumption close to this must have been made; or else why would the three year old say "gooses" and "foots"?

There is much evidence that children's early sentences result from the use of some sort of "rules" — and not simply from the haphazard imitation of adult sentences.

Imagine that you are in a kitchen with a two year old and his mother. The child is seated in his high chair eating. Suddenly he bangs his cup on the high chair tray and says, "Mommy milk," "Mommy milk." We assume from the context — his gesture with the cup and so forth — that he means something like, "Mommy, get me some more milk." If we have spent much time around this child, this may seem like one of his typical sentences: "typical" for one thing in that we have rarely heard him utter sentences with more than two words in them.

On reflection, we may be struck by what a good sentence it is for a two-word sentence! If we had to pick two words to convey the idea in "Mommy, get me some more milk," we could not improve on "Mommy milk." A lot of young children's sentences are like this; that is, they are of a uniform shortness, starting out at one-word sentences. Later as children mature a bit, they begin to use two-word sentences and then move up to three-word sentences and so on. Most early sentences are like this sample sentence, too, in that children show a knack for picking the most important words to convey their meanings. "Mommy milk" packs a lot of information; "get more" conveys less. Early sentences use informative words and leave out in-between words such as "and," "to," "with," "should," "have," "will," "the," "very," and the like. We assume that the limits to the number of words children can put in their early sentences has to do with biology and maturity. But the nature of their choice of words and the order they put them in reveals some deliberation: some rules.

Another piece of evidence for the operation of rules in early speech is seen when a child is asked to imitate adult sentences. Normally, young children cannot correctly imitate a sentence that is more complicated than one they could produce on their own. The following exchange between a psychologist and his young daughter illustrates this point[3]:

*Child:*    Want other one spoon, Daddy.
*Father:*   You mean, you want the other spoon.
*Child:*    Yes, I want other one spoon, please Daddy.
*Father:*   Can you say, "The other spoon"?
*Child:*    Other . . . one . . . spoon.
*Father:*   Say "other."
*Child:*    Other.
*Father:*   "Spoon."
*Child:*    Spoon.
*Father:*   "Other spoon."
*Child:*    Other . . . spoon. Now give me other one spoon?

Similar difficulty was encountered by a researcher who attempted to lead another child away from an incorrect use of a past tense of the verb "hold":

*Child:*   My teacher holded the baby rabbits and we patted them.
*Adult:*   Did you say your teacher held the baby rabbits?
*Child:*   Yes.
*Adult:*   What did you say?
*Child:*   She holded the baby rabbits and we patted them.
*Adult:*   Did you say she held them tightly?
*Child:*   No, she holded them loosely.[4]

This child apparently is not going to say "held" until she changes the rule in her head that produced that form. And language rules, like rules in other aspects of human life, take some time in the changing!

Children do not trade in their immature speech for mature speech all at once. They always go through a sequence of stages of language use, moving from simple to complex. Thus, we hear a child at two years of age say "Why you singing?" and we note that all of her questions are of the same form. At two years, four months, we hear her ask "Why you are singing?" and other questions of this more complex form. Just before the age of three, she arrives at the standard form for the English question, "Why are you singing?"[5]

It is obvious that this child is not learning to talk simply by memorizing sentences or sentence types. She is rather formulating her own rules to help her understand sentences she hears around her and to produce sentences like them. Once she formulates a rule, she uses it confidently until she begins to notice differences between her sentences and the sentences adults use around her. Then she will gradually add to and amend her rules so that they are able to produce sentences more like adults'. She doesn't junk her old rules altogether; this would be too disruptive. Feature by feature she makes her rules more and more like those adults must be using to produce mature sentences.[6]

Remarkably, children usually go through the same *sequence* of rule-learning as they mature in speech production. A study by Brown[7] showed that three separate children started using major grammatical features in roughly the same order:

| | |
|---|---|
| present progressive | I rid*ing* |
| plural nouns | two skate*s* |
| linking verbs | I *am* big |
| articles before nouns | *the* birds |
| past tense marker | we skat*ed* |

Child language researchers are not sure why children tend to acquire language rules in the same order, although one theorist has suggested that it may be because children are born "prewired" to learn language in a certain way.[8]

The uniformity of order surely has nothing to do with what we teach them. The language they hear around them cannot be much different from age one to age two, or from age two to age three — though their own language changes dramatically during that time. Whatever the explanation turns out to be, it is bound to be related to language-learning processes going on inside the child.

Not all of children's early speech is different from adult speech. Sometimes we do hear two and three year olds repeating phrases — learned by imitation — that seem more advanced somehow than their normal speech for that age. We sometimes hear "Why *dincha* tell me?" at two and a half, but later, oddly enough, the child reverts to a less mature form: "Why *you didn't* tell me?" Eventually he will come to use the "correct" form, "Why *didn't you* tell me?"

The implication is that some imitated but unassimilated forms may be used for a time as *formulas* — that is, as whole structures that the child hasn't analyzed and for which rules have not been found that will generate them. But as language development advances, the rules invade the formulas; the utterances produced by formula disappear, and they may not be heard until the rules have been developed to produce them.

If children construct their own rules to use and understand language, how is it that we all wind up speaking English instead of each her or his own private language?

We sometimes do hear of sets of twins who — being raised in isolation from others or in other unusual circumstances — make up a private idiomatic language that makes no sense to anyone but themselves.[9] But that doesn't happen very often. Every year millions and millions of children learn to speak English (and, in their respective settings, hundreds of other languages) through their own efforts, without being taught. That is the normal pattern of things.

Clearly, when children construct language rules, they are attempting to find rules or patterns that account for the language used by others in their presence. It is as if they were carefully feeling and probing the language to find its joints and seams, its outer shape and its inner workings.

Children's early hunches about the way spoken language works can be wrong, of course. An area of language where this is sometimes seen is in naming things. We have an example in our young friend, Will, who produced voluminous speech throughout his second and third year. Except for a few words, most of it was unintelligible to his parents or other adults. One of Will's recognizable words was "bupmum," used to refer to his favorite vehicle, the family's Land-Rover (a British-made jeep). According to Will's father, "bupmum" was a pretty fair rendering of the sound the exhaust made popping out of the Rover's rusted tailpipe. When the family sold it and bought a Volkswagen, Will reflected the change in his name for the new car: "mummum" (a smoother sound for an air-cooled engine!). Later, he used "mummum" to refer to all cars and trucks. Still later, an element of the name showed up in his name for motorboat: "boatmum." At four, Will now speaks standard English. But before, it seemed to those who knew him that he was seeking names for things in the sounds that emanated from them — a perfectly sensible strategy, really, but not one around which English is organized.

Thus far we have observed some basic notions of how children come to string words together grammatically and name things correctly. But there is more to the language than this, as the reader may have already objected. An altogether different but highly fruitful way to look at language learning is to examine what children use it for; that is, we can examine the different functions to which children learn to put language.

Michael Halliday, an English linguist, has noted that children can direct their utterances to serve different functions before they use any recognizably grammatical utterances.[10] A certain kind of baby's cry or coo, for instance, can clearly be meant as a request (or demand) for some thing or some service from a parent. It may mean "Pick me up" or "Put me down" or "Feed me, I'm hungry" or "Change me, I'm wet." This cry or coo will be altogether different from another coo which is done apparently for the sheer pleasure of hearing the sound in the air and feeling the sounds in the mouth. The baby will intend the utterances differently and the parent will understand them differently.

Altogether, Halliday has identified seven different functions for which children use language. They are summarized here, and a characteristic utterance appears beside each one for easy reference.

| | |
|---|---|
| *Gimme!* | (The instrumental function): Language is used to get something for the speaker. Language is used as an extension of the hand; hence, this is called instrumental language use. |
| *Stop that!* | (The regulatory function): Language is used to get somebody else to do something, to regulate somebody else's behavior, though not for the direct benefit of the speaker. |
| *You know?* | (The interactional function): Language is used to build a "we-ness," a sense of closeness or group membership between the speaker and his listener or listeners. "How do you do?" and other such utterances that lack literal meaning have |

|  |  |
|---|---|
|  | this interactional function and are important for the bond they create between the speaker and others. |
| *I love you.* | (The personal function): Language is used to share inner material. The speaker's feelings and attitudes toward things and other people, and the speaker's understanding of himself are put into words and shared verbally. |
| *What's that?* | (The heuristic function): This is language used to ask questions and find things out. "Heuristic" means "related to discovering things" ("eureka" is a cousin word). Children and others use the heuristic function when they use language to learn things or to satisfy their curiosity. |
| *Baa Baa Black Sheep.* | (The imaginative function): Language is used in this mode for the pure fun of it: to amuse the speaker and perhaps also the listener. Speakers using the imaginative function play with sounds, rhythms, and associations in language. |
| *It's snowing!* | (The representative function): Language is used here to communicate facts about the real world, to convey information. Such language represents reality with words. |

These functions of language are not limited to preverbal children. They can be identified in the speech of people of all ages, although in older speakers one utterance may serve several functions at once. For instance, a statement like "I think you're terrific!" may be at once personal and instrumental (instrumental in that the speaker hopes to get a compliment in return).

It is important to note that when children learn to talk they do not learn an isolated skill. Halliday's discussion of the functions of language demonstrates that there are at least seven different areas of spoken language at which a speaker must become adept. Child psychologists, following Halliday's lead, have noted that children do not develop evenly in the seven functions, and that children's home circumstances will have a great deal to do with the functions of language which they do develop. For example, children with few opportunities to talk and be listened to will often come to school limited in the language mode used to find things out — simply because their questions at home so often go unanswered. Children develop the ability to use language across the full spectrum of its functions only if they are given the chance to use language meaningfully for a variety of purposes.

Space does not permit a more extensive discussion of children's oral language acquisition in these pages. We can summarize the points we have made in our brief discussion this way:

1. When children learn to talk, they appear to be constructing for themselves a set of rules that enable them to produce and understand sentences.
2. The rules children use gradually change — are added to and amended — as children gain experience and maturity.
3. There are biological controls on the timetable of oral language learning, but experience in hearing and using language is involved in making progress through the stages of language acquisition.
4. Though children may make some complicated utterances at an early point in their development, this usually turns out to be the result of verbatim memorization; at a later stage such utterances will regress to a more primitive outer form as they become subject to the use of rules. Still later they will emerge stably in the correct form.
5. In the process of constructing rules for English, children sometimes try approaches which are not English at all, before finding rules that *do* produce English.
6. Learning to use language is not to grow in one ability but in a cluster of abilities. Language has at least seven demonstrably different functions for which it is regularly used, and a speaker must learn to use each one by having experience in that function.

To some extent learning to talk and learning to write follow similar dynamics. For the present, we do not understand if they are both enabled by some master capacity in the human brain. The similarities between the two processes suggest that they might be. In any case, the learning of spoken language and written language have at least the following points in common:

1. Children normally take a great deal of the initiative both in learning to talk and in learning to write.
2. Children must be surrounded by language used in meaningful ways if they are to learn to talk; the same is true of written language if they are to learn to write (and read).
3. Children learn to talk by formulating tentative rules about the way language works, trying them out, and gradually revising them. At first, they make many mistakes in speech, but they gradually correct them. In writing we see errors of letter formation, spelling, and composition occurring as children make hypotheses about the rules that govern the writing system; errors give way to other errors before they arrive at correct forms.

4. Children generally do not start using correct forms of speech as a result of direct teaching; speech forms change only gradually. In writing, too, spelling forms and composition strategies will not be immediately improved by corrective teaching but through gradual conceptual learning that is controlled by the child as much as by the teacher.

5. Children learn to talk to meet a range of personal needs, and they learn to vary their use of language as their needs and purposes change and as they have opportunities to use language functionally. Writing serves different purposes, too; and there are unique forms of writing for each function. Children must have opportunities to use writing meaningfully to serve different purposes in order to develop complete literacy.

6. Any spoken language is an immensely complicated thing; no one yet has succeeded in writing down all of the rules that explain how any natural language works. Thus, it is absurd to suppose that we could teach our children to talk by explaining the language to them — we don't understand the language well enough ourselves to do that. People somehow learn spoken language on a working level, but this does not enable them to explain their knowledge of it to others. Written language has never been fully and satisfactorily described, either. None of us understands writing well enough to explain to someone else how to write, unless that other person exerts his powers to learn for himself.

This last point needs some discussion. None of us can describe the knowledge inside someone's head that enables that person to read and write. But we know enough about writing to understand what an amazingly complex thing it is. It is important to try to visualize something of what a writing system is in order to appreciate the range of choices open to a child who undertakes to gain control over written English. In the world today there are several very different kinds of writing in daily use, a fact which makes it all the more amazing that American children can wind up writing English, given the little encouragement and the incomplete and often inaccurate information we supply them about our own written language.

## How Writing Systems Are Organized

When you and I write, we employ letters of the alphabet to represent words. The letters represent "parts" of words — the individual sounds that make them up. But this is not the only way we *could* write if we chose to use letters in a different way. There are other approaches to writing — to the representing of words with symbols — that have been used by different peoples. There is no reason to believe English-speaking children are genetically programmed to use symbols for the sound components of words. So we should consider some different ways to write in order to clarify the alternatives that are open to a child when she decides to represent a spoken message with written symbols.

One approach to writing is to let each symbol stand for an idea, in the manner that a road sign ⟨⟨ ⟩⟩ conveys the idea to motorists that a winding road lies ahead.

*Symbols for ideas: ideographic writing*

Chinese writing is a modern system based on the principle of using a single symbol to represent an idea. In ancient times the symbols were pictures of the things they represented. Through constant usage, the symbols came to look less like pictures, and the meanings became abstracted from the original concrete things that the symbols stood for.

The ancient drawing 业 used to stand for "fire," by representing its jumping, dancing quality. The modern character for fire has changed to 火. By abstraction, two fires, 炎, means "brilliant."[11]

The ancient drawing for "sunrise" depicted the sun between the branches and the roots of a tree 東. Gradually the symbol was changed to 東, and the meaning was extended to include the direction "east," since that is where the sun is seen to rise.[12]

As a result of the abstraction of both symbol and meaning, modern Chinese writing has evolved as an elaborate and versatile system capable of representing approximately the same range of ideas that English writing can. The pictorial basis of Chinese writing gives it one advantage that alphabetic writing systems do not have: Chinese writing can be read and understood by people who speak dialectical versions of Chinese that are so different that speakers of some different dialects cannot understand each other.

> Both a Peking man and a Cantonese will understand 日 means day, and 月 means moon. But a Peking man will pronounce the words r and ywe, while the Cantonese will pronounce yat and ut. . . . If the Peking man reads to the Canton man, the Canton man will not understand one word. If each man reads a text for himself, he can understand it, completely.[13]

This is so because the Chinese symbol is independent of the *sound* of the word, and represents directly the *idea* that is conveyed by the spoken word. Because the symbols represent ideas and not spoken words, they have come to be called *ideographs,* which means, simply "idea-writing." We use a few of them in our own writing system: $, ¢, &; the number symbols 1, 2, 3, 5; and the mathematical operation signs ×, ÷, −, and +. Note that these symbols are found in languages other than English and are paired with different words: 1, 2, 3 can stand for: one, two, three in English; *uno, dos, tres* in Spanish; *eins, zwei, drei* in German; and *moja, mbili, tatu* in Swahili.

Writing words with a single symbol then, is a perfectly workable approach to writing.

*Children and ideographic writing*

Children who are first working on the *sign principle* (see Chapter Four) are producing something that could be called ideographic writing. Note the use of the Valentine shape in five-year-old Jessie's sample (see Figure 1–2).

At age four, Annabrook used her mother's initial (F) and her father's (C) to symbolize her parents standing beside her as she appeared as a bride, or is that a dazzling princess? (see Figure 1–3).

**FIGURE 1–2**
*Jessie* (left)
*Age 5*
*A somewhat ideographic message*

**FIGURE 1–3**
*Annabrook* (right)
*Age 4*
*A more clearly ideographic message*

*Symbols for syllabic: syllabic writing*

A few thousand years ago an Egyptian scribe thought up a joke that eventually revolutionized writing. His language had had a hieroglyph ⮕ that stood for the Egyptian word for arrow called *ti*. There was another Egyptian word, also called *ti*, that meant "life," an idea not easily represented by a picture. The scribe's joke was to represent *ti* meaning "life" with the hieroglyph ⮕ which stood for "arrow."[14] With that pun he invented the phonetic principle — the principle that relates symbols with words on the basis of *sound*.

For an illustration of the sort of writing that resulted, consider rebus — the picture writing found in many young children's prereading books. We write 🐝 4 for "before" and intend that the reader would ignore the honey-gathering insect and the numerical quantity of "four"

and think only of the sounds of their respective names. This is a phonetic use of hieroglyphics.

With this first use of the phonetic principle the scribe may have been using symbols to spell whole words, but it is more likely that he was using them to spell syllables. After the invention of the phonetic principle, Egyptian hieroglyphics spelled syllables of words. That writing system has been obsolete for centuries; but the system of syllabic writing lives on in modern Japanese.

The Japanese language makes use of forty-six different syllables. Combinations of syllables from those forty-six make up every word in the language. A Japanese writing system, called *kana,* provides a symbol for each of the forty-six syllables. The syllable *ro* is written ⬭ ; the syllable *ku* is written ⁊ . The word for "green," *roku,* may thus be written ⬭⁊ . If we know that ⁊ represents the syllable *tsu,* then we can write the word *kutsu* "to bend" ⁊⁊ . Note that the syllable symbols ⁊ , ⬭ , and ⁊ mean nothing in themselves. They gain significance only by representing the sounds of the syllables of Japanese words.[15]

There are few syllabic writing systems besides Japanese in active use nowadays. But in ancient times these systems were widespread.[16] Just as ideographic writing systems mostly gave way to syllabic systems, the latter mostly evolved into alphabetic writing systems or disappeared altogether.

*Children and syllabic writing*

Do our young spellers in English attempt to produce syllabic writing? Sometimes we see writings that have words represented at the level of the syllable.

In one kindergartner's sentence (Figure 1 – 4), the number 2 and the letter T in DELTKO represent syllables.

## LSNT WE    WNT 2 DELTKO

**FIGURE 1–4**
*Melanie Kindergarten Syllabic use of "2" and "T"*

The next sample is another kindergartner's response to the question: "If you could go anywhere in town for lunch, where would you go?" (see Figure 1 – 5). The B and Z in Bonanza also serve as syllables.

Both of these samples differ from true syllabic writing, because they have other symbols in them that represent units smaller than syllables. Few children seem to spell consistently at the level of the syllable — though, as we shall see in Chapter Five, they occasionally do represent syllables with single consonants, a practice which standard English spelling does not allow.

**FIGURE 1 – 5**
*Annabrook
Kindergarten
Syllabic use of
"B" and "2"*

**Symbols for
smaller units
of sound:
alphabetic
writing**

The use of the alphabet as we know it was a Greek invention. Five thousand years ago the Greeks discovered that the syllabaries in circulation at the time did not fit their language. The word *anthropos*, meaning "man," was rendered *a-to-ro-po-se* by an early syllabary. "The crown," *ton chōron*, was written *to-ko-ro-ne*. It wouldn't do. What was plainly needed was a writing system that would let the scribes choose what combinations of consonants and vowels they wanted.

So they made some changes in the syllabaries. Instead of representing a whole syllable (a vowel plus a consonant) the new Greek symbols would represent either a consonant or a vowel but not both. Thus the alphabet, and the alphabetic principle, were born.[17]

It may be that some children who seek to understand how English writing works reject the syllabic approach for the same reasons the Greeks did. English *could* be spelled syllabically, if the names of the letters of the alphabet could be associated with syllables in words — but it wouldn't work very well.

English is better suited to the alphabet than it is either to ideographs or to syllables. It has too many words for an ideographic system. A large dictionary has more than 130,000 entries: if we used ideographs, we would have to learn or look up that many! English is not suited to any syllabary either, because — unlike Japanese — the syllable patterns in English are many and varied, and would require a large number of characters to represent them. The twenty-six letters of the alphabet can, in some combination, represent all of the sounds contained in all 130,000 plus words in a large English dictionary. No other writing system offers such economy.

The match between our alphabet and the sounds of our words is far from perfect, however. English has forty-four sounds, but only twenty-six letters. A few of the letters, moreover, are redundant: the letters K and C can represent the same sounds, as can S and C, and Y and I. Some letters represent many different sounds, and some sounds may be spelled with many different letters. All of these features have consequences for learning to write in English.

That is enough about writing systems. To review, we have briefly described three major types of them: the ideographic system (which uses symbols to represent whole words or ideas), the syllabic system (which uses symbols to represent syllables), and the alphabetic system (which uses symbols to represent individual speech sounds, or "phonemes," as linguists call them). All three are in use today.

There is no inherent reason why children who speak English should expect writing to work by the alphabetic principle. It is reasonable to suppose that children's early suppositions about the way writing works might for a time light on ideographic and syllabic writing, as well as on alphabetic writing. In fact, alphabetic writing requires that writers be able to break a word into its individual speech sounds before they can write it (assuming they are inventing the spelling). This breaking out of speech sounds is a sophisticated language act; far more sophisticated than breaking sentences into words (as ideographic writing requires) or words into syllables (as syllabic writing requires). These matters will be given a more thorough discussion in the ensuing chapters.

From our discussion of writing systems, one point should be clear: discovering how to write in English involves making choices from a very large range of alternatives. Children may very well be more aware of the alternatives than adults are, because our long experience with alphabetic writing tends to blind us to the possibility that there may be ways of representing words with symbols that are different from the way we do it.

**Activities**

Sit down with a four year old and ask her or him to draw a picture of something exciting. When the child is finished, ask her or him to write something about the picture on the paper. The child may object: if so, what does he or she say? You may be able to persuade the child to write, anyway: if so, what do you say?

Once you succeed in getting the child to write something (and it will not look like what you would normally call "writing") examine it carefully. Ask the child what he or she has written, and to tell you what marks say what words. Ask the child to tell you what writing is; what do people do when they write? Why do people write? What is the difference between writing and drawing a picture? If the child answers to the effect that writing is putting down marks to stand for words, how exactly do the marks stand for the words? Following all of this interrogation, try to describe to yourself as thoroughly as you can this child's conception of what writing is.

Repeat this interview with a three-year-old child; with a five year old; with a six year old. Or, if you are reading this book in conjunction with a class, have different members of the class interview different ages of children. When the interviews are completed, compare the results. How did the children differ in:

- their willingness to write
- the nature of what they wrote
- their statements about what writing is and what it is for
- their notions about the way writing represents language?

**References**

1. Carol Chomsky. "Invented Spelling in the Open Classroom." *Word* 27 (1971): 499 – 518.
2. Noam Chomsky. *Language and Mind.* Enlarged ed. New York: Harcourt Brace Jovanovich, 1972.
3. Martin Braine. "The Acquisition of Language in Infant and Child," in C. E. Reed (ed.), *The Learning of Language.* New York: Appleton-Century-Crofts, 1971. (Quoted in Aitchison, *The Articulate Mammal.* London: Hutchinson, 1973, p. 74).
4. Courtney Cazden. *Child Language and Education.* New York: Holt, Rinehart and Winston, 1972. (Quoted in Aitchison, *The Articulate Mammal,* p. 72.)
5. Jean Aitchison. *The Articulate Mammal.* London: Hutchinson, 1973, p. 88.
6. Jill DeVilliers and Peter DeVilliers. *Language Acquisition.* Cambridge: Harvard University Press, 1979.
7. Roger Brown. *A First Language.* Cambridge: M.I.T. Press, 1973.
8. Chomsky. *Language and Mind.*
9. Catherine Gorney. " 'Gibberish' Language of Identical Twins Still Baffles the Experts." *The Houston Chronicle,* 29 July 1979, sec. 10, p. 4.
10. Michael Halliday. *Explorations in the Functions of Language.* London: Edward Arnold, 1973.
11. Diane Wolff. *An Easy Guide to Everyday Chinese.* New York: Harper Colophon Books, 1974, p. 121.
12. Ibid., p. 123.
13. Ibid., p. 3.
14. Ignace Gelb. *A Study of Writing.* Chicago: University of Chicago Press, 1963.
15. Florence Sakade (ed.). *A Guide to Reading and Writing Japanese.* Rutland, Vt.: Charles E. Tuttle, 1961.
16. Gelb. *A Study of Writing.*
17. Ibid., pp. 154 – 183.

# 1
# The Beginnings of Writing

When does writing begin? Is it when the child composes a readable message to serve some communicative purpose? Is it when the child uses letters to spell words with some approximate degree of accuracy? Or is it when the child makes some wiggly lines on paper, and pretends that she is writing?

It is clear that much writing development unfolds in children well before they spell or compose.

The earliest tasks in learning to write concern making marks that look like writing — whether they be long wiggles that fill a page the way writing does or smaller shapes that resemble letters. Thanks to the work of Eleanor Gibson, Linda Lavine, Emilia Ferreiro, and Marie Clay, we can list and describe the concepts and principles children must master in order to make marks that *look* like writing. We turn to these matters in the next three chapters.

# 2

# *The Precursors of Writing*

A four year old was bent over a piece of paper, deeply engrossed in the act of making the marks shown in Figure 2 – 1 when her older sister, a first grader, entered the room.

"Jessie, what are you doing?" asked the sister.

"I'm writing," she replied.

"No, you're not."

"Yes, I am."

"You can't be. I don't see any letters!"

Jessie's sister is certainly a realist, a clear-sighted spotter of naked emperors. But we rather agree with Jessie. Her marks *do* contain many of the rudiments of writing. Our purpose in this chapter and in the two succeeding ones will be to demonstrate the growth of writing — starting with youngsters who "write" as Jessie does and continuing until we see the children beginning to spell.

**FIGURE 2 – 1**
*Jessie*
*Age 4*
*Early writing*

**FIGURE 2 – 2**
*No Name
Kindergarten
The child called
this writing*

**FIGURE 2 – 3**
*No Name
Kindergarten
This, too, was
called writing*

Consider the samples in Figures 2 – 2 and 2 – 3.

How is it possible to examine samples like these and find elements of writing in them? Real writing is composed of combinations of discrete symbols which stand in some socially agreed upon relation to language.[1] These scribbles do not meet this definition by any stretch of the imagination. Indeed, as Jessie's sister pointed out, they don't even have letters in them. How can we see writing in scribbles that don't have letters in them?

**Early Writing and a Theory of Perception**

People who know how to read and write, even newcomers to this endeavor like Jessie's sister, think of writing as something composed of letters and words. Learning to write, it would seem, is nothing other than learning to make letters and to combine them into words. But studies of writing development carried out against a theory of perceptual learning have suggested that young children learn to write through a process that is really quite the opposite. Rather than learning to write by mastering first the parts (letters) and then building up to the whole (written lines), it appears that children attend first to the whole and only much later to the parts. But what is there to be attended to in the "whole" of written language if not words and letters?

Let us now explore the process of perceptual learning for a bit to establish a background for an answer to these questions (our discussion will draw mostly from Eleanor Gibson[2]). Imagine a newborn baby just home from the hospital, lying in a crib in his nursery. What does he see? At first his eyes are closed in sleep much of the time, and for several months he cannot focus on objects more than a few feet away from his face. But from the time he opens his eyes he is bombarded by sensations: light, shadow, and dark; objects that loom into view and withdraw; and objects that do not move.

What does he hear? There is the constant sound of his own breathing, the sound of voices — some loud and distinct (voices of people close by) and some less loud and echoing (voices of people further away). He may hear sounds of traffic outside, sounds of lawnmowers, sounds of birds chirping and dogs barking. The child is surrounded by a bustling confusion of sights, sounds, and feelings.

At first we may imagine that the sensations are all undifferentiated — that is, the baby has no way to distinguish one sight, sound, or feeling from another. But soon he must begin to do some basic sorting. Things that move can be distinguished from things that are static. Human voices can be separated from other nonhuman noises, such as passing motorcycles, ringing telephones, and barking dogs.

These first gross distinctions can be taken further. Things that move can be sorted into parts of the baby himself, and other things that move. Or they can be sorted into things that move on their own accord, and other things that move (people and animals versus balls and mobiles). Sounds can be carried to further distinctions, as voices that are close by are distinguished from voices that are far away, a woman's voice from a child's, and so on.

This process of sorting and classifying is the child's way of finding out about the world and getting some control over it. The process continues throughout childhood and adult life, though it never again reaches the intensity of the first four years.

When the child begins to use words to stand for things, we begin to get a clearer idea of how this sorting process works. Take the case of Annabrook, for example. The first word uttered by this little girl was "dog." During that phase of language development when all of her sentences consisted of a single word, she delighted in pointing to the family beagle and sagely pronouncing him, "dog." But the beagle was not the only animal to qualify for that label. Goats, sheep, cats, and even an occasional cow (she lived on a farm) were all pronounced "dog." During this period it happened that Annabrook was taken to a circus. She and her family had taken their seats and were arranging themselves when a large elephant appeared at the back of the circus tent and swayed into the center ring. "Dog!," cried Annabrook, and in fear and amazement she clapped her hands over her eyes.

It seems that what Annabrook had been doing was lumping together several objects in the world into the category which she labeled "dog." She did the lumping on the basis of features these objects had in common. "Dogs" apparently were four-legged, self-propelled living things. Chickens, having two legs, were never called "dog." Annabrook must have been aware that there are differences in the appearance of dogs, sheep, goats, cats, and certainly cows. For the time being, she chose to ignore the differences and group them together because of the features they did have in common. When she saw the elephant, however, she seemed to realize at once that her category for "dog" must be amended to take *size* into account. In other words, she found it necessary to add another *distinctive feature,* size, to the set of features that defined "dog."

Distinctive features are central to an understanding of perceptual learning. They are the necessary set of features or attributes that we use to define a category of things. For Annabrook, "four-legged," "living," and "self-propelled" appeared to be the distinctive features that made up her category "dog." Distinctive features are acquired with experience. In general, the more experience we have in the world, the more distinctive features we add to our categories. Then two things happen: membership to a particular category becomes reserved to fewer varieties of objects, while at the same time we set up new categories to include those items that were not adequately described by our earlier categories.[3]

To summarize our points about perceptual learning, we can say:

1.  Our environment presents us with a humming totality of potential sense data all of the time. The task of perceptual learning is to carve out classes of objects and events from the undifferentiated confusion around us — classes of things that somehow act or can be acted upon in the same way.
2.  The differentiation of things in the environment usually starts with gross categories defined by gross distinctions and then proceeds to finer categories defined by finer distinctive features.
3.  We assign things to categories on the basis of distinctive features that the things share. In doing this, we initially ignore some differences. However, if the differences become important enough, we will create a new category and assign some things to the new category that will not fit the old, or vice versa.

**How Children Perceive Writing**

If the perception of things in the environment starts with gross distinctions and moves progressively to finer ones, it stands to reason that letters — being the fine elements of writing — would be the last elements to be differentiated. The theory of perceptual learning would lead us to believe that children should first discover gross differences between writing and other similar objects. When children first become aware of writing as a separate thing, they must have some rough set of distinctive features to help them decide when something is writing and when it is not. As they gain experience, they should become aware of finer and finer distinctive features that separate writing from other kinds of graphic displays.

In recent years there have been several productive inquiries into the question of what children think writing is — that is, into the distinctive features children use to define writing for themselves at different points in childhood. These inquiries have been carried out in two ways. First, there have been experiments in which children are asked to make distinctions between several different sorts of graphic displays. Second, children's own productions, which they themselves call writing, have been examined for the features that they have in common. The findings of the first kind of experiment will concern us through the remainder of this chapter. The second kind of experiment will be discussed in Chapter Three.

Several years ago, Eleanor Gibson, a psychologist at Cornell University, put forth the hypothesis that children might come to know about writing through its features — not through its letters.[4] She stated that we might expect children's progress in learning about writing to proceed from the discrimination of gross shapes on to the discrimination of letters themselves. Gibson then proceeded to conduct a long program of experiments, using young children as subjects, to test her ideas of how they might think about writing. One of the most elaborate of these experiments was carried out by her doctoral student, Linda Lavine.[1,5]

Lavine sought to find out what sorts of graphic forms children of different ages classify as writing and which sorts they reject from that classification. She designed a set of cards, each featuring a graphic display of some sort (see Figure 2 – 4). Then she made up a game which she played with her three-, four-, and five-year-old subjects. Showing them the cards, she told the children to decide which cards had writing on them. The ones that did they were to place in a toy mailbox. The ones that did not have writing on them were placed in another round box where cards that had things other than writing were to go.

**FIGURE 2 – 4**
*Cards from Lavine's experiment*

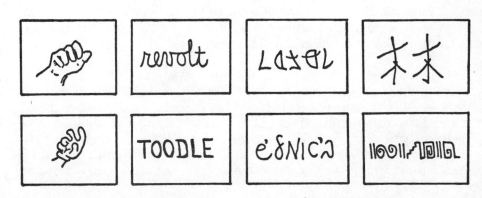

On the cards Lavine had printed four kinds of graphic displays (see Figure 2 – 4). The first consisted of pictures: pictures of familiar and unfamiliar objects and of geometric designs. The other three kinds she designated as follows:

- Class I dealt with real English writing, such as might be found in the child's environment. This included both cursive and printed letters and words.
- Class II was made up of writings that looked very much like Roman letters (that is, the writing shared many distinctive features with Roman letters), but the writing was not of a sort that was found in the children's environment. For Class II writing Lavine used Hebrew characters.
- Class III consisted of designs which neither looked like Roman letters nor were found in the children's environment. These were Chinese letters and a Mayan design motif.

All the types of figures were presented in several formats to contrast the different features that children might respond to. The normal presentation was horizontal, linear, six units to a line (see Figure 2 – 5). But variations were single-unit presentations (see Figure 2 – 6), presentations that repeated the same unit six times (see Figure 2 – 7), and nonlinear arrays of varied units (see Figure 2 – 8).

When the responses of the three age groups — three, four, and five year olds — were tallied and compared, they showed some very interesting patterns. No one said the pictures were writing — not even the three year olds. Only the youngest subjects called the Class III figures writing (these were the Chinese and Mayan figures). But all the age groups called both Class I (real writing) and Class II (Hebrew characters) writing. Class II figures shared features with Roman letters, but they were not Roman

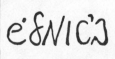

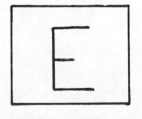

**FIGURE 2 – 5**
(left)
*Horizontal, linear, six units per line*

**FIGURE 2 – 6**
(right)
*Single-unit variations*

**FIGURE 2 – 7**
(left)
*Variations with
the same symbol
repeated*

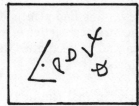

**FIGURE 2 – 8**
(right)
*Nonlinear
variations*

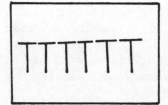

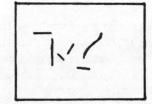

letters and they were not likely to have been seen in the children's environment. On this finding, Gibson's hypothesis was supported: Children did seem to be using *features* of the writing system and not just an inventory of known letters as the basis for making judgments as to whether or not a display could be called writing.

The younger children appeared to use both linearity (whether the figures were presented in a straight horizontal line) and variety (whether there was a composition of different sorts of figures rather than one figure repeated) as distinguishing features of writing. That is, unlinear and unvaried displays were usually rejected by the younger subjects. But the older subjects tended to ignore such features as linearity and variety and focus instead on the appearance of the individual figures. Thus they tended to class unlinear or unvaried arrays as writing, so long as the figures that composed them were Roman letters or Roman-like letters (see Figure 2 – 9). This finding, too, was in accordance with Gibson's hypothesis: Gross features such as linearity and variety were distinctive in the judgments of the younger subjects. But finer features such as the details of the letters themselves were distinctive for the older subjects.

**FIGURE 2 – 9**
*Linearity and
variety were dis-
tinctive to youn-
ger children
(left) and Roman
letters were dis-
tinctive to older
children* (right)

Lavine's study supported the supposition that children come to know about writing through the process of perceptual learning. Children appear to identify distinctive features that they use to separate writing from other graphic displays. Moreover, they progressively refine the sets of distinctive features they use to define writing.

Lavine reasoned from her experiment that several distinctive features must be included in children's categories of "writing." The features apparently considered distinctive by even the youngest subjects were:

1.　*nonpictoriality* — whatever is considered writing may not be a picture;
2.　*linearity* — the figures must be arrayed horizontally in a straight line;
3.　*variety* — figures in a display should vary from one another;
4.　*multiplicity* — writing consists of more than one figure.

The features used by the older subjects appeared to be:

5.　*"Roman-likeness"* — the individual units of writing should share the distinctive features of letters in the Roman alphabet (what these features are was not detailed in this experiment); and
6.　*being Roman letters themselves* — writing is composed of letters we can recognize from our knowledge of individual letters.

**Conclusion**

"What looks like writing to you?" That, essentially, was the question Lavine asked her subjects. In their answers, the children revealed the distinctive features that they considered to define writing at their respective ages. And since these features differed from the younger children to the older ones, these findings were interesting indeed.

We may still want to ask what all this has to do with children's writing. Judging designs to be writing or nonwriting is one thing; producing designs that look like writing may be quite another. That objection is reasonable, but Lavine's study nevertheless tells us much that is important. For one thing, it is likely that the features to which the children in her study responded parallel the features children notice in the writing they find in their environment. With repeated exposure to print — in books, on billboards, in buses and subways — these features may become more and more important to children and more stable in their minds.

When children make their own early attempts to produce designs that look like writing, we might expect features similar to those identified by Lavine to emerge in their designs. In the next chapter, in which we look closely at the first writings children produce themselves, we will see whether or not this prediction is borne out.

**References**

1. L. Lavine. *The Development of Perception of Writing in Pre-Reading Children: A Cross-Cultural Study.* Unpublished Ph.D. dissertation. Cornell University, 1972. Xerox University Microfilms, 73 – 6657.

2. E. Gibson and H. Levin. *Psychology of Reading.* Cambridge: M.I.T. Press, 1975.

3. J. Bruner. "On Perceptual Readiness," in *Beyond the Information Given.* New York: Norton, 1976.

4. E. Gibson. *Principles of Perceptual Learning and Development.* New York: Appleton-Century-Crofts, 1969.

5. L. Lavine. "Differentiation of Letterlike Forms in Prereading Children." *Developmental Psychology,* 13 (1977): No. 2. 89 – 94.

# 3

# *Features of Children's Early Writing*

Jessie crept up beside one of the authors as he ate his breakfast and put down the strange message shown in Figure 3–1. "Read it!" she said. He knew from previous occasions that it wouldn't do to protest that she hadn't written anything readable.

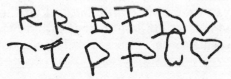

**FIGURE 3–1**
*Jessie*
*Age 4*
*Early writing*

"Rrrbuhdow!," he said. This was just what she wanted. She disappeared into her bedroom and returned almost at once with four more sheets of the same.

"Read it!" she demanded.

In this chapter we are going to look closely at writings by children like Jessie. These are children whose written productions have stopped being pictures but have not yet become writing (if by "writing" we really mean spelling — using letters to represent words *by their sounds*). We will study the features that emerge in children's productions — the features which make their productions more and more like writing.

Following the example of Marie Clay,[1] a New Zealander whose research forms the backbone of this chapter, we will cease to use the term "features" and now speak of "principles." The reason for the shift is this: When children sort writing from nonwriting (as we observed in the previous chapter), they do it on the basis of the visual features of the graphic displays — horizontally, variety of figures, nonpictoriality, and so on.[2] But when children produce early pseudowriting, they appear to be trying to discover and manipulate principles that can make their productions look like writing. Hence, *principles* and *features* are active and passive versions of the same thing. When we produce writing, we employ principles; when we discriminate writing, we use features.

In the following pages we will describe the *recurring principle,* the discovery that writing uses the same shapes again and again; the *generative principle,* the discovery that writing consists of a limited number of signs in varied combinations; the *sign concept,* the idea that print stands for something besides itself; and the *flexibility principle,* the idea that there is a limited number of written signs, and a limit to the number of ways we can make them. Finally, we will describe a number of principles related to the way print is arranged on a page, *page-arrangement principles.* All of these principles must be learned by children before they can be said to write. And many of them may be seen emerging in children's scribbles before anyone notices that they are trying to produce writing.

## The Recurring Principle

Study the picture and the handwriting sample in Figure 3 – 2. On a very general level, what makes the writing look different from the picture? You may notice several differences. The writing is arranged in rows across the page, while the picture makes more use of two-dimensional space. If you squint your eyes and look at the writing and the picture, the individual letters lose their identity. Now you may notice that the writing seems to be composed of loops and tall sticks repeated over and over

**FIGURE 3 – 2**
*Picture and words for the same idea*

There was a house. It had a chimney with smoke coming out, and two flowers in the yard. There was a bird and a cloud in the sky.

again. Children's early attempts to imitate writing often have this characteristic repetition of loops or sticks or circles.

Clay applied the label *recurring principle* to the idea that writing consists of the same moves repeated over and over again. She noted that children derive a great deal of satisfaction from filling whole lines or pages by repeating the same moves over and over.

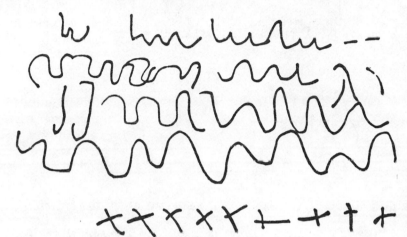

**FIGURE 3 – 3**
*Carlene*
*Age 4*
*Recurring*
*principle*

**FIGURE 3 – 4**
*Matt*
*Kindergarten*
*Recurring*
*principle*

The displays in Figures 3 – 3 and 3 – 4 were produced by children who said they were writing. Note how each gives evidence of the recurring principle.

When recurring moves such as these are arranged across a page in lines, they are sometimes called linear mock writing.

It is possible to fill an entire page with repetitions of the same basic mark. That is what the child in Figure 3 – 5 has done. But as we saw in the previous chapter, children learn early on that the same character repeated over and over again is not writing. To be called writing, there must be variety in the arrangement of marks.

**The Generative Principle**

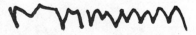

**FIGURE 3 – 5**
*No Name*
*Age 3*
*Filling a line*
*with the same*
*form*

It *is* possible to create writing with just a few characters, *but they must be repeated in different combinations.* Every book written in English simply combines and recombines fifty-two letter symbols (see "The Flexibility Principle"). The writer in Figure 3 – 6 uses considerably fewer, but it is clear that she has discovered the same principle around which English writing is organized: a limitless amount of writing can be generated by using a small set of letters, provided they are combined in

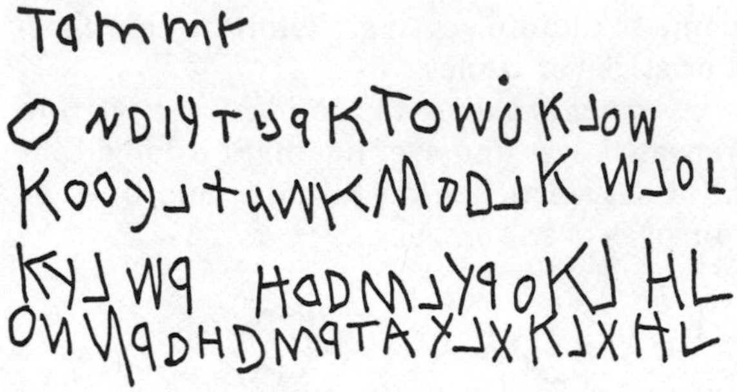

**FIGURE 3-6**
*Tammy*
*Kindergarten*
*Generative*
*principle*

Tammy

O ᴎDIᴚTᴜqKToᴡÜᴋᴊow
Kooᴊ᭙ᴜᴡᴋMoᴅᴊK ᴡᴊoL
Kᴚᴊᴡq HoᴅMᴊᴚqoKᴊHL
oᴎᴠqᴅHᴅMqTAXᴊXᴋᴊXHL

**FIGURE 3-7**
*No Name*
*Age 4*
*Generative*
*principle*

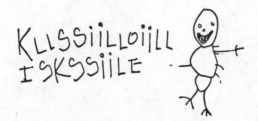

KLISSiiLLoïᴊLL
I SKSSiiLE

different ways. This is what Clay calls the *generative principle* (see Figure 3-7).

The generative principle may be employed with words, too. In Figure 3-8 note how Wes has recombined a small repertoire of words to make a list of sentences covering a whole page.

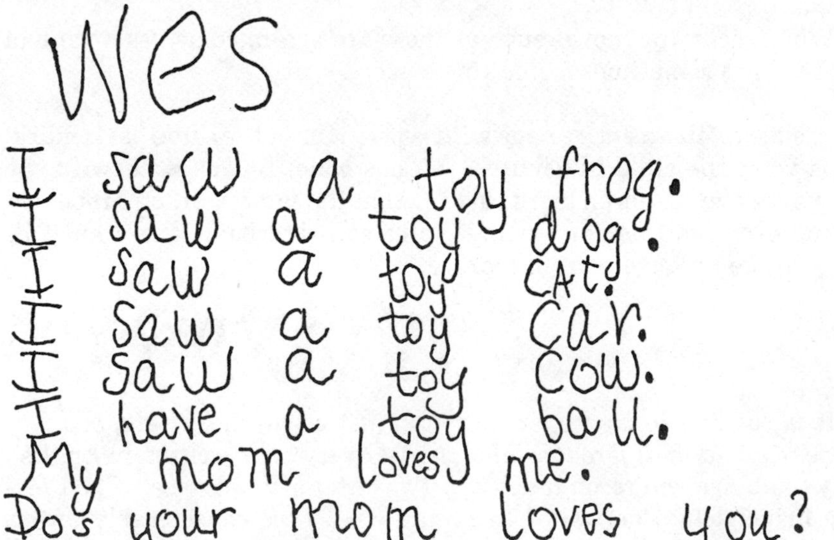

**FIGURE 3-8**
*Wes*
*Grade 1*
*Generative prin-*
*ciple applied to*
*sentences*

Wes

I saw a toy frog.
I saw a toy dog.
I saw a toy cat.
I saw a toy car.
I saw a toy cow.
I have a toy ball.
My mom loves me.
Dos your mom loves you?
this mom reall loves me.

All of the items in Figure 3 – 9 could be called "graphic displays." But only some of them could be called "signs." Figure (1) is a picture, not a sign. Figure (2) is a design, such as might decorate the hem of a skirt; it is not a sign either. Figure (3) *might* be a sign to someone who read Chinese (the author made it up!). Figure (4) contains three signs: the graphic configurations for the letters a, b, and c, respectively. Figure (5) contains the three signs, c, a, and t; collectively these make up the sign cat, the English word for a small feline animal.

**The Sign Concept**

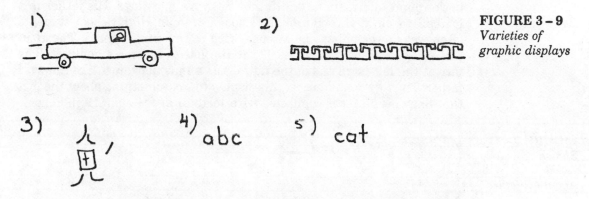

**FIGURE 3 – 9**
*Varieties of graphic displays*

What is a sign? A sign is a display that stands for something else. In writing, signs are arbitrary — that is, there is no reason why a particular graphic display *has* to stand for what it does. There is no particular reason why a sideways hook should stand for the letter C. Generations of readers and writers of English have simply agreed that it does. This is what separates *writing* from *pictures*: writing represents something arbitrarily, while drawing does not.[2] The relation between the graphic display in Figure 3 – 10 and the idea "truck" is *not* arbitrary. The graphic

**FIGURE 3 – 10**
*"Truck"*

display shares many features (wheels, back and front, steering wheel, window, etc.) with the object it represents. But the written word *truck* has none of these things in common with the object "truck." The written word can represent the object only because the community of literate English speakers agrees that the word stands for the thing, and the letters stand for the word.

At some point in their development as writers, all children must come to understand that writing uses graphic displays to stand for something else. This understanding is called the *sign concept*. Children have the sign concept when they intend, even in play, to have the things they put on paper to stand for words, ideas, or messages.

The sign concept seems to be present when children make marks that begin to look like writing. Note the evidence of the sign concept in the piece by Shawn, a four year old (see Figure 3 – 11). We need some background information to interpret Shawn's markings. His father is a football coach at Stroman High School. Stroman High School students often wear sweatshirts emblazoned with a Teutonic letter S. The H in this passage probably stands not for the letter, but for a goalpost. The face at the left-hand end of the figure has a mustache, just like Shawn's father. Thus we can interpret this display to say something about the fact that Shawn's father is connected with football at Stroman High School.

**FIGURE 3 – 11**
*Shawn*
*Age 4*
*About his father*

Shawn's signs are not arbitrary. Perhaps he is showing us that it is natural for a beginning writer to think of concrete relations between signs and the things they stand for. Emilia Ferreiro has argued that this is the case.[3] Her ideas will be discussed in Chapter Four.

Most beginning writers are willing to *pretend* that the marks they wrote stand for something — leaving the relation between the marks and the things they stand for up to the reader's imagination. Note the grocery list written up by Susan, at her mother's suggestion (see Figure 3 – 12). After she had written down her marks for each item, her mother went back and asked her what each one was. Typed to the left of each mark is her answer.

Where does the sign concept come from? Children who grow up in homes where literacy is practiced have many indications that writing stands for things. Children whose parents read to them hear a certain story come from a certain book with certain pictures and print. And although for a time they may believe that the story is somehow contained in the picture, it eventually dawns on them that the print is the source of the story.[4] Perhaps they notice that a variety of spoken comments may be induced by a picture, whereas an exact story line is stimulated by print. Recognition of the sign potential of the print is certainly made easier when parents occasionally run their finger along with the print as they read.

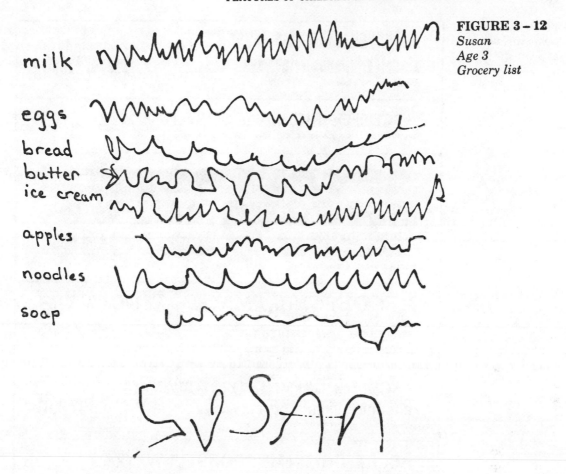

**FIGURE 3–12**
*Susan*
*Age 3*
*Grocery list*

milk

eggs

bread

butter

ice cream

apples

noodles

soap

Even if children are not read to, there are other indications available to them of the sign potential of print. Logos on popular restaurants, such as McDonald's, Burger King, and the like, are quickly picked up by children. A three year old at home who is shown a McDonald's hamburger wrapper may easily say, "McDonald's!" No wonder such businesses so jealously protect their logos from use by competitors!

**The Flexibility Principle**

In our discussion of the sign concept we noted that signs stand for things on the basis of social agreement. Hence, the figure D stands for the letter D, and the figure P stands for the letter P; we know this because it is taught in school and used consistently in any society where English is read and written. It follows that signs must be used *carefully*. In writing there is a limited set of agreed-upon signs. To write English, we *have to* use the agreed-upon signs and no others. On the present author's typewriter there are fifty-two of these: abcdefghijklmnopqrstuvwxyz,

**FIGURE 3 – 13**
*Some variations of print style*

ABCDEFGHIJKLMNOPQRSTUVWXYZ. Some scripts add *a* and *g* to total fifty-four. If we use any other figures than these as signs for letters, we must not assume that others will know what we mean by them.

On the other hand, we know that letters are made up of combinations of a limited number of features. All of the letters we use are made up of lines that are horizontal, vertical, and diagonal; of loops that face left or right, up or down; or loops that are closed; and dots. These ten shapes account for all fifty-four of the letter forms in English. We can say that writing English letters is a matter of writing correct or allowable combinations of those ten basic shapes.

Once children begin to experiment with writing, a period of months or years may go by before they know all of the letter forms. During that time, they may be constantly surprised that letters they know can be varied to produce new letters. For example, the letter d may be turned upside down to make a letter p, or flipped around to make a letter b. If we add two horizontal bars to the letter L, we get E; if we take the lower bar off E, we get F. Children can discover ways to make letters they didn't previously know how to make. But in the process, they are likely to invent letters that do not exist.

Clay has referred to this whole problem as the *flexibility principle*. The flexibility principle might be stated as follows: By varying letter forms that we know, we can produce letters that we didn't know how to make. But we must be careful, because not all of the letter forms we produce in this way are acceptable as signs. There is one more aspect of the flexibility principle which is of great importance to beginning writers. That is the fact that the same letter form may be written many different ways. Depending on the reading matter a child picks up, he may see quite a variety of printed forms for the same letters (see Figure 3 – 13).

Observe in Figure 3 – 14 how Carlene, a four year old, came upon the flexibility principle. Which of her figures are allowable letters? Which

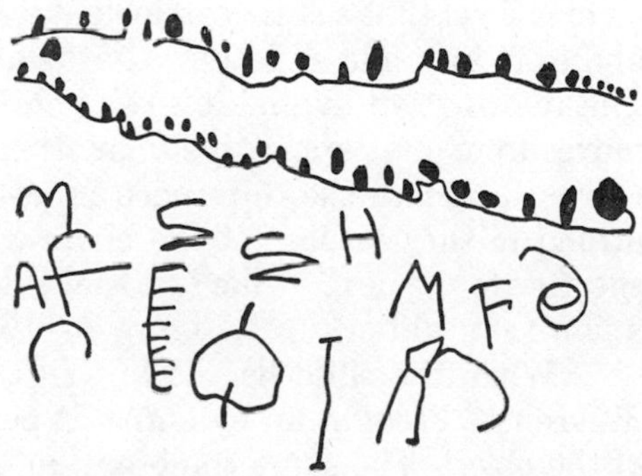

**FIGURE 3 – 14**
*Carlene*
*Age 4*
*Flexibility*
*principle*

are unallowable variations? Which ones are allowable forms that she might have invented? That is, has she produced some allowable letters by accident?

Jessie's figures all appear to be allowable letter forms (see Figure 3 – 15). But what might have influenced her to put the loops on her letters? The embellishments Jessie puts on her letters may be her attempt to imitate the serifs on standard type that she sees in books.

**FIGURE 3 – 15**
*Jessie*
*Age 4*
*Flexibility*
*principle*

When young children explore the flexibility principle, this should be considered a positive sign.[1] In this way children gain active control over the features or principles of print. It is only speculation, but it seems likely that children who explore the flexibility principle will be better able to respond appropriately to varieties of print types encountered in their reading than children who memorize letter configurations one at a time. This is because practice with the flexibility principle helps children attend to the defining features of letters, to consider what features constitute a letter and what features make it something else.

**Linear Principles and Principles of Page Arrangement**

Perhaps one of the hardest things for young children to grasp in approaching early writing is the fact that the direction in which written characters face is so important. Psychologists of perception have taught us to marvel that a child can look at a chair from the top, from the bottom, and from any side and know that what she is looking at is still a chair.[5] The information available to the child's eyes changes markedly as she moves from one perspective to another vis-à-vis the chair. Still, the child learns to ignore the difference imposed by changes in perspective and attend to the features of the chair which do not change from one perspective to the next — the fact that it has four legs, a horizontal platform, and a vertical back (see Figure 3 – 16).

When the child begins to write, the rules change. Now the visual differences brought on by shifts in perspective change the very identity of the object! The same combination of circle and stick can be the letter b, p, d, or q, depending on its arrangement in space. Writing is one of

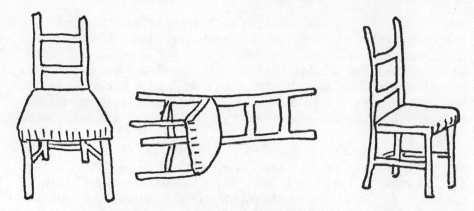

**FIGURE 3 – 16**
*A chair is still a chair, regardless of perspective*

very few areas of our experience where identity changes with direction. The orientation of letters gives children problems for months and even years as they begin to write (see Figures 3 – 17 and 3 – 18).

Directionality is also an important issue with regard to the arrangement of print on a page. When we write in English we start on the left-hand side of the page at the top, proceed straight across to the right side,

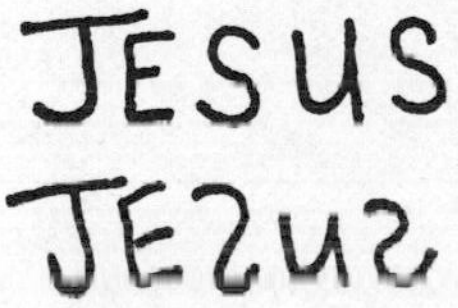

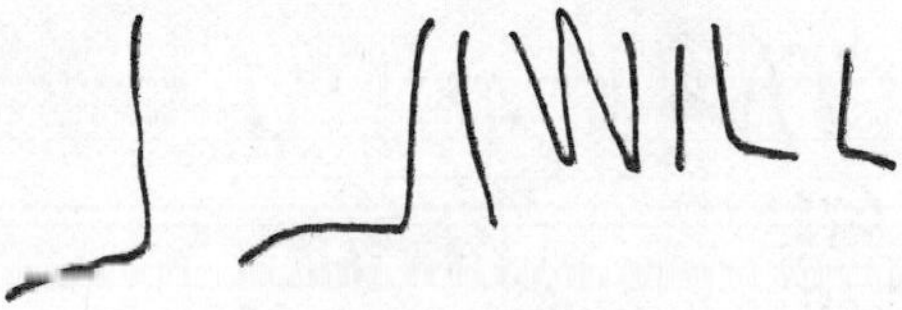

JESUS
JEZUS

**FIGURE 3 – 17**
*Jessie* (left)
*Age 5*
*Letter direction problems*

**FIGURE 3 – 18**
*Will* (right)
*Age 4*
*Started with "W" and went both ways*

return to the left, drop down one line, and proceed to the right again. This fairly complicated directional pattern is arbitrary, and it does not extend to all writing systems. Hebrew readers read across from right to left. Chinese readers read top to bottom and right to left. Ancient Greeks used to read from left to right on the first line, then right to left on the second line, then left to right on the third line. Our English pattern of left to right and top to bottom is one set of choices selected arbitrarily from many possibilities.

Clay found in a study that directional problems were common in the five and six year olds she studied in New Zealand. Most of her five year olds and many of her six year olds had not yet settled on the left-right-top-bottom pattern. Her subjects read from right to left, from bottom to top, or from the middle of the line out to either end.[1] She also noted that children continue to have directional difficulty in writing well after this issue is settled in reading.

If children draw a picture first and then write, the direction in which they arrange their print is often a matter of the best use of the space available on the page. The child in Figure 3 – 19, for instance, glued a picture onto her page first, and then wrote the text in the vertically extended space that was left over.

**FIGURE 3 – 19**
*No Name*
*Kindergarten*
*Page arrange-*
*ment variations*

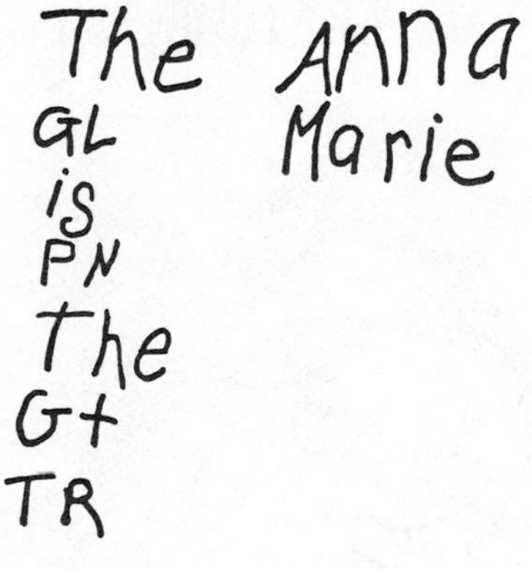

Young children's habits of directionality are remarkably fluid. Adults cannot easily write their names backwards, but many beginning writers appear able to do this with little trouble (see Figure 3 – 20).

During the time when their notions of directionality have not yet been cast solidly in favor of left-to-right, top-to-bottom, we should avoid exercises with writing that violate this principle. Note, for example, what happened to the kindergartner in Figure 3 – 21 when she was given a commercially printed worksheet to complete. The worksheet asked that she fill in the letters of the alphabet in their proper order in the cells of the snake (or is it a tapeworm?). But since the snake meandered from left to right, then from right to left, then from left to right again, the girl

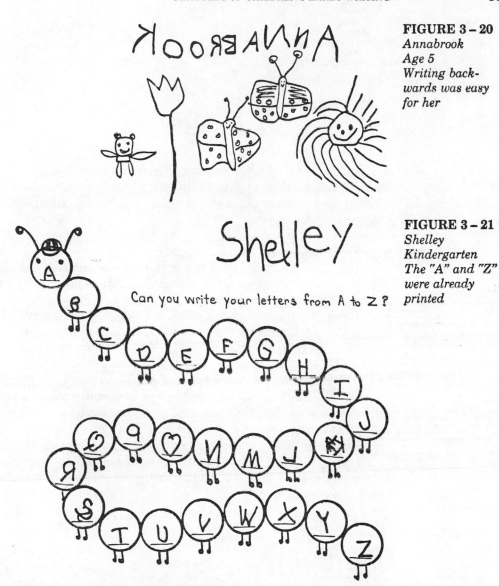

**FIGURE 3-20**
*Annabrook
Age 5
Writing back-
wards was easy
for her*

**FIGURE 3-21**
*Shelley
Kindergarten
The "A" and "Z"
were already
printed*

Can you write your letters from A to Z?

took her cue from the snake's orientation and wrote those letters backwards that were to fill the blanks running from right to left. Then she
straightened out and pointed them correctly when the snake ran from
left to right again. This was a thoughtful response to a confusing exercise.
Children deserve materials that are more sensitive to the real problems
of learning to write than this sheet was.

When children violate directional principles in writing, part of the
reason must be their tendency to focus on one letter or word at a time —
they do not appear to give much forethought to the question of how the

**FIGURE 3 – 22**
*Karan*
*Grade 2*
*Page Arrange-*
*ment problems*

whole page is to be arranged (see Figure 3 – 22). It is therefore a good idea for the teacher to give them some guidance here. In an exercise where they are drawing a picture first and then writing about it, the teacher might first

- Fold the papers from side to side so as to leave a crease separating the top of the page from the bottom. Then instruct the children to draw their picture on the top (or the bottom) and do their writing on the bottom (or the top).
- Put a green arrow on the left-hand side of the page, pointing to the right, to remind the children where to begin and which way to arrange their writing.

**Spaces
Between
Words**

In Chapter Seven of this book, in which we discuss early spelling behavior, we raise the question of whether or not beginning readers and writers know what a word is. One reason that the question comes up is that so many beginning writers give no indication of what their word units are. Or when they do, they sometimes do so incorrectly (see Figure 3 – 23). Our writing system routinely indicates word boundaries by leaving spaces between the word units in print. Beginning writers quite often fail to leave these spaces.

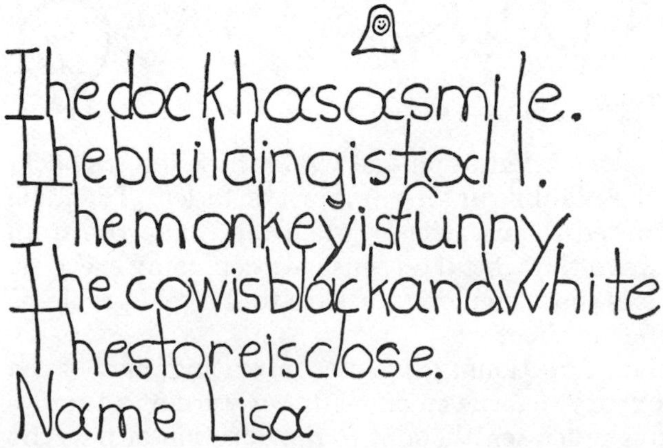

**FIGURE 3 – 23**
*Lisa*
*Grade 1*
*Word spacing*
*problems*

Thedockhasasmile.
Thebuildingistall.
Themonkeyisfunny.
The cowisblackandwhite
Thestoreisclose.
Name Lisa

Nevertheless, a child's failure to leave spaces between words should not be taken too quickly to indicate that she doesn't know that the words exist as separate units. It happens that leaving spaces is a highly abstract procedure for children to manage. The present writer remembers his difficulty some years ago when reading an introductory book on architecture. The book called attention to the use of positive and negative space in building design. Positive space is what you put in; negative space is what you leave out. At the time, negative space seemed a very difficult concept to work with. The space left between words is negative space, and the concept probably causes difficulty for children, also. Many children appear to prefer inserting periods between words rather than leaving spaces. It seems that they prefer to manipulate positive rather than negative space (see Figure 3 – 24).

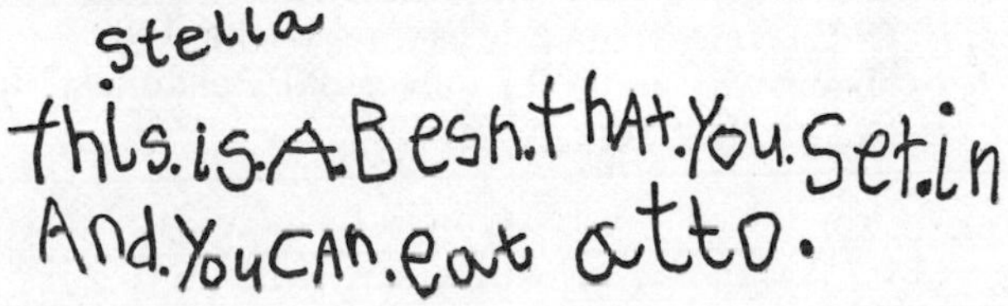

stella

this.is.A.Besh.that.You.Set.in And.YouCAn.eat atto.

**FIGURE 3 – 24**
*Stella*
*Grade 1*
*Indicating word*
*spacing with*
*periods*

The features of early writing which children use to distinguish writing from nonwriting (see Chapter One) parallel very closely the principles and concepts that are displayed in the early writing children produce themselves.

**Conclusion**

Lavine's feature of *nonpictoriality* — that pictures are not writing — shows up as Clay's *sign concept* — that signs represent objects or ideas but not directly the way pictures do. Lavine's *variety* feature — that writing consists of strings of different letters, not the same one repeated over and over — is much like Clay's *generative principle* — that a few letters can be made to look like writing if they are written over and over in varied order. Lavine's *multiplicity* feature — that writing must consist of many characters — reminds us of Clay's *recurring principle* — that a simple move may be repeated over and over and strung across a page to look like writing.

There are more parallels as well as some differences — these especially being related to the greater difficulty involved in producing forms that look like letters compared to the task of discriminating writing from nonwriting.

A more important difference between Lavine's work and Clay's is that Lavine associated certain features with greater levels of maturity in writing development. Clay made no such distinction but rather suggested that as more of her early graphic principles showed up in a child's writing, the more mature he was likely to be as a writer.

Future research may allow us to draw firmer conclusions about children's writing development from the examination of the emerging principles in their productions. At present, all we can say is that these principles do turn up in all the young children's writing we've seen. They seem to be signs that the child is actively exploring the writing system. This exploration normally leads to progress in writing.

**References**

1. Marie Clay. *What Did I Write?* Exeter, N.H.: Heinemann Educational Books, 1975.
2. Linda Lavine. *The Development of Perception of Writing in Pre-Reading Children: A Cross-Cultural Study.* Ph.D. dissertation, Cornell University, 1972. Xerox University Microfilms, 73 – 6657.
3. Emilia Ferreiro and Ana Teberosky. *El Sistema de la Escritura en el Desarollo del Niño.* Mexico City: Siglo XX, 1979.
4. Marie Clay. *Reading: The Patterning of Complex Behavior.* 2d ed. Exeter, N.H.: Heinemann Educational Books, 1980.
5. Jerome Bruner. "On Perceptual Readiness," in *Beyond the Information Given.* New York: Norton, 1976.

# 4

# What Children Do with Early Graphics

In the previous two chapters we have observed that children learn about writing not by acquiring letters one after another but by first becoming sensitive to the features of written language. Before children use a selection of letters with any stability, we see first a slow revelation of certain graphic principles in the children's scribbles — principles such as *directionality, flexibility, generativity*, and *recurrence*. With repeated writing practice children produce marks which more and more closely resemble the writing they see in the print around them. This learning proceeds not letter by letter but feature by feature. But *why* do children go through this learning process in the first place? What are children trying to do when they make scribble after scribble, only gradually producing letter forms that look like those of adults?

It will be our task in this chapter to consider children's purposes for their earliest writing. We will first try to understand what children are trying to get done when they commit marks to paper, considering both the reasons behind the marks they select and the overall communicative purposes. Then in a later section we will discuss ways that parents and teachers of young children can aid children in making a beginning in writing, by providing appropriate help but not pressure.

In Chapter Three, we noted a basic difference between pictures and writing. We observed that writing uses signs to stand for things in an arbitrary way; we must refer to some previously agreed upon social meanings of written signs in order to interpret them correctly.

Children are capable of making signs on paper before they develop a concept of the way the signs represent things. It is interesting to examine children's early writing to determine how they think writing might

**Children Write on Their Own**

*The sign concept, revisited*

43

**FIGURE 4 – 1**

*The way writing represents language for fluent readers*

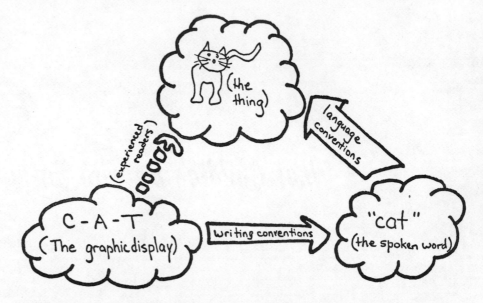

represent things. Some of the most interesting research into this question has been performed by Emilia Ferreiro,[1] an Argentine psychologist. In order to understand Ferreiro's ideas, let us begin with an illustration. In the English that we adults read and write, we may say that written figures represent letters that combine into representations of words, which stand for real or imaginary things. We may illustrate this series of relationships by means of the diagram in Figure 4 – 1.

Some children who are new to writing hypothesize relations between writing and language which are different from the relations we described in Figure 4 – 1. Emilia Ferreiro worked with some four- and five-year-old children in Argentina who had some exotic notions about how writing represents language.

One little boy named Javier said "cat" could be written O i A,

while "kittens" could be written OAi OAi OAi.

Ferreiro concluded that he had the following hypotheses about the relation between writing and the things represented by writing:

1. written words for similar things should *look* similar, even though the spoken words for those objects may not *sound* the same; and
2. when characters refer to more than one object, the child uses *more* characters to represent them.

Ferreiro found many children who thought there might be a concrete relation between written marks and the things they stood for. She suggested that there may be a developmental continuum that would have children looking first for concrete relations between graphic characters and the things they stood for *without reference to sound.*

At a later stage, the relation between graphics and language became based on sound. Specifically, the children put the same number of letters in a graphic display as the number of syllables in the spoken word for which the graphic display stood. Thus, "chicken" was written ⌠ ∕ and "fencepost" ♪ ↘ . There is no relation between the graphic characters and the individual speech sounds in either word. Letters are used as syllable counters only, in this sort of writing.

In terms of the diagram in Figure 4 – 1, Ferreiro's finding was that children first —

1.  look for a concrete relation between $A$ and $C$ (see Figure 4 – 2),
2.  and only later for a *sound* relation between $A$ and $B$ (see Figure 4 – 3).

Ferreiro gathered her findings from work with children who came from both uneducated and upper-class families in Argentina and Mexico. As a group, the subjects from uneducated families probably had less exposure to print than children in the United States. Perhaps that ex-

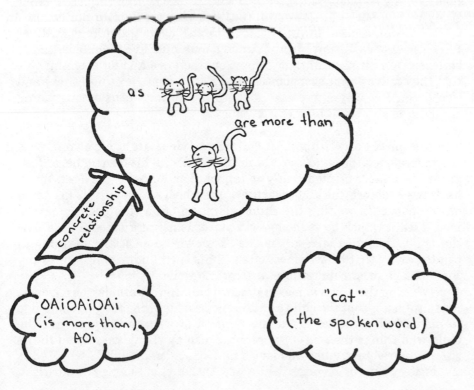

**FIGURE 4 – 2**
*Concrete relation
of letters to
language*

FIGURE 4–3
*Sound relation-
ship of letters to
language*

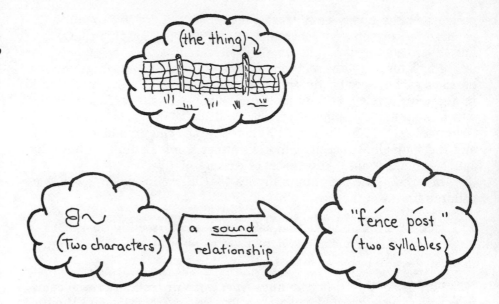

plains why we the authors have seen so little evidence of Ferreiro's findings in four year olds we have worked with. This whole issue needs further
study with children in other cultures, including the United States.

The *sign concept* in American children's early graphics is still not
fully understood in any depth. Among four and five year olds, many
children think it natural that graphic characters stand for something —
that they convey some sort of message. Exactly *how* they think sticks and
circles could convey a message, if there is any consensus among young
children, is still something of a mystery.

### Writing your own name

The first pieces of writing most children produce are their own names.
In kindergarten the child's coat bin is marked with his own name. In first
grade his name is printed neatly on tagboard and taped to his desk. When
he draws a picture, his kindergarten or preschool teacher prints his name
on the paper. In writing the child's name so often the teacher may be
motivated as much by management concerns as instructional ones. For
the child, though, the result is that his own name is the meaningful
printed array that he sees most often in his surroundings. It is certainly
the message most children first attempt to write.

Writing their own names may teach children several lessons at once.
Ferreiro[1] notes that the child's own name provides the first real challenge
to his early hypotheses about the relation of writing to language. The
child who thinks the *size* of the graphic display should be related to the
size of the referent must wonder as he looks at name labels why Ted is
the biggest boy in the class, while he, Anthony, is among the smallest.

In a similar vein, the child who relates the number of characters in a graphic display to the number of syllables in the word for which it stands will wonder why "Ma-ry" has four letters while "Keith" has five.

The children's early hypotheses cannot explain the spelling of their own and their classmates' names. So they look for new hypotheses. As we shall see in Section Two of this book, children's thinking about spelling will go through many interesting changes before the children learn to spell correctly.

Learning to write one's own name carries with it another advantage for the learner. The name becomes a repertory of known letters. That is, letters that one gains in the course of learning to write one's own name can be recombined to form other words. Note in Figure 4 – 4 how Annabrook, age six, used many of the letters in her name to write two additional words. The child's own name as a repertory of known letters also pays off in a more abstract sense. As we noted in our discussion of Clay's *flexibility principle,* a beginning writer can start with a standard letter and embellish it until it becomes another letter. Thus, the letter L with a few more horizontal lines becomes ⊾, E, Ɛ, and F, two of which are standard letters. Knowing how to write his own name may give a child a fairly good variety of letter forms, a point of departure for coming up with still other letter forms by means of the flexibility principle.

ANNABROOK

SHOOK

A BOOK

**FIGURE 4 – 4**
*Annabrook*
*Grade 1*

Learning their own names is a trailblazing event in children's writing for another reason. The process by which children learn to write their own names may be repeated to enable the children to write other words.

Clay[2] points to three common processes children use to begin writing words and longer messages. The processes are *tracing, copying,* and *generating.* It is not claimed that children will always employ each of these processes in the order used here. However, tracing does seem to be the easiest of the three, with copying being the next most difficult, and generating being the most difficult process. Some children trace, then generate. Others copy, then generate.

Many children trace spontaneously, without being instructed to. Carlene, age 4:4, traced first, then copied. Her sample gives an indication of the relative difficulty of the two tasks (see Figure 4 – 5).

**Strategies for Early Writing**

**FIGURE 4–5**
*Carlene*
*Age 4*

**FIGURE 4–6**
*Carlene*
*Age 4*

Note in Figure 4–6, however, that she was generating letterlike graphics at the same time she produced Figure 4–5. Her generated products are more abundant than those she either traced or copied, but they are not limited to standard letters. This conforms to a finding of Clay's; namely, that copying may be a shortcut to accuracy, but most children prefer to generate letter forms on their own over copying. Her subjects stayed at the task much longer when they were generating, rather than copying.

Which strategy is best? Ultimately, we want children to be able to write letters on their own without having to rely on a model of correctly formed letters to copy. On the other hand, they must eventually learn to produce standard letter forms — not just invented ones. Generating letters is the process children should aim for, but they should pay attention to the details of standard letters. In our schools many children need to be encouraged to take risks — to rely on their own devices and generate writing even if it's "wrong." Nevertheless, there are a few children who are less mindful than they should be of the ultimately conservative nature of the writing system; that is, that there *is* a right way to make each letter. Teachers can safely encourage children to generate, knowing that they will copy anyway. With an occasional child it may be necessary to encourage copying. In our opinion, copying is probably encouraged far more often than need be.

Children's own names are usually the first objects of print to be traced, copied, and eventually generated. But after performing these feats with their names, the children do not hesitate to carry them out with other words, known or unknown.

Clay noted that "until I observed five year olds closely I had no idea that they took stock of their own learning systematically."[2] She was referring to what she called the *inventory principle:* the widespread tendency of beginning writers to make ordered lists of letters or words they can write. Next to writing their own names, then, are listed *inventories* as objects of children's first writing efforts.

*The inventory principle*

Jessica's first compositions consisted of inventories of letters she could write. These were the sole content of her writing for some months. Another first-grade child offered inventories when her teacher asked the whole class to write something about a picture. She did not feel free to compose on that topic, apparently, so she listed her known words instead (see Figure 4 – 7).

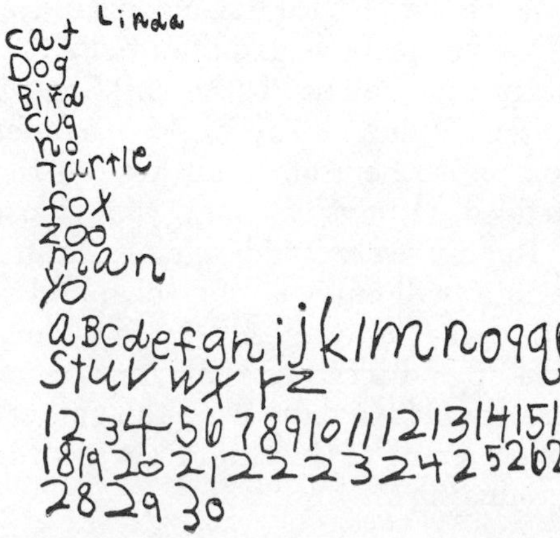

**FIGURE 4 – 7**
*Linda*
*Grade 1*

**Parents and Teachers Encourage Early Exploration of Print**

In the present section we will discuss ways that parents have found to encourage their children to explore early writing. These ways take the form of adding drawing and play writing to the things children naturally explore during their day.

The kind of encouragement children can profit by is of three types:

1. having plenty of models of print at children's height around the house;
2. having materials that the children can write upon, and utensils with which to write; and
3. asking an occasional question, or setting up an occasional challenge, that will lead the child to emulate print.

*Providing models of writing*

Probably the best way to encourage children to explore writing — by which we mean both the act of writing and the writing that is produced — is to have plenty of models of both senses of writing around for children to imitate. The obvious starting point for showing children models of print is to read to them. Reading to children on at least a daily basis is a necessary nutrient for their growing literacy. This is true for many reasons, one of which is that the children gain, by being read to, a notion that print is somehow a means to a desirable end — a good story. When reading to children, it is a good idea occasionally to point to the words as you read. Marie Clay has found that many children entering school do not realize that in a storybook it is the print and not the pictures that provides the words that mother or father reads. Given a storybook that has both a picture and an array of print on a page, she tests this understanding by asking the child: "Put your finger where I should read." She observes to see whether he puts his finger on the print or on the picture.[3]

There are other good models of print, too. Labels on things around the house are good sources of print. If the child draws a picture that the parent wants to hang on the refrigerator, it is useful to put the child's name on the picture (for older children the parent can ask the child to "name" the picture, and then write the name on the picture for him, too). Things that belong to the child can be labeled, also. A toybox can be painted, "Jimmy's Toybox." With older children, making signs on paper and taping them on items around the house, the labeling idea can be extended without reducing your house's resale value! "Jimmy's room," or "Tommy's secret hiding place," can be written around in places where the child will enjoy seeing them and enjoy telling others what they say. Print makes messages. Print is arranged in horizontal displays. Print is made up of discrete graphic units some of which are repeated, but never more than two right next to each other. All of these concepts can be brought home to the child from meaningful print that is displayed in his surroundings.

Another sort of modeling that is extremely valuable to children who may wish to explore writing is to have someone else write in their presence. Is writing a worthwhile activity? If it is, then adults should be seen doing it. Is writing a regular and important part of human communication? If it is, then adults should be seen doing it. For many adults, writing is a source of pleasure, an opportunity to reflect and think clearly. It is sometimes an occasion of frustration and hard work. Do children get a chance to see adults and older brothers and sisters approaching writing seriously? The ones who do are likely to be eager to get started becoming writers, too.

The spouse of one of the authors was writing a children's book one year, at a time when their daughters were four and six years old. Everyday the mother would go into her bedroom and sit down before the big drafting table. There for one to two hours she would write and draw, throw away, and rewrite and redraw. Occasionally the rest of the family got a glimpse of what she had produced. The children were captivated by the mystery of the quiet room where mother would go and create, and enthralled by the fragments of story and flashes of colorful pictures mother would share with them from time to time.

Soon the four year old had taken to stealing away quietly to her bedroom, too. She would stay sometimes for twenty or thirty minutes at a stretch, after which she would bring out writings for the rest of the family to read (see Figure 4–8). Though more than two years have passed, and the girl's writing has picked up rules of spelling and composition, she has really never stopped writing since the day she decided to imitate her mother.

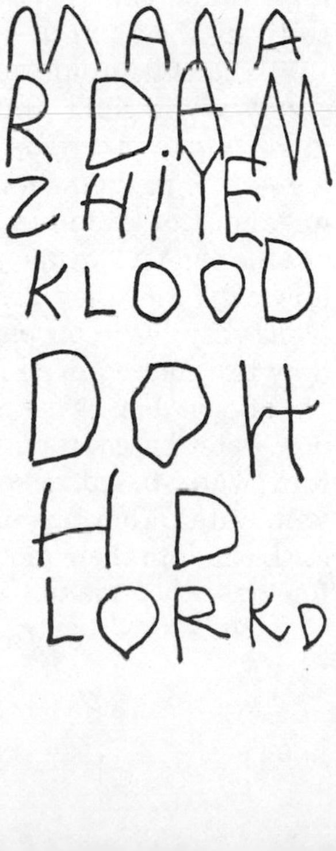

MANA
RDAM
ZHIYE
KLOOD

DOH
HD
LORKD

**FIGURE 4–8**
*Jessie*
*Age 4*

The central message parents put across to children when they write in front of them is that writing is important; it is a worthy use of time. But there must be other messages as well. All of the *dynamic* principles of writing must be observed in process to be understood. If writing proceeds from left to right, then children must see someone doing it to comprehend this point. If writing can record a message and convey it to a distant receiver, then children must participate in the family drama of remembering absent friends, thinking of a message for them, writing the messages down, sealing them up, and mailing them out. The purpose of all of this is made especially clear if the child is invited to slip in a message of her own, and even more so if she receives something back.

**Writing materials in the home**

There are some people reading these pages who must be saying to themselves: "Hey! My problem is not to get my baby to write, but to keep him from writing all over everything!" If we consider the child's early communicative attempts with the medium of strained asparagus, it does seem odd to take up space here to describe materials children can use to write on in the home. Almost anything will do, the only guiding considerations being (1) the safety of the child; (2) the well-being of your wall and furniture; and (3) cheapness and convenience.

In order to protect your house — to take that point first — it is a good idea to get your child in the habit of asking for paper to write or draw on and then to be generous with it when she *does* ask. In this way the child is not in the position to try to decide for herself what is or is not an allowable surface for writing. Most preschool children cannot always be trusted to pass up a newly painted wall, or the back of your automobile registration papers, when they have the urge to write. So it is best to cultivate the habit of asking, and to provide paper when they do.

The child's safety would militate against giving a sharp pencil to a very young child. But very young children do not sustain an interest in writing anyway. By the time children do become interested in writing — say, in their fourth and fifth years — a standard-sized pencil is a fine thing for them to write with. We normally hear that children should use the big, fat "primary pencils" first. But the children seem to find them unwieldy, and they are disappointed by the faint and indistinct silver trails they leave on paper. Our children prefer a *pencil* pencil, though they like colored marking pens even better.

Colored marking pens come in all shapes and sizes, too. Markers are now water based, though the first ones on the market were the indelible sort. Water-based markers leave writing that can be washed off walls with water. They are also not harmful to the children if they happen to stick one into their mouths. The children like the colors and the distinct fine lines they make.

For safety's sake, it is a good idea to make a rule against children running with pencils in hand, or roughhousing when they have pencils, or generally crowding up too much on each other when they are writing. Writing is inherently a quiet and solitary activity, and writers know it. These rules are more necessary to enforce for the nonwriters in your family or preschool than the writers; that is, you sometimes have to point out to other children not to leap on the back of a child who is writing.

Practically any sort of paper is good for children to use to explore writing. It is probably best if it is not lined. Dealing with the proper height and staying on a horizontal line are unnecessarily difficult concerns to a child who is simply fooling around with the letter forms. The lines do not seem to help at first and may even be a hindrance. Therefore, there is no reason why parents or preschool teachers should buy paper for children to write on. The back side of practically any paper will do. Old memos from the office are perfect. Maybe even better is computer paper, since the big format seems to invite big ideas. Any university computing center and most businesses have tons of used computer paper around.

In addition to modeling writing and providing writing materials, a parent or teacher can lead children to find challenge and delight in writing by means of a well-considered and timely suggestion. The best of these suggestions seem to be situational. That is, a person who spends time with a child or a group of children will know of things that interest them and can often extend this interest into writing with a good suggestion.

*Making good suggestions to children to get them writing*

A friend of ours invites her child to write each time she writes herself. When the mother is writing out a grocery list, she hands her daughter a piece of paper and asks her to make out a list of things she wants to buy, too.

Another parent works writing into the children's play. If a child comes to her and complains that her brother is not picking up his shoes from the living room floor, the mother says: "I'll tell you what. You be the policeman and write him a ticket. You can leave the ticket in his shoes."

Of course these writings will be unreadable by a stranger, but in the context of the situation they were written in they have meaning. And they are fun ways for children to begin to explore writing.

As already mentioned, children like to be invited to slip a note into a letter that their parents are writing to a friend or relative. Contributing a note — whether it is on a separate piece of paper or is written on the bottom of someone else's page — is less responsibility than writing the whole letter, even if it is understood that the child doesn't really know how to write. The child knows that the parent can explain what the child meant to say; but it *is* an added pleasure to the recipient of the letter to hear directly from the child.

Another suggestion that works in some households is for the parent to hand the child some paper and some markers and invite her to write something. For many children, that is all that is needed to get them started. But occasionally a child will not write. Perhaps it is reluctance to do something he knows he does not do correctly. After all, a child who has seen models of print around him in books recognizes immediately that what he himself writes on paper looks almost nothing like what he sees in books. (That is another reason why the parent's own writing is a very important model for children who would be beginning writers.) How do we get such children started? The first advice is for the mother and father to write themselves in the child's presence — and then invite the child to try it. But if that doesn't work, the parent might show the child a page from this book. Show the child another child's bold efforts to make things that look like writing. We've known children to say: "Oh, I can do better than *that!*" and then write up a storm.

## Conclusion

The earliest stage of writing is a sort of make-believe: children make designs that look like writing, but are still a long way from the real thing. Like other kinds of children's play, this make-believe writing is serious business — it is experience from which children learn.

As Ferreiro has shown us, children may be speculating on the ways in which written marks can represent ideas. They also seem to be experimenting to see where writing comes from: whether it is most efficiently produced by tracing, copying, or by generating marks of their own.

Finally, as in many other areas of endeavor, early writers are forming attitudes and behavior patterns. Some approach the task of writing with curiosity, energy, and confidence; others do not approach it at all. Some seek to make their own sense of how the writing system works; others wait to be shown. Some children experiment boldly and make mistakes; others do not experiment for fear of making mistakes. Some of the difference between children is attributable, no doubt, to deep-seated differences in personality. But to a degree, children's daring, initiative, and enthusiasm can be encouraged by parents and teachers. In the case of writing it is certainly in their interests to give them this encouragement.

## References

1. Emilia Ferreiro and Ana Teberosky. *El Sistema de la Escritura en el Desarollo del Niño*. Mexico City: Siglo XX, 1979.
2. Marie Clay. *What Did I Write?* Exeter, N.H.: Heinemann Educational Books, 1975.
3. Marie Clay. *Concepts about Print Test*. Exeter, N.H.: Heinemann Educational Books, 1975.

# Exercises for part one

1. The cards in Figure 1 are taken from Lavine's early writing experiment. Which *distinctive features* of writing are present in each of
   the cards? Which are missing?

2. When Lavine asked children to decide which of her cards contained
   "writing" and which did not, there were differences between the
   responses of the three year olds and the five year olds. The younger
   children said some types of graphic displays were writing which the
   older children said were not, and vice versa. Write a number 3 beside
   each of the cards in Figure 1 that you believe the three year olds

**FIGURE 1**

but not the five year olds would have considered to be writing. Write
the number 5 beside each of the cards that you believe the five year
olds but not the three year olds would have called writing. Explain
your choices.

3.  In Figures 2 to 7 see how many examples you can find of:
    • the recurring principle;
    • the generative principle;
    • the sign concept;
    • the flexibility principle;
    • letter-orientation principles; and
    • page-arrangement and word-spacing principles.

**FIGURE 2**

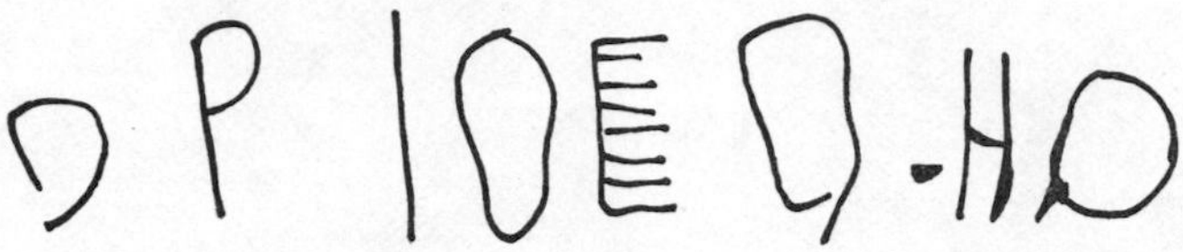

**FIGURE 3**

**FIGURE 4**

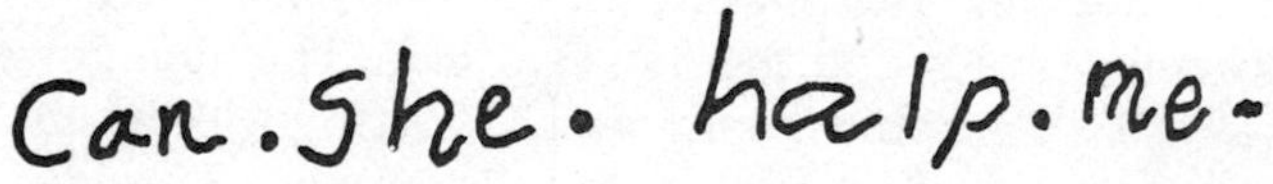

**FIGURE 5**

**FIGURE 6**
**(left)**

**FIGURE 7**
**(right)**

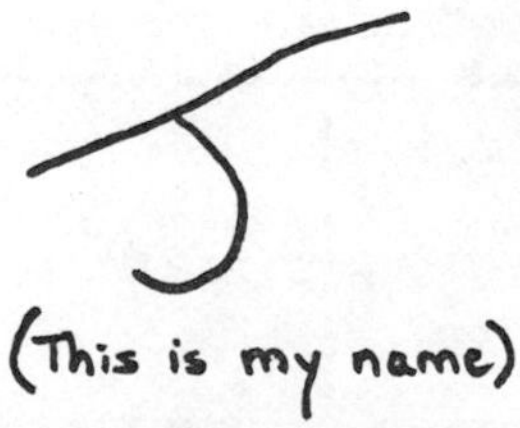

(This is my name)

# II

# The Beginnings of Spelling

A four year old produces a string of letterlike forms that looks like writing (see Figure 1). A five year old deliberates carefully, inscribes a sparse collection of letters on the page, and claims it says: "Our car broke down." (See Figure 2.)

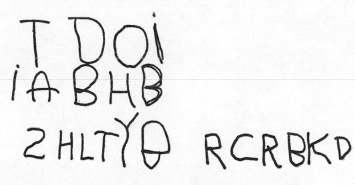

**FIGURE 1**
*Jessie* (left)
*Age 4*
*These letters represent no sounds*

**FIGURE 2**
*No Name* (right)
*Age 5*
*This says, "Our car broke down."*

These two presentations differ in more than appearance. The four year old is trying to make forms that look like writing, but the five year old is trying to make her letters do what writing does.

Writing uses marks to represent words. The marks represent words according to a socially agreed upon set of relationships. In some writing systems like Chinese the relationship holds between symbols and whole words. In others like Japanese it holds between symbols and syllables. In alphabetic systems like English it holds between symbols and individual speech sounds, or "phonemes" as they are called. Anyone who wants to write must know what unit of language written symbols represent.

57

The would-be writer must also know how the symbols do the representing. In our English language particularly, weathered old tongue that it is, the relations between symbols and phonemes have become somewhat peculiar — knowable, but peculiar. Beginning writers of English seem to proceed like this: they first discover the unit of language the symbols are to represent (word, syllable, or phoneme); they invent a plausible way for the symbols to represent language units; then they revise their invented spelling in favor of the standard spelling used around them.

# 5

# *Invented Spelling*

Some years ago George Bernard Shaw, the British playwright, told of an acquaintance of his named Fish, who did not like the conventional way of writing his name and came up with the spelling GHOTIUGH. This spelling, he argued, found precedent in the spelling of common English words. The letters GH for the sound of *f* in his name was established in the spelling of the word "tou*gh*"; the O for the short sound of *i* is found in "w*o*men"; the TI for *sh* is heard in words like "ini*ti*al," "ter*ti*ary," and "spa*ti*al"; finally, the letters UGH are silent, as in "tho*ugh*."

This story points out some of the more bizarre relations that seem to obtain between sounds in English words and the letters that represent them. And if each letter in a word is to have a clearly identifiable sound, some disappointment is inevitable. Just look at the spellings of some of the following words: What is the sound of the *i* in "complaint"? Of the *e* in "failure"? Of the second *l* in "spellings"? Of the *a* in "each"? And of the *h* in "paragraph"?

A large portion of the words in English contain letters that do not themselves directly represent sounds.

Look, however, at the words in the sentences in Figures 5 – 1 and 5 – 2, written by the beginning speller, Annabrook.

Every one of Annabrook's letters represents a sound. There are no "silent" letters, no extra letters at all.

The early spellings that children produce on their own — we call them invented spellings — observe the same dictum: "letters talk." Any letter that a child puts in a word is intended to represent some sound.

Why children select the letters they do to represent sounds presents a problem. Why is Virginia spelled FRJEYE? Why does it begin with the

**FIGURE 5–1**
*Annabrook*
*Grade 1*
*Invented spelling*

I   GOT BET
BAT M SKED A S
AN ET HRT.

**FIGURE 5–2**
*Annabrook*
*Grade 1*
*Invented spelling*

I   EM GONE
TO FRIEY E AN
I  HAVa HECAC

letter F? Why are the last two vowels E's? Why is "bit" spelled BET and not BIT? Why does "it," ET, follow the same pattern? As we shall see in this chapter, there are usually very good reasons why young spellers choose the letters they do to represent sounds. Seen together, these reasons constitute what has been called a system of spelling "logic."[1] Our purpose in this chapter will be to make this logic explicit, so that the reader can understand invented spelling the same way a child does.

**Letter-Name Spelling**

Recall the sample we saw in Chapter One: YUTS A LADE YET FEHEG AD HE KOT FLEPR. ("Once a lady went fishing and she caught Flipper.") This sample fits the pattern we have just described: Every letter in the sample stands for a sound, and no letters are supplied unnecessarily. Let's try to determine why the child chose the letters she did to represent the sounds in those words.

Notice the spelling YUTS for "once" and YET for "went." Why the letter Y for the sound we normally represent with a letter W? The answer lies in the names by which each letter is known. The letter Y is called "wye" and W is called "double-yu." Which name sounds more like the beginning sound in "once" and "went"?

The child who wrote YUTS A LADE . . . is apparently using a letter to spell a sound if the name of the letter closely resembles the sound. This technique for spelling has been called the *letter-name strategy*.[2] The letter-name strategy accounts for the spellings of almost all the letters in YUTS A LADE YET FEHEG AD HE KOT FLEPR.

Two factors influence the use of the letter-name strategy in determining which letters will represent what sounds in a word. The first factor is the availability (or lack of it) of a good letter-name-to-sound match. The English alphabet has twenty-six letters, but the English language has forty-four standard sounds, or "phonemes." Some of the sounds children wish to spell have ready matches in letter names. For others no direct letter-name matches exist. In these latter cases children will select the nearest fit and have good reasons — albeit subconscious ones — for the selections they make.

The second factor involved in the choice of letters for spellings has more to do with the sounds in words themselves. As we noted above, when speech sounds come together in words, some odd things happen to them. Some sounds are changed around, and children perceive changes that we don't and tend to spell what they hear. Some are overshadowed by others and not heard distinctly. Let's consider a range of possible sound and letter combinations and see what happens when children put the letter-name strategy into practice.

As Daryl's sample shows (Figure 5 – 3), initial consonants, consonants that come at the beginning of a word, usually find close matches to letter names. The name "ell" has in it the first sound in the word "live." "Tee" for "Texas" is clear enough, as is "em" for "my." Note that "gee" does not match the initial consonant sound in "Goliad," which begins like "gold." Neither does the letter name "aitch" sound anything like the beginning sound of "house." Daryl has learned that letter G represents the beginning sound of "gold" and that the letter H represents the "huh" sound in the beginning of "house."

*Initial consonants*

IL NgL eADTX S

**FIGURE 5 – 3**
*Daryl*
*Grade 1*
*Early invented spelling*

The letter N in Daryl's sentence stands for the word "in" — a reasonable procedure since the name of the letter sounds the same as the word.

A sample of Daryl's writing taken a month after the first shows the initial consonants still being unambiguously represented, and his words filled out in other ways, too (see Figure 5 – 4).

**FIGURE 5–4**
*Daryl*
*Grade 1*
*Later invented*
*spelling*

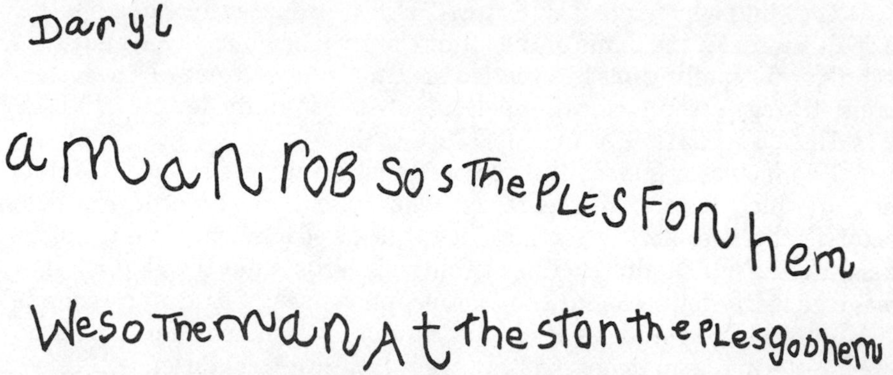

Daryl

a man rob sos the ples for hem

weso ther man at the ston the ples goo hem

In this sample, the G's and the H's are used correctly — not as letter-name matches, but for their representational value.

What sort of problems do beginning consonants present young spellers? Which ones work by letter name, and which ones by an arbitrary presentational relationship?

Table 5 – 1 lists all the consonants that have a stable and predictable letter-name match.

**TABLE 5 – 1**
*Letter-name matches for consonants*

| Sound | Letter | Examples |
|---|---|---|
| *b* as in bat | B | BBGON (B B gun) BABE (baby) B (be) BEG (big) BLW (blue) |
| *p* as in pat | P | PEC (pick) PAT (pet) PLAG (playing) POGOSTECK PANS (pants) |
| *f* as in fat | F | FEH (fish) FES (friends) FEN (friend) FOWS (flowers) FAS (face) AFTR (after) |
| *v* as in very | V | HAV (have) LUV (love) LEV (live) VOT (vote) |
| *m* as in man | M | MI (my) HOM (home) MENEKDE (manicotti) GAM (game) MOTR (mother) |
| *n* as in note | N | NAM (name) NIS (nice) EN (in) BLON (balloon) NAW (now) |
| *t* as in tan | T | TXS (Texas) TIM (time) DOT (don't) WUT (what) SURT (shirt) |
| *d* as in Dan | D | DOT (don't) GLEAD (Goliad) DESES (dishes) TODA (today) |

| Sound | Letter | Examples |
|-------|--------|----------|
| *s* as in sun | S | BICS (bikes) HAS (house) SCIEY (sky) SIK (sick) SUMS (swims) |
| *k* as in kick | K | SIK (sick) WRCK (work) KAT (can't) SKIY (sky) SEK (sick) TAK (take) |
| *j* as in joke | J | JOPT (jumped) JEP (jeep) |
| *z* as in zoo | Z | PLEZ (please) ZB (zebra) |
| *l* as in lay | L | LETL (little) LAS (last) PLES (police) PLANS (planes) BLON (balloon) LAT (let) |
| *r* as in ray | R | RETTE (ready) RAD (red) GRAON (ground) STOR (store) |

Other consonants, like G and H, do not have a letter-name match with the sounds they normally represent. Nevertheless, they regularly represent one sound, and they appear frequently enough to be learned easily by children. Table 5 – 2 shows these "representational" consonants.

Spelling like WRRX for "works" and HAWS for "house" are so strange to the eye it is safe to conclude that the children who created them were not imitating anyone else, or dimly remembering a standard spelling they had seen somewhere. These are 100 percent original! Yet as far from standard spelling as they are, they do employ the consonants C, G, H, W, and Y to represent their standard sound values. So the

| Sound | Letter | Examples |
|-------|--------|----------|
| *k* as in kick | C | CENT (can't) PEC (pick) CUM (come) CLAS (clouds) CADY (candy) |
| *g* as in good | G | GUD (good) GAM (game) GLEAD (Goliad) GOWE (going) GIT (get) |
| *h* as in hay | H | HOO (who) HED (head) HEM (him) HAS (house) HORS (horse) |
| *w* as in way | W | WUT (what) WET (went) WEO (will) WERRE (wearing) WEH (with) WRRX (works) |
| *y* as in yes | Y | YALO (yellow) YOR (your) YASEDA (yesterday) YIU (you) |

**TABLE 5 – 2**
*Representational consonants*

children must have learned something about spelling from someone out-side of themselves; these relationships cannot be invented.

There is another type of consonant representation that children have more difficulty mastering. This is the spelling of consonant digraphs.

**Consonant digraphs**

Anyone who trains as a reading teacher comes across the terms *consonant blend* and *consonant digraph*. After a few years of teaching, though, a person is likely to have forgotten the difference between them. Knowing the difference between a blend and a digraph is probably not necessary to successful reading instruction. But digraphs do present serious challenges to young spellers.

The word digraph comes from the Greek, meaning "double writing." It describes a single sound spelled with two letters. The "ph" in "digraph" is a digraph, since the two letters together spell a single sound (which is often represented by the letter F).

The *gr* sound in the word "digraph" is not a digraph but a blend. Blends occur when the letters which represent two or three distinct consonant sounds are pronounced closely together. *Cl* in "closely" is a blend, as is the *bl* in "blend." Blends differ from digraphs in that it is possible to hear each of the sounds which make up a blend, if you pronounce the blend slowly. The same is not true of digraphs. No matter how slowly you pronounce the word "digraph," you will never hear separate sounds for the p and h.

Young spellers seem to perceive correctly that digraphs represent one sound. What they do not know is that digraphs have to be spelled with two letters and not one. So invented spellers are forced to puzzle out which individual letters are best suited to represent digraphs. Note in Figure 5 – 5 what one first grader did with the digraphs.

**FIGURE 5 – 5**
*Joey*
*Grade 1*
*Note spellings of*
th

FIDI I SOR THE BLA AJLS
TA R APRLNS TA CRT IHOVR
AO FOL UP NTU VE CLALS

The digraph *th* received three different spellings. "The" was correct, but it is likely that Joey had memorized the spelling of this word as a whole. In "they" he spelled it T, twice. In "each other," IHOVR, he spelled it V — and he used the same spelling for *th* the second time he wrote "the."

Note, too, his spelling of the digraph *ch* in "each other": IHOVR. In both digraphs, *th* and *ch*, Joey's tendency was to represent the single sound with a single letter.

On what basis did he choose the letters to represent the sounds? Again the basis seems to be the similarity between the sound to be represented and the name of a letter of the alphabet. The spelling of the H in I*H*OVR is an interesting example of this. Say to yourself the letter-name H ("aitch"). Note the *ch* sound contained in that name. If you sound out the names of all the letters of the alphabet, you will not find another that contains the sound *ch*. Of all the single letters that could spell the digraph *ch,* the letter H is the best choice.

There is no such clear candidate to represent the digraph *th*. The child made two inventive entries: T and V. In order to understand why those two consonants should both be good choices to represent the sound of *th,* we must digress for a moment to explore the question of how we make consonant sounds.

**How We Make Speech Sounds: A Long but Necessary Digression**

To begin: It won't surprise anyone to hear that breath is the substance of speech. But there is more to speech than breathing. We direct our breath through the vocal bands in the throat, and the resulting vibration of these vocal bands makes the sound that we call our voice. Stretching or loosening these bands makes our voice go up or down.

Breath and vocal bands, however, still do not give us speech. The activation of those two alone will enable us to (1) cry and (2) ooh and ah. (No wonder these are children's first utterances!) But we still cannot *say* anything without adding something more.

What we add is the *shaping* activity of the tongue, lips, teeth, mouth, and nasal passages. How do all these "shapers" work together to form speech sounds, like the ones represented by the letters B, Y, A, Z, CH, and so on?

When we breathe through our vocal cords and set them vibrating, and then allow the sound to pass uninterrupted through the mouth and out into the air, we have produced a vowel. Say "ahhhh" and you will see that this is so. All languages employ several vowels. We produce different ones depending on the position of the tongue when the vibrated air passes through the mouth. After saying "ahhh" say "eeeee"; if you pay attention to your tongue, you will see that this is so. We will say more about vowels later.

Consonants are made when we use the shapers in the mouth to interrupt the flow of vibrating air through the mouth. For example, when we say "ahhh," and then open and close the lips repeatedly, we produce a series of *b*'s: "Ababababab . . ." If we stop the air flow by repeatedly raising the back of the tongue against the roof of the mouth, we get a series of *g*'s: "Agagagag." And if we stop the flow by hitting the tip of the tongue against the fleshy ridge right behind our upper front teeth, we get a series of *d*'s: "Adadadad." Try it and see.

Consonants are produced by interrupting the flow of vibrated air through the mouth. But *which* consonant we make depends on three further concerns: (1) the *place* in the mouth where we make the interruption; (2) the *manner* of the activity that produces the interruption;

and (3) whether or not the vocal cords are vibrating while the interruption is being made (*voicing*).

The three consonants we just produced, *b*, *g*, and *d*, were alike in the *manner* in which they were made: all three temporarily stopped the air flow — in linguistic parlance they are therefore called *stops*. They also were alike in that the vocal cords were vibrating as we made them —they are therefore said to be *voiced*. They differed only in the *places* they were made: the *b* on both lips, the *g* between the back of the tongue and the rearward roof of the mouth, and the *d* between the tip of the tongue and the ridge behind the front teeth.

Now let's try some variations. Hold your fingers over your Adam's apple and say "Abababab" again. With your fingers still in place, now substitute in *p*'s: "Apapapap." Notice the difference? The sound of the letter *p* is like *b* in both *place* and *manner;* it differs only in being *unvoiced* — that is, the vocal chords don't vibrate as it is made. Try alternating "Agagagag" with "Akakakakak" — *g* and *k* are alike except that *k* is *unvoiced*. The same is true of *d* and *t*, *z* and *s*, *ch* and *j*, the *th* in "thin" and *th* in "their." All of these pairs are alike in the *place* and *manner* in which they are made, but different in *voicing*. These facts have consequences for children's spelling.

Try another variation. Say the sound of the letter D — "duh." Notice the spot on the fleshy ridge behind your teeth where your tongue tapped. Now hold your tongue just short of touching that spot and blow air out through the constricted space over your tongue. You should hear a sound like that of the letter S. Now, if instead of blowing out, you say "ahhh" while you raise your tongue to that same spot (raise it until you hear a whistle, but don't let it touch), you should hear a sound like that of *z*. You will be saying "ozzzzzz . . ." Two points: first, we have demonstrated that the sounds of *s* and *z* are alike except for *voicing*. Second, we have demonstrated another manner of making consonants — by restricting the air flow so that we hear a sort of whistling friction.

The name *fricative* is applied to consonants made in this manner. Let's make some others. Say "ozzzzzzzzzzz" again. While you are saying it, slide your tongue forward and down, until it is behind the upper front teeth themselves and almost — but not quite — touching them. You should hear the sound *th* of "*th*en." If you'll leave off saying the "ahh" part and just whistle air through that space, you will hear the other *th* of "*th*in." The two *th*'s, *th*en and *th*in, are voiced and unvoiced fricatives, respectively.

Here's another pair of fricatives. Place your lower lip against your upper teeth in Bugs Bunny fashion. Now say "ahhh" again, and you should hear a *v* sound: "Ahhvvvvvv . . ." If you turn off the voicing and just blow air out through the space, you should hear a long *f* sound. The sounds of *f* and *v* are alike in the *place* and *manner* in which they are made, but different in *voicing*.

There are other manners in which consonants are made and other places also. But our brief exploration should enable us to answer an important question: Suppose a child wants to represent a sound in spelling a word, but he cannot find a perfect fit with a letter name. He chooses to find a "near fit" — a letter name that is *somewhat* like the sound he wants to represent. In what specific ways can sounds of letters be *like* each other or *unlike* each other?

Our discussion of consonants provides a way of answering. Speech sounds — for instance, sounds of consonants — can be like each other in the *place* and *manner* in which they are made, and perhaps in *voicing*. With these features in mind, let's return to our examination of digraphs.

Digraphs present a special problem in invented spelling because children don't accept the notion that two letters can represent one sound.

*A return to digraphs*

So they are forced to search for a single letter whose name sounds most like the sound they wish to spell, a sound which adults represent with a digraph. This sometimes causes them to make some strange-looking substitutions.

In Figure 5 – 5, Joey represented the *th* sound of "then" (the *voiced* sound) five times. He spelled it once correctly in "the," a word he probably had memorized. Twice he spelled it with the letter T, and twice with the letter V. His inconsistency is strange, but his choice of letters makes sense.

Remember that the *th* sound is made by placing the tongue behind the front teeth and vibrating ("fricating") forced air between the tongue and the teeth. To make the sound *t,* we touched the tongue to the fleshy ridge just behind the front teeth — a place very close to the place where *th* is made. The sound of *t* stops the air, though, and it is unvoiced. But we can say *t* is quite similar to *th* in the *place* where it was made.

The letter V for the sound of *th* appears to be a stranger choice. But recall that the sound of *v* is made by a frication, just as *th* is, and that it is voiced just as *th* is. These two facts, plus the fact that *v* is made in the forward region of the mouth, make the sound *v* fairly similar to *th* and hence justify the spelling V for the *th* sound.

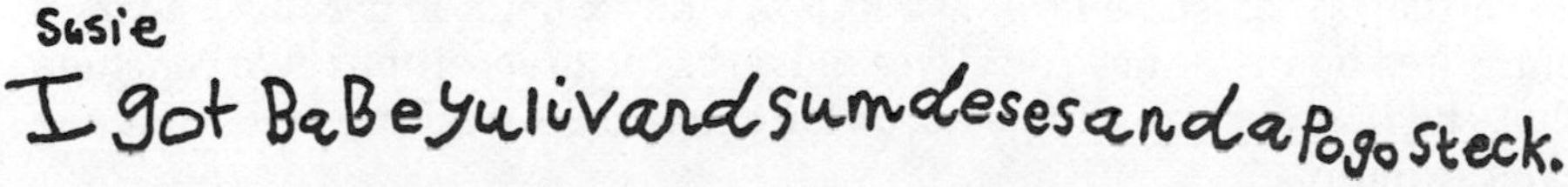

Susie

I got BaBe yulivard sumdesesanda Pogo steck.

FIGURE 5 – 6
*Susie*
*Grade 1*
*Note spelling of*
*"dishes"*

The sound represented by the digraph *sh* gets various spellings in children's inventions. The spelling S for it, in Figure 5 – 6, is frequently offered. The letter S seems to be a clear enough choice, first because it is one of the letters of the digraph *sh* and the child may have remembered seeing it in other words. But the letter S is a good choice, too, because it is identical in *voicing* and *manner* to the sound of *sh*, and very near it in the *place* in which it is made. If you make a long hissing stream of S's, then change to make the *shhhh . . .* sound without stopping the air flow, you'll find that your tongue simply moved back a fraction of an inch along the roof of your mouth while you continued to blow the air through.

When children invent spellings, they virtually always come up with something other than standard spellings for consonant digraphs. Table 5 – 3 shows some frequently offered inventions for them.

**TABLE 5 – 3**
*Digraph consonants*

| Sound | Letter | Examples |
|-------|--------|----------|
| *ch* as in chip | H | HRP (chirp) IHOVR (each other) TEHR (teacher) |
| *sh* as in ship | H | FIH (fish) FEH (fish) HE (she) |
| *sh* as in ship | S or C | SOS (shoes) COO (show) SES (she's) |
| *th* as in the | T | BATEG (bathing) TA (they) MOTR (mother) GRAMUTR (grandmother) |
| *th* as in the | V | IHOVR (each other) VE (the) VU (they) |

"But," you may ask, "surely children do not deliberately set out to find consonants that are alike in place, manner, and voicing — what five year old ever used these terms?"

Let us remind you of our earlier discussion of language development. There we said that children learn to talk by developing a system of language rules that enables them to understand and produce speech. We see evidence, for example, in the three year old's statement, "I got tiny foots," that the child has formed a *rule* to the effect that plurals are formed by adding the letter S to a noun. We doubt, though, that a three year old would give you a definition of the word "noun" or "plural" or even "word." Nevertheless, on some level she knows what a noun is because she only. pluralizes nouns — not adjectives, adverbs, or prepositions. We conclude that she knows some things about language on a working level that she can't explain.

The same is true of spelling. If you watch a youngster invent spellings, you will see and hear him exaggerating the production of speech sounds: whistling her S's, stabbing repeatedly at her D's, choo-chooing her H's. On a working level she is exploring place, manner, and voicing. But if you ask her what she's doing —

"Writing you a letter," she says!

When children invent spelling they do so by breaking a word into its individual sounds and finding a letter to represent each sound. This point, we hope, has been made abundantly clear. But if children represent sounds they hear, how do we account for the peculiar case of N and M? These sounds quite often go unspelled, even by children who have otherwise demonstrated a keen ear and an inventive hand. Note, for example, the omission of the N's in

YUTS A LADE YET FEHEG AD HE KOT FLEPR.

Surely a child resourceful enough to think of using the letter Y for the sound *w* and the letter H for the sound of *sh* could find a spelling for an *n* sound if she wanted to. Notice, too, that *n* and *m* sounds are often spelled by children in some words. Sometimes on the same paper *n* and *m* will be spelled in one spot and left out in another, as in Figure 5 – 7.

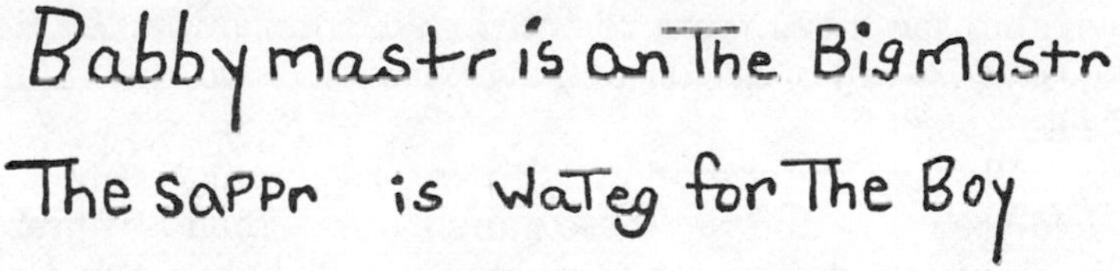

Babby mastr is an The Big mastr

The sappr   is waTeg for The Boy

**FIGURE 5 – 7**
*Melissa
Grade 1
Note omissions
of n's.*

What factors might there be in the *position* of the *n* and *m* sounds in words that would lead to their being spelled in one place and not spelled in another? Study Figure 5 – 7 again and see if you can answer this question. The factor that decides whether an *n* or *m* sound will be spelled or not is what follows it. If a vowel comes after an *n* or *m* sound or if either comes at the end of a word, these consonants will be spelled. Accordingly, the sound of *n* is spelled in NIS ("nice"), SNAK ("snack"), and the M is spelled in SMIL ("smile").

On the other hand, when the sounds of *n* or *m* are followed by some other consonant, they often go unspelled. Thus, the letter N is omitted from YET ("went"), AD ("and"), FEHEG ("fishing"), and YUTS ("once"). Knowing where the N's and M's are omitted, however, does not explain why they are. We might venture a guess that the following consonant somehow overshadows the N or M, so that the child doesn't *hear* it, and hence, omits it. But is it the case that he doesn't hear the sound? We can easily test this out. Just ask a three year old to point to your "*lap*," and then to point to your "*lamp*," and see if he can distinguish the two. If he can, he can hear the *m* sound. The same test could be made with the words "land" and "lad," "crowd" and "crowned," "stained" and "stayed." If the child can tell the difference between the two words, he can hear the *n* and the *m* sounds. As it turns out, children can hear *n* and *m* in these environments well before the age when they begin to create invented spellings.

**TABLE 5 – 4**
*N and M before other consonants*

| Sound | Letter | Examples |
|-------|--------|----------|
| *m* | M | LAP (lamp) BOPE (bumpy) LEP (limp) STAP (stamp) |
| *n* | N | RAD (rained) WET (went) GOWEG (going) CADE (candy) AJLS (angels) |

If they know how to spell *n* and *m* sounds in other positions, and they can hear these sounds when they are followed by consonants, then why don't they spell them in such cases? How *do* we account for the spellings YET for "went" and YUTS for "once"?

When we pronounce the *n* sound, we place the tongue in the same spot where *d, t, j,* and *ch* are made: the fleshy ridge behind the front teeth. In fact, when the sound of *n* is followed by any of these latter consonants, it is impossible to tell from the activity inside the mouth whether the *n* is present or not. You can demonstrate this by repeating these pairs of words over and over: "witch – winch," "plant – plat," and "dote – don't."

We *hear* the *n* sound in these words, though — so how is it made? Hold your nose and say these pairs again. When *n* is present in a word, the air is resonated out through the nose while the *n* and the vowel preceding it are pronounced. When *n* is followed by a consonant made in the same place, the nasal resonance is the only feature of the *n* that is heard.

Since the nasalization is more of an influence on the vowel than on the consonant, in such cases many beginning spellers seem to assume that what they hear in "plant," "went," and "once" is a peculiar vowel, not an extra consonant.[3] As we shall shortly see, children adjust early to the idea that a single vowel letter may spell variations of a vowel sound. Thus in YET for "went," the E may be intended to stand for both the sounds of *e* and *n.*

The sound *m* works the same way, except that it is made on both lips, where *p* is also made. When *m* occurs before *p,* as in "lamp," it is typically not spelled, because the *m* then acts as a nasalization of the vowel preceding the *p.* You can demonstrate this by pronouncing "lap – lamp," "stomp – stop," and "chip – chimp."

Some common examples of omitted nasal consonants — N and M — are presented in Table 5 – 4.

**Invented spelling of long vowels**

"Long vowels say their names." That useful piece of first-grade lore is true enough. Judging from their writings, though, this rule need not be pointed out to many children; they know it already (see Figure 5 – 8). Of course, when long vowels occur in words, correct spelling usually will not

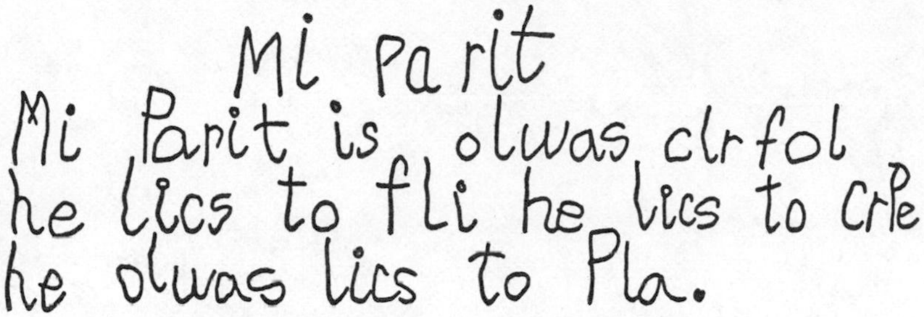

**FIGURE 5 – 8**
*Ronnen*
*Grade 1*
*Note long vowel*
*spellings*

let them stand alone and still say their names. They can in "A" and "I" and also in "he," "she," "go," and "so." But "stay," "late," "bone," "see," and the like require that the vowels be *marked* to indicate their longness. Inventive spellers leave off these markers, and this is one indication that they are inventing. The spellings that result are like those shown in Table 5 – 5.

| Sound | Letter | Examples | |
|---|---|---|---|
| ā | A | LADE (lady) PLA (play) TA (they) NAM (name) | **TABLE 5 – 5** *Long or "tense" vowels* |
| ē | E | PLES (police) MNEKDE (minicotti) | |
| ĭ | I | MI (my) FLI (fly) TRID (tried) SLIDEG (sliding) BIT (bite) | |
| ō | O | JOD (Jody) DOT (don't) | |
| ū | U, O | SOS (shoes) NTU (into) | |

Short vowels do not say their own names, or provide any other very good hint as to the way they should be spelled. Nevertheless, children often do figure out a consistent strategy for spelling short vowels. This strategy, like the omission of nasal consonants, reveals a surprising ability to hear and to make judgments about speech sounds.

**Invented spelling of short vowels**

In the samples in Figures 5 – 9 and 5 – 10, how are the children solving the problem of spelling the short ĭ sound? These two children consensed on a spelling of E for the ĭ sound. Why did they?

The best explanation for children's representing the ĭ sound with the letter E is provided by Charles Read.[4] Read's explanation starts with the letter-name strategy for matching speech sounds with written letters. When children spell "fish" FEH, they use the letter E for the sound of the letter's name, which is long — ē. They use the letter name E because they perceive a similarity between the *long sound of ē* and the *short sound of ĭ*.

**FIGURE 5 – 9**
*Jody* (left)
*Grade 1*
*Note spelling of* I

**FIGURE 5 – 10**
*No Name* (right)
*Kindergarten*
*Note spelling of* I

JOD     ETS  sprng.     The LaTisoGekeg

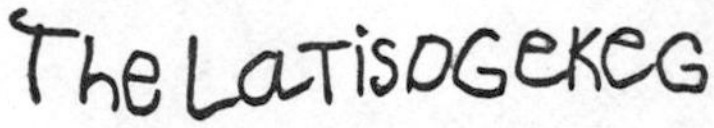

Let's see how inventive spellers solve the problem of spelling the short ĕ sound. As in the word "pet" the short sound of ĕ does not have an exact match in the names of any letters of the alphabet. Actually it *is* contained in the letter names for F, L, and S; but children rarely use consonants for vowel sounds in this way. Note in Figures 5 – 11 and 5 – 12 how these children spelled the short sound of ĕ.

The letter these children used, we see, was A. Again our hypothesis is that they used the letter A for the long sound in its name.

In children's invented spelling, short vowels are sometimes spelled correctly, presumably because children learn or are told their correct spellings in some words. But when they are spelled incorrectly, the most frequent substitution is E for short ĭ, A for short ĕ.

These substitutions create spellings that look very little like adult spellings for the same words. They sometimes lead us to the erroneous

**FIGURE 5 – 11**
*Susie*
*Grade 1*
*Note spelling of*
ĕ

Susie Lewis
Do You have A Dog. No I dot DoYou no.
Butt I Wosh I had One Do You have A Cat.
Yes I Do have A cat Butt he ran away.
All I have is a h Urs e I Dot have A Pat.
My Dad Wot lat me have A Pet. the end

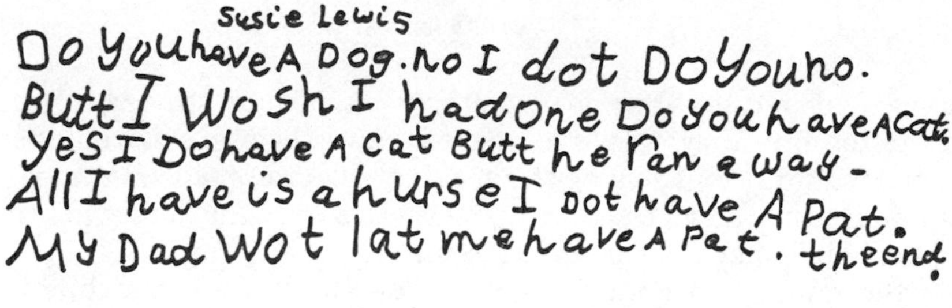

**FIGURE 5 – 12**
*Brian*
*Grade 1*
*Note spelling of*
ĕ

My feh is rad

conclusion that children don't know what they are doing when they produce spellings like ALVADR for "elevator." What are they thinking? By what process do they arrive at these spellings? Again we must consider the way speech sounds are made, and again our source is Charles Read.[5]

This time, let's consider vowels. If you open your mouth wide and vibrate your vocal cords, you will make a vowel: probably "ahhhh." If you pronounce a drawn out "ahhhh" and switch abruptly to "eeee," note what happens in your mouth. You may be aware of two things: first, your jaw raised slightly on "eeee," but even more obvious was the raising of the tongue in the front of the mouth. Now try this: pronounce "aaahh," and then change *very, very slowly* up to "eeee." You probably heard some other sounds you could recognize as vowels in between. What were they? Where was the tongue when they were made?

**How Vowels Are Produced**

Pronounce the *u* sound of "fruit," stretching it out. Then shift to "eeee" again. Now back to *u*. What does your tongue do? You may have noted that it went up at the front of the mouth for "eeee," but that it went up at the *back* of the mouth for *ū*. If you didn't feel it go up in the back for *u*, try saying ŏŏ (as in "took") in alternation with *u* (as in "new"): ŏŏ—*ū*; ŏŏ—*ū*; ŏŏ—*ū*. This should help you become aware of a movement of the back of the tongue up toward the back of the roof of your mouth.

We make vowels by holding the tongue in certain positions as voiced air passes through the mouth. Essentially the placement of the tongue is along two planes: it can move from front to back, and from high to low — or into intermediate positions between high and low and front and back. We could diagram the positions of the tongue with a grid as in Figure 5 – 13.

Let's demonstrate the *front* vowels. Try saying these sounds, gliding

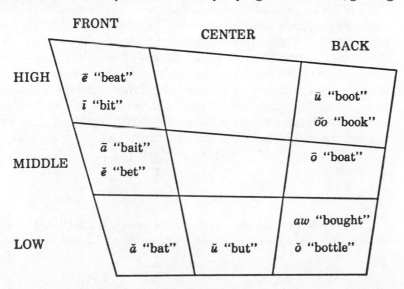

**FIGURE 5 – 13**
*A diagram of tongue positions as different vowels are produced*

smoothly from one to the other: $\bar{e}$ (as in "beet"), $\breve{\imath}$ (as in "bit"), $\bar{a}$ (as in "bait"), $\breve{e}$ (as in "bet"), $\breve{a}$ (as in "bat"): $\bar{e}, \breve{\imath}, \bar{a}, \breve{e}, \breve{a}$. Do it three times and pay attention to what your tongue does. Now try it in reverse: $\breve{a}, \breve{e}, \bar{a}, \breve{\imath},$ $\bar{e}$. You probably noticed your tongue started high and went low in the first series, and that it started low and went high in the second series. You also may have noticed that this movement took place in the front of the mouth (although $\bar{e}$ is somewhat further forward than $\breve{a}$).

Note that the sounds $\bar{e}$ and $\breve{\imath}$ were positioned next to each other: that is, from $\bar{e}$ the next position you came to in the first series was the $\breve{\imath}$ sound, as you went from high to low. The sounds of $\bar{a}$ and $\breve{e}$ were also quite close in the position of the tongue. In the vowel grid in Figure 5 – 13 these vowels appear close together.

Actually, they are even closer than the vowel grid makes them appear. The sounds of $\bar{e}$ and $\breve{\imath}$ are formed in almost the same place in the mouth. They differ in what has been called "tenseness/laxness." Hold your fingers against the flesh on the underside of your jaw and alternate pronouncing the vowels, $\bar{e} - \breve{\imath}, \bar{e} - \breve{\imath}, \bar{e} - \breve{\imath}$. You may feel the muscles in the floor of your mouth becoming tense with the pronunciation of $\bar{e}$, and lax with pronunciation of $\breve{\imath}$. You should feel the same tensing and laxing with $\bar{a}$ and $\breve{e}$, respectively. Some language scientists consider $\bar{a}$ and $\breve{e}$ to be alike in the place in which they are sounded, and different mainly in tenseness and laxness.[6] That is, they are tense and lax versions of the same vowel. The same is said of $\bar{e}$ and $\breve{\imath}$. The child who wrote FEH for "fish," and LATR for "letter" must have sensed this pairing of the tense and lax vowels by position.

Let's quickly recapitulate the argument. Remember that children who are inventive spellers represent sounds in words according to the similarity between the sound in the word and the sound of the name of some letter of the alphabet. All of the vowel letters of the alphabet have long vowel sounds in their names. All of these long vowels, it turns out, are produced by tensing the tongue and floor of the mouth (therefore, all the vowels you think of as "long" are also tense: $\bar{a}, \bar{e}, \bar{o}, \bar{u}$ — we'll get to $\bar{\imath}$ in a minute!). No short vowel sounds find *exact* matches with the names of any vowel letters, for a good reason. All short vowels are *lax* — produced by relaxing the tongue and floor of the mouth — while the sounds of all vowel letter names are *tense*. If you are getting confused, pronounce these sounds and check for tenseness:

$$\bar{a} \qquad \breve{e}$$
$$\bar{e} \qquad \breve{\imath}$$
$$\bar{o} \qquad \breve{o}$$
$$\bar{u} \qquad \breve{o}\breve{o}$$

The vowels marked long should have felt tense (though $\bar{o}$ and $\bar{u}$ tense the tongue more than the floor of the mouth). The vowels marked short should have felt lax.

When children seek to spell a long or tense vowel, they have no trouble finding a letter to represent it, as we have seen, because the names of the vowel letters A, E, I, O, U are long or tense themselves. But when they want to spell a short or lax vowel trouble ensues, because there are no short or lax letter names. The strategy most children employ in such a case is to *find the long (tense) letter name that is made in the same place in the mouth as the short (lax) vowel they wish to spell.*

This is sometimes called the "vowel pairing strategy," so-called because it pairs in spelling the tense and lax vowels that are pronounced in the same position in the mouth. It results in some other strange matches beside *ē – ĭ* and *ā – ĕ*, although these two are the most consistent. Another match that is often seen is *o* for *u*: as in BBGON ("BBgun"). Still stranger is the case of the long *ī* sound.

The long *ī* is actually made up of two sounds: *ŏ* and *ē*. If you pronounce it slowly, you will feel your tongue start low and back and then move high and front while the vowel is still being made: *ŏ – ē*. Children sometimes notice this short *ŏ*, or broad *ä* (as in "ahhhh" with a physician's tongue depressor) element contained in the letter name I, and make use of it to spell *ŏ* (as in BIDM for "bottom" and WIS for "wants").

Why do the spellings produced by children's vowel pairing strategies (*ā* with *ĕ*, *ĕ* with *ĭ*, etc.) appear strange to us? For a very good reason: although standard spelling pairs vowels, it pairs them differently from the matches that inventive spellers work out for themselves. Standard spelling pairs "long" and "short" A: *ā*, as in "bay," with *ă*, as in "bat." It pairs "long" and "short" I: *ī*, as in "by," with *ĭ*, as in "bit." It pairs them because they are represented in spelling by the same letter — not because they sound the same, or because they are made in the same place in the mouth. The pairing of *ā* and *ă*, *ī* and *ĭ*, *ē* and *ĕ* are second nature to us adults, simply because of our years of reading and writing experience. But this system of pairing vowels does not seem natural to beginning spellers.

Table 5 – 6 summarizes the vowel pairings that Read identified, with examples from writings we have collected from children.

| Sound | Letter | Examples |
|---|---|---|
| *ĕ* | A | FAL (fell) RAD (red) PAT (pet) TALUFO (telephone) |
| *ĭ* | E | FEH (fish) HEM (him) BET (bit) VESET (visit) |
| *ŏ* | I | WIS (wants) BIDM (bottom) |
| *ŭ* | O | JOPT (jumped) MOD (mud) SOPR (supper) FOTIME (funtime) |

**TABLE 5 – 6**
*Pairing of lax (short) vowels with letter names*

**Syllables**
**without**
**vowels**

Children who produce invented spellings often show surprising acuity not only in learning speech sounds but in categorizing them together on the basis of very subtle features. Why is it, then, that they leave out so many vowels, as in Figure 5 – 14?

We note two things in the circumstances of the vowel omissions: They happen before certain consonants: L, R, M, S; and they happen in certain places, mostly the ends of words, in unstressed syllables. The consonants before which vowels are omitted sound much like vowels themselves. The sound of *r* is made without any complete closing of the "shapers" in the mouth, and consists largely of the vibration of the vocal cords to make themselves heard. The sound of *l* is made with the tongue against the roof of the mouth; the vibrated air is passed around the sides of the tongue for the *l*. The sounds of *m* and *n* both close off the mouth, but pass the vibrated air out through the nasal passage. All of these consonants are *voiced*; that is, the vocal cords vibrate while they are being made. All of them also allow the vibrated air to pass uninterrupted out of the mouth or the nose. Hence, of all the consonants, they are the most like vowels — because vowels are uninterrupted passages of voiced air.

**FIGURE 5 – 14**
*Daryl*
*Grade 1*
*Note omission of*
*vowel before* r

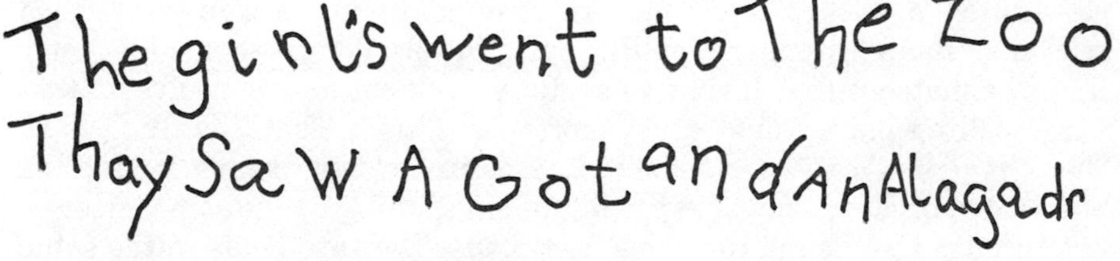

The girl's went to The Zoo Thay Saw A Got and An Alagadr

When vowels occur in syllables that are unstressed, they are said to be "reduced." Say these words aloud: "table," "wonderful," "lentil," and "infernal." The last syllables you pronounced probably all the same way — *ŭl* — even though they were written four different ways. In normal speech, the individual vowels in these unstressed syllables are unrecognizable — they are all reduced to a common — *uh*.

When the vowellike consonants occur in these unstressed syllables where one cannot hear any distinct vowel, children tend to let the vowellike quality of the consonant serve for whatever vowel is needed. By children's logic, any vowel letter that they *did* write in such a place would say its name clearly — giving us "litteel" if they wrote LETEL or "bottoam" if they wrote BIDOM. This is not what the children intend, so they leave the vowel out.

Some common examples of syllables without vowels are given in Table 5 – 7.

| Sound | Letter | Examples | |
|-------|--------|----------|---|
| ŭl | L | LETL (little) BISECL (bicycle) TABL (table) AJLS (angels) | **TABLE 5 – 7** *Syllables without vowels* |
| ŭr | R | TEHR (teacher) GRAMOTR (grandmother) PECHRS (pinchers) SOPR (supper) | |

Sometimes invented spelling diverges from standard spelling because children perceive oddities of pronunciation which adults do not. Words like "tree," "train," and "trick" are commonly pronounced as if they began with "chr." We read *tree* and say "chree" — but we adults don't believe we say "chree" because we have seen the "tr" in print and we have a strange hidden conviction that what we've been seeing is what we've been saying. But children are not easily taken in. They will sometimes spell *tr* CHR.

**CHOO CHOO CHRAN**

They will do a similar thing with *dr*. When we pronounce "drink," "drive," and "dragon," we often say "jrink," "jrive," and "jragon." When children spell these words the way they hear them, they often use letters G or J at the beginning of the word.

Often, too, they omit the letter R after the T or D. Children seem to have a bias toward simplicity in their pronunciation.[7] They say "jink" for "drink." It may be that the bias for simplicity carries over into spelling, too. We notice that many consonant blends get reduced to a single letter even when they *could* be puzzled out by the letter-name strategy.

Figures 5 – 15 and 5 – 16 show some samples where the sounds of *dr* and *tr* have been dealt with imaginatively by the children.

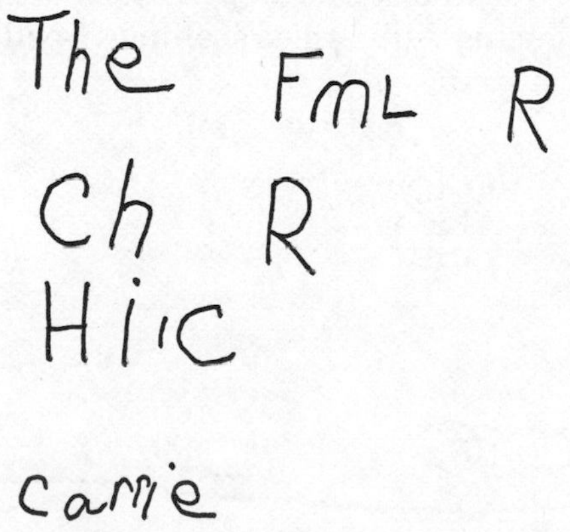

**FIGURE 5 – 15**
*Carrie* (left)
*Kindergarten*
*Note spelling of "drinking"*

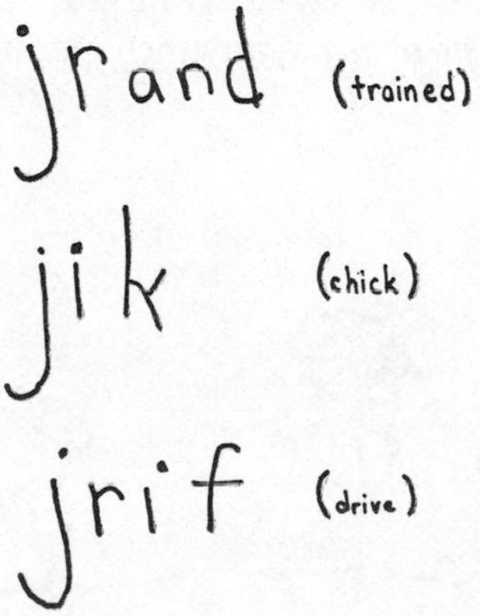

**FIGURE 5 – 16**
*No Name* (right)
*Grade 1*
*Note spelling of "trained" and "drive"*

**The Develop-
mental
Dimension of
Invented
Spelling**

We have covered the most important aspects of children's invented spelling with the letter-name strategy. The spellings we saw in this chapter
are of the most inventive sort that children produce. The children
who wrote them were acting mostly on their own intuitions about
spelling: learned spellings showed up less frequently than invented ones.
In the next chapter this condition will be reversed. Learned spelling will
dominate the children's writing, though invention will still be in evidence
as children employ learned spelling patterns in novel ways. The result
will still be spelling errors, but the errors will be influenced more by
learning and less by intuition than those we encountered in the present
chapter.

The next type of spelling, which we will call *transitional* spelling,
is a developmental step beyond the letter-name spelling. On that subject,
however, there is a developmental aspect of letter-name spelling which
has been lurking in the background of the present discussion. The per-
ceptive reader will have noticed that some of the spelling samples displayed in this chapter were more complete, more filled out, than others.
Consider again the following two samples by Daryl. The first was written
in September of his first-grade year; the second, two months later.

1.     I L N GLEAD TXS     ("I live in Goliad, Texas")
2.     A MAN ROB SOS THE PLES FID HEM.     ("A man robbed shoes.
The police found him.")

Daryl used the letter-name strategy to produce invented spelling in
both sentences. But in the second one he represented considerably more
speech sounds with his letters than he did in the first. This reflects a
widely observed characteristic of children's invented spelling: early in
their career as spellers, children represent far fewer speech sounds or
phonemes with their letters than they do later in their development.

As we see in Figure 5 – 17, when a child begins to spell by phonemes,
he does not advance instantly to producing well-formed spellings. Spelling

**FIGURE 5 – 17**
*No Name
Kindergarten
Early phonemic
spelling*

words phoneme by phoneme, or phonemic spelling, at first seems to restrict the quantity of a child's written production. Whereas before he may
have scribbled volubly, and produced pages of linear mock writing, his
first efforts at phonemic spelling yield only a trickle of production —
usually only a letter or two for each word he wishes to spell. Clearly this
reduced production indicates that the task of phonemic spelling is hard
for the child and that he must really work at it. What is so hard about
phonemic spelling?

There are at least three sources of difficulty: the need to segment
words into phonemes, the need to have a stable "concept of word," and
the task of choosing a letter with which to represent the phonemes.

To anyone who can read this book, the idea of breaking a word down into
its smallest sounds or phonemes may not seem to be an unusually difficult
task. Our experience with reading written words over the years has made
it natural for us to see words as bundles of phonemes — if we understand
phonemes to be the sounds to which individual letters correspond. Certainly there are exceptions in the correspondences — but the very fact
that we can recognize exceptions and irregularities in the match between
letters and speech sounds is an indication that we have a working sense
of the sound units to which letters correspond.

*Segmenting
words into
phonemes*

Our experience with print may be misleading, however, because
even though letters on the page are distinctly recognizable units, the
speech sounds to which they correspond are not. When we say "bat," we
do not say "buh," "ă," "tuh" rapidly together. No matter how quickly we
pronounce those three sounds, we can never run them together to say
"bat." Laboratory experiments have been conducted to test this point.
Using sophisticated hardware, scientists have taken words like "bat" and
mechanically broken them into their smallest components. Then they
have tested to see if people could recognize the parts of the word. Invariably, people had no difficulty recognizing the vowel sound, but when the
vowel sound was removed from either consonant, they were unrecognizable — people reported hearing a "chirping sound" instead of a consonant![8]

The explanation is that we produce many phonemes together when
we speak in a process called *coarticulation*. If we are able, on reflection,
to separate phonemes out of the speech we hear, it is only because we
have a sense of what we are looking for; the phonemes do not come to us
separately. The task of recognizing the individual phonemes that make
up a word — called *phonemic segmentation* — is more of a complex perceptual operation than it appears. It does not simply consist of recognizing
separate items: it also includes the act of deciding how they might be
separated.

For children, segmenting words into syllables is not very difficult.
But segmenting words into phonemes usually is.[9] In any group of five

year olds, there may be a few who are able to segment phonemes, a larger number who can distinguish only one or two phonemes per word, and a like number who cannot break a word down further than a syllable, if that.

**The concept of word**

Another complication a child must overcome in order to spell is the development of a concept of what a word is and of the ability to think about words.[10] Like phonemes, words come to us all run together in undifferentiated strings. There is not usually any clue in the speech stream we listen to as to where one word leaves off and another begins. As in the case of phonemes, we usually attend to the meaning of words rather than to their sounds. Thus, a bilingual person may not be able to remember in what language a particularly interesting comment was made to her. The idea will be remembered but the words somehow fall away.

But for the child to be able to spell a word, the word must have some reality for him as a unit; he must be able to make it hold still in mind while he operates on it. For in order to spell a word, the child must:

1. say the word mentally to himself;
2. break off the first phoneme from the rest of the word;
3. mentally sort through his repertoire of letters and find one to match with that phoneme;
4. write down the letter he has decided on;
5. recite the word again in his mind;
6. recall the phoneme he has just spelled, subtract it from the word, and locate the next phoneme to be spelled;
7. match that phoneme with a letter of the alphabet, and so on, until all of the phonemes are spelled.

The child must have a very stable image of the word in his mind to be able to switch back and forth between the sound of the word, its phonemes, his repertoire of letters, and the motor act of writing each letter.

We can illustrate the importance of the concept of word in carrying out the tasks of spelling with an analogy. Suppose that in an astronomy class your first assignment is to make a chart of fifty stars in the sky. You go outside on a starlit night, armed with drawing paper and pencil, and look up. You spot a bright star. You look down at the paper to see where its mark should go. You look up to verify its position, but alas! Which star is it? So it goes — every time you isolate a star from the thousands of others, you lose your place in the transition from sky to paper and back.

But suppose later on you studied the constellations. Now when you looked into the sky you could quickly orient yourself to the patterns of stars in the sky. Every time you looked down at your paper you could quickly reorient yourself by the constellations.

For the beginning speller, we expect that a concept of word is akin to our ability to recognize constellations. It serves the same important orienting function when he attempts to spell.

Children generally produce early phonemic spelling in kindergarten or early first grade. Their productions usually look like that in Figure 5 – 18a; normally you will have to ask the child what he wrote soon after he produced it, for you will not be certain how to decipher it otherwise.

**Early Phonemic Spelling**

For the reasons just discussed — because of the child's difficulty with phonemic segmentation, or the instability of his concept of word — he is not able to spell very much of each word. The child almost always spells the first phoneme in the word and may spell one or two others — either the final letter or the most salient. But he invariably gives out before he has spelled more than a beginning or rough contour of the word (see Figure 5 – 18b).

<sub>A</sub> MiBE hotosL      <sub>B</sub> toDasVNtFMim

**FIGURE 5 – 18**
*No Name
Kindergarten
Early phonemic
spelling*

Sometimes the child will spell only the last phoneme in the word and sometimes the child will spell the first phoneme, the last phoneme, and then go back and spell a phoneme from somewhere in the middle.

An early phonemic speller may be conscious that a word should have a minimum number of letters in order to look like a word. Occasionally, a child will exhaust his efforts to spell a word after writing only one or two letters, then add a string of random letters to fill it out.

These early phonemic spellings have a humble appearance, but they demonstrate that the child has already learned quite a lot about writing. She has learned to use letters meaningfully to stand for a message. She has learned that spelling involves the representation of spoken words by means of written letters. She has learned that letters represent phonemes — the smallest sound units of words. She has begun to develop the ability to separate out the phonemes that make up a word. Finally, she is developing a concept of what a word is — so that words will "hold still for her" while she thinks about them, analyzes them, spells them, and gradually learns more about how they are made.

All of the spelling forms and spelling stages we have considered in this chapter have one important feature in common: they result largely from children's invention, from their untutored assumptions about the way

**Conclusion**

spelling works. In succeeding chapters we will see what happens as children begin to learn the patterns of standard spelling. For now a pair of questions remain to be answered about invented spelling.

Do all children invent spelling? If every child spontaneously wrote out invented spelling at the kitchen table, the phenomenon would be as widely known a writing behavior as baby talk is a speech behavior. But they don't and it's not. Many children do not explore writing before they enter school, and there they usually practice writing only words they have memorized. However, if these children were ever to write words whose spellings they had not memorized, it is probable that they would employ the strategies we have described in this chapter.

For a time, it seems that children's memories tell them one thing, and their reasoning about spelling tells them something else. In order to learn to spell, children must adjust their concepts about spelling so that the words spelled by reason — by invention — follow closely the same patterns as the words they know from memory. "To," "two," "too," and the like will always have to be remembered, but people can reduce the burden on memory by using refined concepts of spelling structure.

Should all children invent spelling? Yes, children will learn to spell correctly and to write fluently if they are encouraged — but not forced — to express themselves in writing as soon as they feel the urge, and as best they can. They should never be *taught* incorrect spellings, however, because that runs the risk of committing incorrect forms to memory. All that is needed is encouragement to "spell it the way you think it should be spelled," along with some reinforcement like "yes, that could say dinosaur." More on this in Chapter Seven.

**References**

1. James Beers. "Developmental Strategies of Spelling Competence in Primary School Children," in Edmund H. Henderson and James W. Beers (eds.), *Developmental and Cognitive Aspects of Learning to Spell*. Newark, Del.: International Reading Association, 1980.
2. Ibid.
3. Charles Read. *Children's Categorization of Speech Sounds in English*. Urbana, Ill.: National Council of Teachers of English, 1975.
4. Ibid.
5. Ibid.
6. Ronald Langacre. *Language and Its Structure, Some Fundamental Concepts*. 2d ed. New York: Harcourt Brace Jovanovich, 1973.
7. Jill DeVilliers and Peter DeVilliers. *Language Acquisition*. Cambridge: Harvard University Press, 1979.
8. A. M. Liberman, F.S. Cooper, D. Shankweiler, and M. Studdert-Kennedy. "Perception of the Speech Code." *Psychological Review* 74 (1967): 431 – 461.
9. I. Y. Liberman and others. "Explicit Syllable and Phoneme Segmentation in the Young Child." *Journal of Experimental Child Psychology* 18 (1974): 201 – 212.

10.  Darrell Morris. "Beginning Readers' Concept of Word," in Edmund H. Henderson and James W. Beers (eds.), *Developmental and Cognitive Aspects of Learning to Spell.* Newark, Del.: International Reading Association, 1980.

# 6

# *Learning Standard Spelling*

Susie wrote the writing samples shown in Figure 6 – 1 during the fall of
her first-grade year. The writing in Figure 6 – 2 she wrote in the spring.
The difference between her spelling at the two times is striking. Her first
efforts are strange to the eye, while her later ones are familiar; she seems
to have moved out of some exotic, foreign way of writing and into English
writing. Her later words look like they *could* be English words.

How do we account for the difference? It does not reside in the way
she sounded out the words she spelled. In both types of writing each word
appears complete with all of its phonemes represented. What is different
is the *way* she represented the phonemes in the word. She has largely
given up her original letter-name basis for spelling. In its place she has
begun to employ features of standard English spelling. But although she
has begun to notice and employ features of standard spelling in her writing, she does not use them correctly. She is in a stage of experimentation
with standard spelling forms, a stage which we call *transitional spelling*.

**FIGURE 6 – 1**
*Susie*
*Grade 1*
*Susie's letter-*
*name spelling*

84

> Susie
> Can I go Play with Billey mom
> I like to Play withe Billey.
> We are goweg naw. are You comeg
> I will be ther in a minit.
> I like to go to grane's haws.
> Dad is home mom I will be ther in a minit.
> Can I Play With You.
> Bill wont let me Play mom.

**FIGURE 6–2**
*Susie*
*Grade 1*
*Susie's transitional spelling*

With practice and learning, she will move directly from this stage into correct spelling; but for now she must come to grips with the system of generalizations that make up standard spelling.

What system of generalizations are we talking about? English spelling often draws complaints for being *unsystematic* because it frustrates the expectation of simple letter-to-sound relationships. The letter A, for example, can represent a dozen different sounds, and the sound *ā* can be spelled as many different ways. The patterns of regularity in English spelling are complex, but they do exist, nevertheless.

The patterns that relate English spelling to the spoken language necessitate recourse to such things as *marking systems* — in which combinations of letters, some of them silent, represent sounds of words; *grammatical considerations* — in which parts of words which contain grammatical information, such as verb tense markers and noun plural markers, are spelled in one way while they are pronounced in several ways; considerations of *pronunciation* — which copes with the normal changes that speech sounds undergo when they occur next to other speech sounds; and finally, patterns that stem from spelling changes made by medieval scribes.

Before we describe these aspects of English spelling in detail, and then discuss the ways that they show up in children's spelling, we should say a word about how English spelling came to take its present form.

**How English Got Its Strange Spelling**

The alphabetic system of writing was introduced into England by the Romans. They spoke and wrote Latin, of course, but their writing system and alphabet was put to early service of the Anglo-Saxon or Old English language that was spoken on the island. Old English manuscripts have been found dating back to the eighth century, A.D.

England does not occupy a large piece of geography, nor are there many natural barriers on the island. But early peoples living in different regions had very limited contact with each other. Thus each region had a markedly different dialect of English. When speakers of these dialects occasionally came together, their dialects influenced each other in strange ways to give rise to new ways of speaking. Gradually the whole language was propelled forward with changes of speech and usage unevenly spread across the land. By the time the printing press was imported to England, the language had evolved into what is called Middle English — the language of Chaucer.

There were great varieties in Middle English; but we know that in general when Middle English was written down: most letters, especially vowels, had one pronunciation; and almost all the letters that were written in a word stood directly for a sound.

It was in 1476 that William Caxton set up the first printing press in England. Up until his time each scribe had had his own style of spelling. With printing that changed: the printer became the final arbiter of spelling, and variations of spellings for individual words greatly diminished. Caxton selected the London dialect of Middle English as the basis of his spelling, and succeeding printers usually followed his example.

In the few centuries before Caxton, England had been invaded and ruled by the French from Normandy. Though French was widely spoken, Latin was the language of the church, the school, and of the court. Through the seventeenth century, literate people read more Latin than they did English — and also a good deal of French. At this time, when occasional attempts were made to "reform" the spelling of English, the reforms actually moved spelling away from sound so that English words would look more like their Latin and French cousins. *Dette*, for example, was changed to "debt" in order to make it resemble the Latin form *debit*.

To complicate matters further, it seems that many of the early printers were from Germany and Holland. Some were not good speakers of English or French, and so they introduced several peculiarities into our spelling out of error!

From the fifteenth century through the eighteenth, the English language changed so much that a speaker from the later period could not have understood a speaker from the earlier one. But spelling changed relatively little during the same time. The seventeenth and eighteenth centuries saw several efforts to reform English spelling along phonetic lines. The most influential man of letters of the eighteenth century, however, would have none of it. Dr. Samuel Johnson published his famous *Dictionary* in 1755 and established from that time to this the historical, or etymological, basis of English spelling instead of the phonetic.

English spelling is today considered "historically phonetic": it is spelled roughly the way it sounded 500 years ago. In all these years many differences have occurred between spelling and sound. There are two such differences that stand out above all of the others.

One source of difference between spelling and sound is the "great vowel shift." In Old English there was not the same distinction between long and short vowels (by which we really mean tense and lax) that we have today. But in Middle English vowels came to have relaxed pronunciations when they occurred in unstressed syllables. The letter E was at that time pronounced $\bar{a}$ in stressed syllables, and $\breve{e}$ in unstressed syllables. Thus the word "bete" would have been pronounced "bāteh." The letter I was pronounced $\bar{e}$ in stressed syllables and $\breve{\imath}$ in unstressed ones, giving bēēteh for "bite." The respective pronunciations for the letter A in stressed and unstressed syllables were $ah$ and $\breve{a}$.

Between the fifteenth and sixteenth centuries a very peculiar thing happened: the pronunciation of each of the above vowels in stressed positions were changed around, while the unstressed vowels kept their original pronunciations. The stressed letter E went from $\bar{a}$ to $\bar{e}$; stressed letter I went from $\bar{e}$ to $\bar{\imath}$; and stressed letter A went from $\bar{a}h$ to $\bar{a}$. Thus, the two vowel sounds that were represented by each vowel letter became remote from each other, as we can see in pairs such as "mate–mat," "bite–bit," and "Pete–pet."

The second major change that occurred in the relation between spelling and pronunciation was the appearance of silent letters. Words in Old and Middle English had almost no letters that did not stand for some sound. Thus "bite" was pronounced "beeteh," and "light" was pronounced "lixt," with the $x$ having a sound akin to the $ch$ in "loch" and "Bach." But with changes in pronunciation, the last vowel in "bite" dropped off, and the $x$ sound in "light," "right," "bright," "sigh," and similar words ceased to be sounded. The spellings for these silent sounds stayed on, however. They came to indicate that the preceding vowel had its long or stressed pronunciation, since the first syllable in a two-syllable word was always automatically stressed. Today they serve as *markers* — letters which are silent themselves but serve to indicate the pronunciation of neighboring letters.

**Some Learnable Patterns of Modern English Spelling**

To account for the relationship between spelling and sounds of words in modern English, it is necessary to consider the historical background of the relationship. But that does not mean that children must become historians of language. It means that they must rather be able to sense patterns of spelling that are old in origin, but which can be perceived today as generalizations governing the relation between spelling and sound.

In the modern English spelling, we can identify four separate types of patterns all of which emerging spellers must contend with as they seek to learn the system. We will refer to them as *rules,* though we must emphasize that they were never deliberately planned as rules and they are rarely explicitly taught in the fashion in which we will describe them. The patterns we will treat are *marking rules, phonological rules, scribal rules,* and *morpheme conservation rules.*

*Marking rules in English spelling*

Marking rules are involved in the sounds that letters represent, given the environment in which the letters occur in a word, and the presence of marker letters in the word.

Marking rules affect both vowels and consonants. When they affect vowels their influence is usually to signal the vowel sound as long or short. In the word "bet," for example, the letter E has its short pronunciation. This is predictable because E occurs as a single vowel followed by a word-final consonant. Vowels in this environment nearly always have their short sound: for example, "bat," "bit," "but," and "not." If we intend for the vowel to have its long sound, we must add a *marker,* as if to overcome the shortening influence of the following consonant. Markers are letters, usually silent in themselves, which indicate how a sounded letter is to be pronounced. Adding letter E's to "bit" and "not" yield "bite" and "note," both having long vowels. "Bat" is lengthened as "bait," "bet" as "beet" or "beat." Though the particulars differ, the principle is the same: We add a vowel which itself represents no sound in order to make the original vowel long.

In English there is a set of grammatical endings which we add to words to indicate such things as noun plurality, verb tense, and so on. These endings sometimes act inadvertently as markers. Adding either the past tense ending *-ed* or the participial ending *-ing* to "mat" changes the pronunciation of the stem from "măt" to māte in "mating." So English has another marking rule that doubles the final consonant in such cases to keep the stem vowel short. Thus we get: mat – matted – matting; bat – batted – batting; bit – bitten, and so forth.

Some consonants need marking, too. The letter C when it occurs by itself may represent either the sound of *s* or of *k*. It represents the sound of *s* before the vowels e or i. It represents the sound of *k* before the other vowels and consonants. The letter G follows exactly the same pattern, alternating between the hard *g* of "got" and the soft *g* of "gesture."

In the word "sage," the final E marks the soft pronunciation of G — and it also marks the long sound of *a* (note the alternation of "sage" – "saga"). The letter E in "face" indicates both the long sound of the vowel and the *s* pronunciation of the letter C.[4]

*Children and marking rules*

To use marking rules correctly, spellers must coordinate several things at once. To be able to spell "mat," for example, they must:

1.  remember that the letter A in English spelling properly spells the sound ă.

2.   recognize that a vowel letter occurring before a word-final consonant will have its short pronunciation; and

3.   recognize that if the first two above conditions are met, then no further marking is necessary.

Beginning spellers do not always coordinate all three considerations at one time.

In Figure 6 – 3 note the spelling of "pick" is PIKE. Elaine correctly paired the vowel sound *i* with the letter I (she has moved beyond the letter-name match, by which she would have paired the sound *i* with the letter E). She also demonstrates an awareness of markers — hence, the silent E she places after the K. But she appears not to know precisely when she should use markers and when the environment (i.e., the two consonants around the vowel) can do the work of marking for her.

But the reader may see that there is another problem. PIK does not spell "pick" (except in advertisers' spelling!). The letter K in word-final

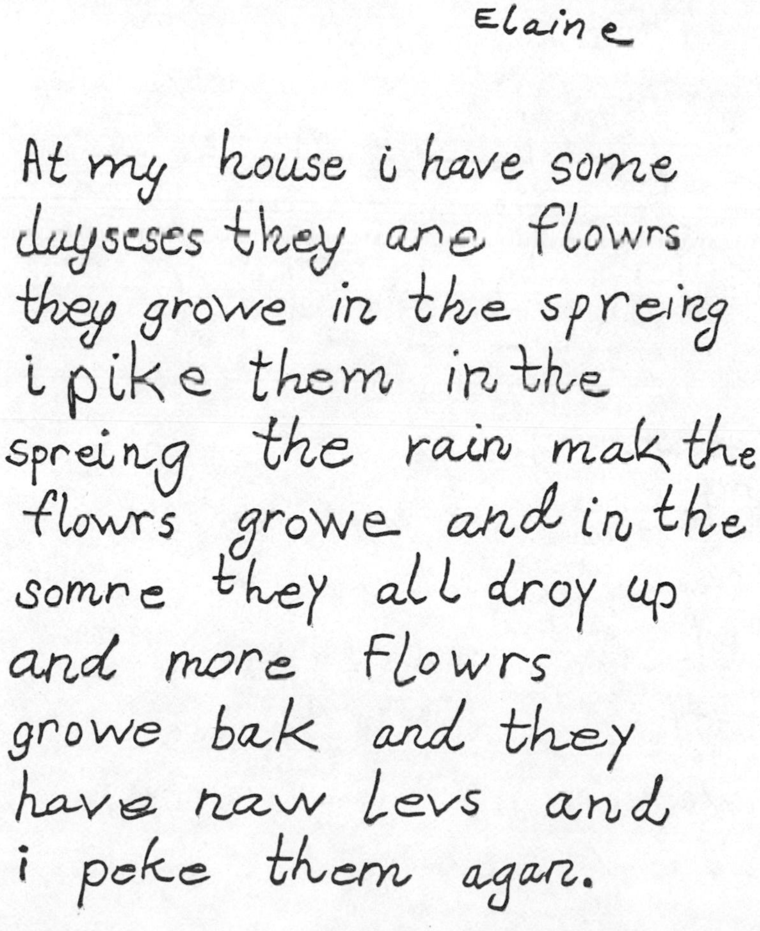

Elaine

**FIGURE 6 – 3**
*Elaine*
*Grade 1*
*Note vowel*
*marking*
*problems*

At my house i have some dayseses they are flowrs they growe in the spreing i pike them in the spreing the rain mak the flowrs growe and in the somre they all droy up and more Flowrs growe bak and they have naw Levs and i poke them agan.

position follows a scribal rule: K can never stand alone after a single vowel without a vowel following. We cannot have PIK, or BAK, or LOK, or DUK. The letter K needs to be accompanied by a preceding C in all such cases. The reason for this goes back to the Middle Ages. At that time it was standard practice to double final consonants after a preceding *short* vowel — "egg" and "ebb" still follow that pattern. But the scribes of the period had an aversion to writing the two letter K's together (we don't know why). So they developed the device of substituting CK for KK. The practice of doubling final consonants to mark a short vowel is long past, but CK is still with us, as a *scribal rule*.[5]

     Elaine may have seen that PIK was not what she wanted, and she may have therefore been put in search of a way of marking PIK to make it right. It would be logical, though incorrect, for her to arrive at PIKE.

     GROWE is another interesting extension of the silent letter E marker. By a certain logic, she is well motivated to put it there. The

**FIGURE 6–4**
*Teri*
*Grade 1*
*Note the mark-*
*ing of ā*

Teri

Can you see snow
flacks they are
verry prtty
they mack me
think of jeuse
weve he was littl
and merry his mothr.

Elaine

I have a ducke. I can drcke wottre. She has baby ducklings. Theye foloe her in a strat line. Theye leve in a barine. Thaye are yellow. Theye can tack a bathe and The un is out. and we play a lot with Theme.

letter W is, after all, a consonant, whose influence on the word is easily felt in the rounding of the lips. By the normal pattern, a vowel between two consonants GR-O-W would have the *short* pronunciation without a final E-marker. So Elaine's E, by this logic, is marking the O long.

Teri has overextended the marking strategy, too (see Figure 6 – 4). But her overextension is just the reverse of Elaine's. She has correctly noted the common juxtaposition of the letters C K, but she employs it for the long vowel marker instead of the short one. This pattern is apparently strong with Teri, since she uses it both for FLACKS (flakes) and MACK (make). The word WENE, on the other hand, has been given a long vowel marker, even though the E is short.

Figure 6 – 5 shows another by Elaine.

Elaine shows very clear signs of experimenting with marking as a strategy in invented spelling. It is not just a half-remembered feature from some other words. From her handwriting, it appears that she first wrote DUCK, and later appended an E to it — perhaps to make it look more like the words that followed! DREKE is a move toward institution-alizing the omission of N before other consonants. With the N omitted, the spelling DREKE probably comes closest to standard spelling of what is left. WOTTRE is another case of an earlier invented spelling that has an overlay of standard practice. At an earlier stage, the letter R would have represented the final syllable by itself. Elaine seems to have sensed that a consonant cannot spell a syllable by itself, so she has inserted a vowel — but in a secondary position, which is what she may have thought it deserved. Meanwhile she seems to recognize the need to double the consonant at the syllable boundary in order to keep the preceding vowel short.

Note that "take" is marked the reverse of the correct way, TACK. Note, too, that this marking business is still not second nature: she spells "straight" by the old letter-name strategy: STRAT.

Marking rules develop as a concept. The concept is applied very generally as a strategy for spelling words when the spellings have not previously been memorized. Sometimes these markers create spellings that can quite easily be read and understood by adults.

For example, Darla's paper (Figure 6 – 6) is easily readable, but she

**FIGURE 6 – 6**
*Darla*
*Grade 1*
*Note marking*
*problems*

Darla

here are the dogs

Ouce a pon a time we bote a
little kitten and you no how
they are win there little
They are little rascules.
But this one Loved to climb
tree and scach pepple He was
a mean rascule.

shows some uncertainty with marking patterns. RASCULES (rascals) and PEPPLE (people) are marked in a fashion just the opposite of standard spelling.

Even when marking rules are taken into account, there are many words in English whose spellings appear to violate the normal relation between letters and sounds.

*Scribal rules in English spelling*

These irregularities can often be traced back to the influence of the medieval scribes. The scribes, acting as the manual forerunners of the printing press, had a monopolistic influence on spelling, just as printers were to have later. Occasionally they made spelling changes to reflect changes in pronunciation. Sometimes their changes moved spellings toward greater consistency across classes of words. HWIC (which) and HWAT had their initial letters reversed to conform to the CH and SH spellings of words like "church" and "ship."

The scribes made some spelling changes to correct confusions among words brought about by the peculiar style of handwriting used in formal documents during the Middle Ages. The Gothic style of the period stressed a repetition of heavy vertical strokes, which reduced the means of discriminating between letters. An example can be seen in the text reproduced in Figure 6 – 7.

The spelling of the word "love" demonstrates the effects of two scribal changes. "Love" violates our expectations of regularity in two ways. First, it has a letter E at the end. This E looks like a marker for a preceding long vowel; but the vowel heard in "love" is short. The second irregularity is the sounded vowel: the vowel we hear in "love" is usually spelled by U, not O. How do we account for these anomalies?

The final letter E is there because since the early Middle Ages it has been unallowable for an English word to end in a letter V. This strange prohibition came about in the days when the letters U and V were not regarded as separate letters. Until the seventeenth century, the letters U or V could be written interchangeably for the vowel or the

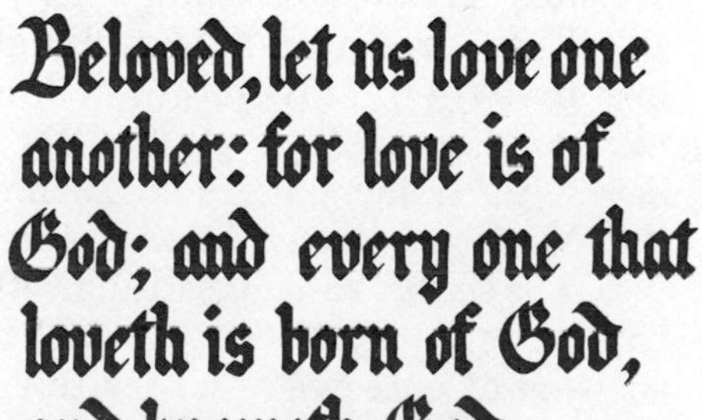

> 𝕭eloved, let us love one another: for love is of God; and every one that loveth is born of God, and knoweth God.
>
> 1 John 4:7

**FIGURE 6 – 7**
*Gothic script u's are difficult to distinguish from* M *or* N

consonant sound. But confusion could be avoided if word-final V, when it stood for the consonant, were followed by the letter E. Thus "you" was spelled YOU, or YOV. But "love," which had earlier been spelled LOU or LOV, came to be spelled LOUE or LOVE. In the seventeenth century, the vowel *u* and the consonant *v* were each stably identified with its own letter, but by then the silent E after V had become so entrenched that it is still with us 300 years later.

But what of the letter O in "love"? This vowel and the same vowel in "above," "some," "son," "one," "come," and "none" took its present form as a direct result of the Gothic script. In Old English, "love," "above," "some," and the others were spelled with the letter U.

The evolutions of their spellings were as follows:

| Year | | | | |
|------|------|-------|------|------|
| A.D. | 1000 | lufu  | bufan | sum |
|      | 1200 | luue  | buuen | sum |
|      | 1300 | lou   | abuue | summ |
|      | 1400 | love  | above | somme |
| MODERN | | love | above | some[6] |

It seems that in all of these words the letter U was changed to O deliberately, because in the Gothic script, with its repetition of bold vertical lines, the letter U was difficult to distinguish from M, N, and of course, from V. In the example of Gothic script in Figure 6 – 7 this difficulty is easily observed.

The Gothic script stayed in active use for centuries. Later typefaces alleviated the discrimination problem, but by the time this occurred, the letter O before V, N, and M was a solid fixture of English spelling.

*Children and scribal rules*

Like the vowel pairings ($\bar{e}/\bar{\imath}$; $\bar{a}/\bar{e}$) we saw in Chapter Five, the presence of scribal rules in English spelling leads to divergences between children's invented spellings and standard forms.

These are apparent in spellings involving a final letter V, as we see in Figure 6 – 8. This child's spelling of the word "of" lays bare some of his thinking on this problem. His spelling UV by itself would be phonetically regular, but his addition of a final letter E shows he is aware that V's never occupy the word-final position without an E.

The scribal rule concerning U/O and V is a central issue in Michelle's paper (Figure 6 – 9). She, too, had arrived at the spelling UVE for "of," showing at once the tendency to spell the vowel phonetically with the letter U and remembering to "cover" the letter V with the following letter E. She used that spelling twice.

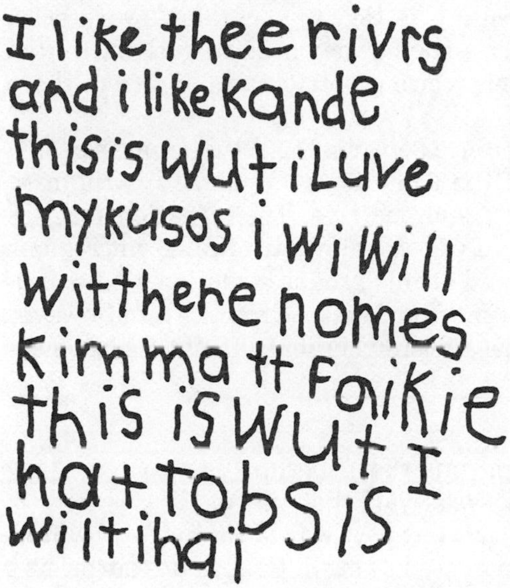

I like thee rivrs
and i like kande
this is wut i Luve
my kusos i wi will
witt here nomes
kim matt foikie
this is wut I
hat tobs is
wiltihai

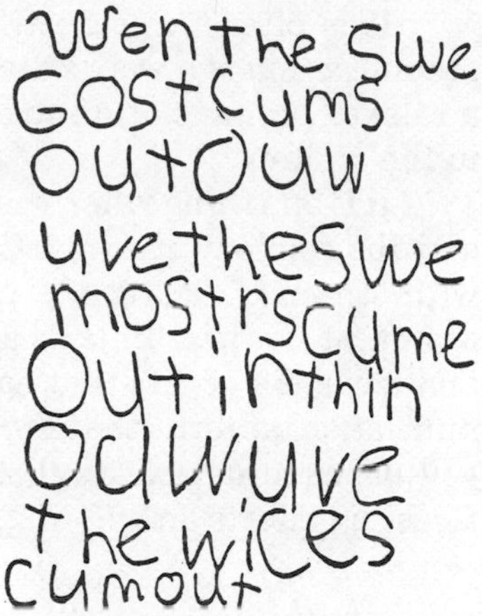

wen the swe
Gost cums
out ouw
uve the swe
mostrscume
out in thin
ouw uve
the wices
cumout

**FIGURE 6–8**
*Ralph* (left)
*Grade 1*
*Note spelling of
word final* **v**

**FIGURE 6–9**
*Michelle* (right)
*Grade 1*
*Note spelling of
"of"*

"Come," however, she spelled two different ways: CUM and CUME. The first of these spellings is phonetic. The second strangely contains the final letter E, perhaps because Michelle remembered seeing an E in the correct spelling.

Sometimes words change their pronunciation when they change their part of speech. Note the shift between "bath" and "bathe," between "teeth" and "teethe," between "strife" and "strive." These differences in pronunciation are reflected in spelling. But other such changes are not. Note the difference between "produce" (as a verb) and "produce" (as a noun; e.g., vegetables), "contract" (as a verb) and "contract" (as a noun; e.g., a document), "recess" (as a verb) and "recess" (as a noun).

*Phonological rules in English spelling*

Some sounds in words change their pronunciation when they occur next to other sounds. Say this sentence out loud, as you would to a friend: "I bet you can't eat the whole thing!" Chances are the end of "bet" and the beginning of "you" ran together as something like "betcha."

There are *phonological rules* that govern these sound changes. They work within words, too. When the sounds of *t* or *s* are followed by the sound *y*, the sounds blend to *ch* or *sh*. Thus we write *initial* but say "inishul." We write *special* but say "speshul." We write *fortune* but say "forchun." It is the coming together of the *t* or *s* and *y* sounds in each of those words that gives way to *sh* or *ch*. And that is a *phonological* phenomenon.

It is often the case that spelling is tied to a careful, overprecise pronunciation of a word: an accurate speller may need to work back from a relaxed pronunciation to an overprecise pronunciation and from there to the spelling.

It is one thing when the difference between the actual pronunciation and the spelled pronunciation is the same for everyone, as is the case with "special," "nature," "initial," and the like. The situation is more complicated when dialects are involved. Inhabitants of different regions and members of different social and ethnic groups sometimes have pronunciation patterns that are different from Walter Cronkite's, or however you define standard English. These pronunciation differences have interesting effects on spelling.

*Children and phonological rules*

Young spellers have no way of knowing that "speshul" is a compact way of saying "spessyal" and that it's "spessyal" that the spelling is tied to. Nor do they know that "nachure" is a compact way of saying "naytyure," and it's "naytyure" that we are supposed to spell. So it is not surprising that their first untutored approaches to these spellings are phonetically based and incorrect.

Note how Stella (in Figure 6 – 10) went about spelling "nature trail." The affricated (*ch*) sound of *t* and *r* rapidly produced was discussed in Chapter Four. Not surprisingly, she heard the *ch* in "nature" also.

Stephanie's spelling of "especially" is also interesting (see Figure 6 – 11). To include the first syllable in "especially" indicates a careful attempt to spell the word, but the C and I in the middle of the word is simply not available even to the most careful reflection.

"Grocery" is another word whose individual sounds are often compacted and changed in normal speech. The letter C is often fricated (see Chapter Five) to yield GROSHRY.

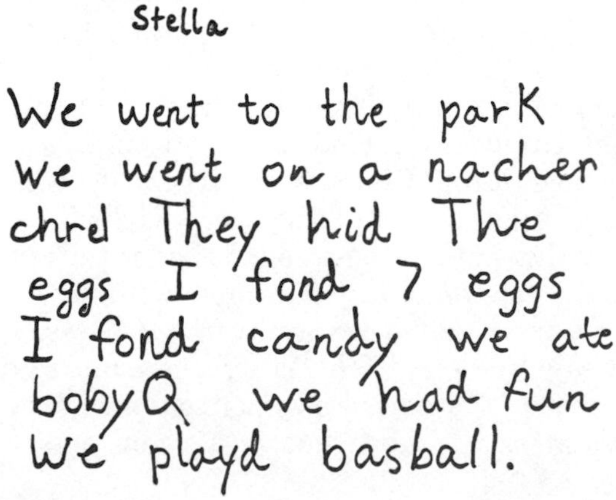

**FIGURE 6 – 10**
*Stella* (left)
*Grade 1*
*Note spelling of "nature trail"*

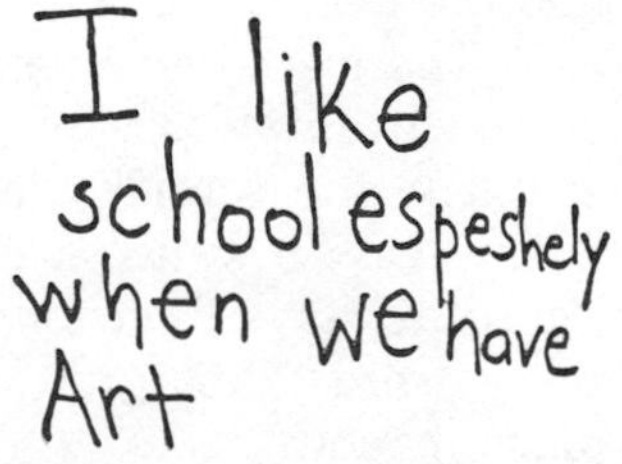

**FIGURE 6 – 11**
*Stephanie* (right)
*Grade 1*
*Note spelling of "especially"*

Stella

We went to the park
we went on a nacher
chrel They hid The
eggs I fond 7 eggs
I fond candy we ate
bobyQ we had fun
We playd basball.

I like
school espeshely
when we have
Art

Susie
I like to go to taun withe you Darla
I like to go to taun withe You to
ask your mon if you can go to
taun withe me Okay can you yes I can
Were are we goweg We are goweg
to the Groshre Stor.

FIGURE 6 – 12
*Susie*
*Grade 1*
*Note spelling of*
*"grocery"*

Susie's spelling of the word indicates the pronunciation usually given in southern Texas (see Figure 6 – 12).

Susie's SH in "grocery" and Stella's CH in "nature" were clever, but not surprising. We adults may sometimes forget what these words really sound like — seeing print biases our ears — but the children hear the sounds in words very acutely as they are spoken. GROSHRY and NA-CHUR are good renderings of what these children hear in those words.

In Figure 6 – 13 Susie shows that her knowledge has gone a step further. In her spelling of "jewelry box" she demonstrates that she is

FIGURE 6 – 13
*Susie*
*Grade 1*
*Note spelling of*
*"jewelry"*

On the holaday.
I went to my gramows house
and we went to mexeco and
I got a dyolreybox and I
honeted ester egg and I got
elem and my bruther fawd
three and my sistder got elevn.

That is us    ester egg

FIGURE 6–14
*No name*
*Grade 2*
*Regional dialects
affect spelling*

> Onece there was two dogs
> he chood on the sofa
> and inee thang he can
> git a hode uv.

aware that the sounds of *j* and of *dy* may alternate with each other. This awareness goes beyond having an acute ear for sounds. Her spelling demonstrates an awareness of phonological rules and of their relation to spelling.

A fine example of the influence of regional dialect on spelling is seen in Figure 6 – 14. This, too, comes from southern Texas.

**Morpheme
conservation
rules in
English
spelling**

Morphemes are words, or else they are parts of words that have meaning yet cannot stand alone. "Word" is a word, and a single morpheme. "Words" is also a word, but it is composed of two morphemes: *word* and *–s*. The letter S has meaning of a sort, because it shows that there is more than one of whatever it is attached to. There are dozens of these "bound" morphemes — thus called because they cannot stand alone: *–ed, –ing, –ly, –er, –ness, –ful, –ity, –ation, un–, re–, dis–, anti–* are some examples.

*Morpheme conservation* gets to the heart of the issue morphemes raise for young spellers. The problem is this: Because of speech habits, some morphemes are pronounced in a variety of ways. But because the different pronunciations all *mean* the same thing, they are usually spelled one way. In these cases we say that letter-to-sound regularity is ignored so that the identity of a morpheme may be conserved or maintained. And that is the *morpheme conservation rule.*

Let's return to *–s.* The *–s* actually represents two morphemes. One is a plural marker, as in "one duck/two ducks." The other indicates the number of the verb, as in "I duck/she ducks." But note the different sounds these morphemes can have:

| *Nouns* | *Verbs* |
|---|---|
| cats | stacks |
| dogs | folds |
| foxes | presses |

There are three possible sounds in *–s: s, z,* and *iz.* Which one it takes depends on the ending of the word it attaches to.

There is a phonological rule (that is, a rule of sound relationships) that summarizes the conditions under which –*s* will take its various sounds.

- Generally, –*s* takes the sound *s* after words ending in the sounds of *f, k, p,* or *t*.
- It takes the sound *z* after the sounds of *b, d, g* (as in "bag"), *l, m, n, r, v,* and *w*.
- It takes the sound *iz* after words ending in the sound of *j* (such as "page"), *ch, sh, s,* or *z*.

This rule is well known on an unspoken level to all native English speakers (it is devilishly tough, though, for foreign speakers of English!). To demonstrate, try pluralizing these non-sense words:

- one *barch*, two _____
- one *pog*, two _____
- one *burt*, two _____

You undoubtedly produced the "correct" sounds for –*s*. The curious thing is that we can do this sort of thing automatically, without being conscious of knowing or using a rule. We may even be surprised that –*s* has three sounds. Is this because the three sounds of –*s* are psychologically the same to us, or because we have so often seen them share a single form in print? It is difficult to say. The task for children, however, is to learn that the various spoken forms have a single written form.

The past tense marker –*ed* is another morphemic ending. Like the ending –*s*, it has one usual spelling, but three pronunciations. The pronunciations depend on the sounds of the word ending to which the –*ed* is attached.

To demonstrate for yourself the three pronunciations of –*ed*, put the following nonsense verbs into the past tense:

Today I will *blog* my yard. Yesterday I _____ my yard, also. Today I *trock* my grass. Yesterday I also _____ my grass. But I won't *frint* the leaves. I _____ the leaves yesterday.

The three endings, as we hope you discovered, are –*d*, –*t* and –*id*, respectively. Here is a summary of the distribution of the sounds represented by –*ed*.

1. Generally, –*ed* takes the sound of *d* after endings in all vowels, and after the sound of *b, g* (as in "beg"), *j, l, m, n, r, v, w,* and *z*.
2. Usually –*ed* takes the sound of *t* after endings in the sounds of *f, k, p, s, ch* and *sh*.
3. Similarly, –*ed* takes the sound of *id* after endings in *d* or *t*.

*Children and morpheme conservation rules*

Since the sounds of *s, z,* and *–iz* all mean the same thing, it is convenient for readers that they be written in a standard way, with a letter S. Children, however, may not be aware that spelling in this instance ignores the various sounds of the *–s* element in favor of its meaning. Thus, they will spell the *–s* ending in a variety of ways that honor the sounds. Examples of this are found in Figures 6 – 15 and 6 – 16.

As readers, we have become accustomed to seeing written words ending in *–ed* whose endings are pronounced different ways. We may even be surprised that these endings *are* pronounced different ways, since we have learned to associate them with one written unit: *–ed.*

**FIGURE 6 – 15**
*Ginger*
*Grade 1*
*Note spelling of "hugs"*

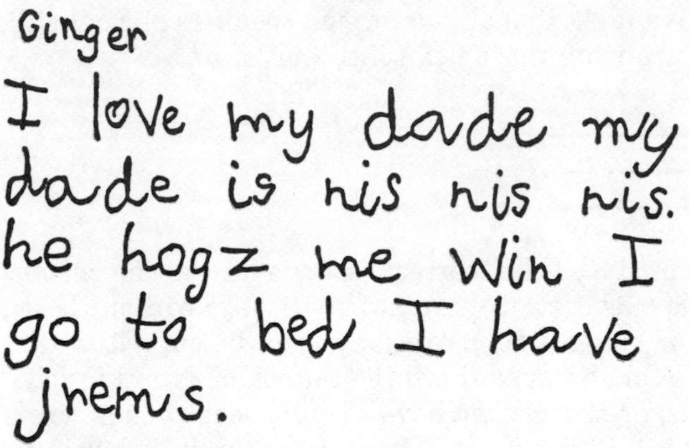

Ginger

I love my dade my dade is nis nis nis. he hogz me win I go to bed I have jnems.

**FIGURE 6 – 16**
*Elaine*
*Grade 1*
*Note spelling of "tadpoles"*

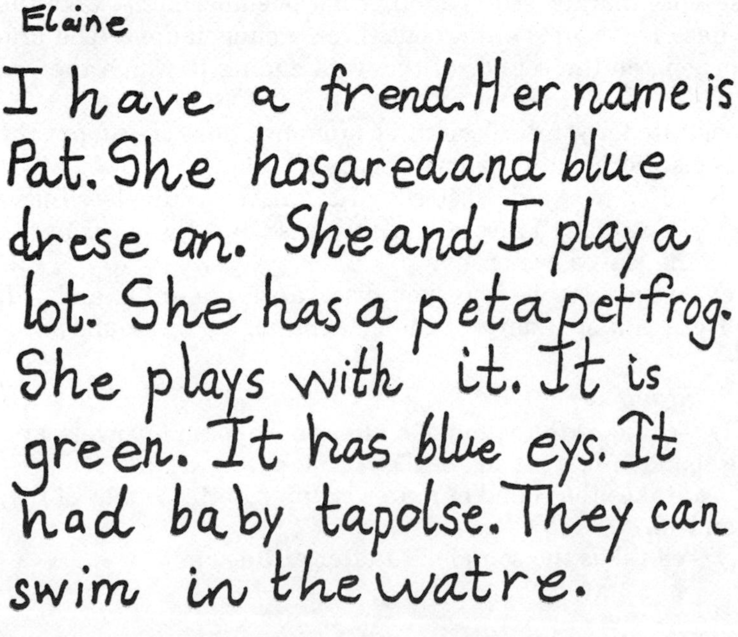

Elaine

I have a frend. Her name is Pat. She has a red and blue drese an. She and I play a lot. She has a pet a pet frog. She plays with it. It is green. It has blue eys. It had baby tapolse. They can swim in the watre.

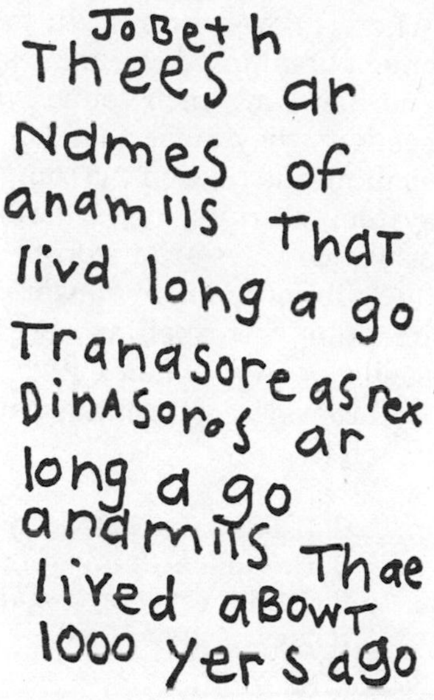

GingerLee

I Wet to The prK.
I SLIEG on TheSLIEg.
I Slide on The Side.
I posht ThemiE<sup>ron</sup>you
and I Rod my bik.
ten. I SpetOnit at<sup>th</sup>
es has ten I cant
Schoo.

JoBeth
Thee's ar
Names of
anamils That
livd long a go
Tranasore as rex
DinAsoros ar
long a go
anamils Thae
lived aBowt
1000 yers ago

**FIGURE 6 – 17**
*Ginger* (left)
*Grade 1*
*Note spelling of*
*"pushed" and*
*"rode"*

**FIGURE 6 – 18**
*JoBeth* (right)
*Grade 1*
*Note spelling of*
*"lived"*

But children who have not learned that different pronunciations are associated with this one written unit are likely to spell these endings different ways. Note in Figures 6 – 17 and 6 – 18 how these children treated the endings.

Teri shows that she has become aware of –*ed* as a morphemic unit that must preserve its –*ed* spelling. She has not figured out how to graft it on properly to the rest of the word, though (see Figure 6 – 19).

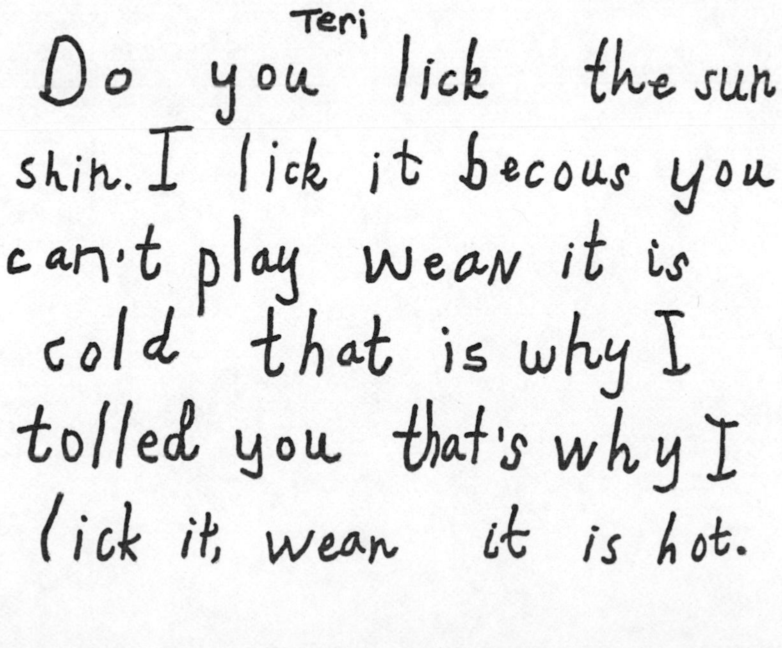

Teri

Do you lick the sun
shin. I lick it becous you
can't play weaN it is
cold that is why I
tolled you that's why I
lick it, wean it is hot.

**FIGURE 6 – 19**
*Teri*
*Grade 1*
*Note spelling of*
*"told"*

**Conclusion**    When children first begin to spell, they seem to perceive their task as one of breaking down their spoken words into individual speech sounds and matching each sound with a letter. As they move toward mature spelling, they must abandon the relatively simple phonetic approach to spelling and take on the complex patterns that are at work in our spelling system. Marking rules, scribal rules, phonological and morpheme conservation rules are involved in some of the more important patterns.

Children become aware of these rules and patterns through experimenting with spelling and comparing their productions with correctly spelled words. When children reach the stage of transitional spelling, well-considered teaching can help, too. This is the topic of the next chapter.

**References**

1.  G. L. Brooks. *A History of the English Language.* London: Norton, 1958.
2.  G. H. Vallins. *Spelling.* London: Andre Deutsch, 1965.
3.  Richard Venezkey. *The Structure of English Orthography.* The Hague: Mouton, 1970.
4.  Ibid.
5.  Vallins, *Spelling.*
6.  *The Oxford English Dictionary.* 13 Volumes. Oxford: Oxford University Press, 1933.

# 7
# *Making Progress in Spelling*

Children's invented spelling changes as they get older. Early spelling strategies give way to later ones, and the changes in strategies are reflected in the way words are spelled. Observe in Figures 7 – 1 and 7 – 2 spellings of the words "dragon" and "purred" offered by five children at different levels of maturity.[1]

| Lorraine 2nd grade | Joyce 2nd grade | Chris 1st grade | Angela Kindergarten | Brian Kindergarten |
|---|---|---|---|---|
| DRAGON | DRAGUN | GAGIN | J | MPRMRHM |

FIGURE 7 – 1
*Developmental changes in spelling*

| Lorraine | Joyce | Chris | Angela | Brian |
|---|---|---|---|---|
| PURRED | PURD | PRD | P | BDRNMPH |

FIGURE 7 – 2
*Developmental changes in spelling*
(Figs. 7–1 and 7–2 by permission of J. Richard Gentry, Ph.D.)

Though these spellings were taken at one time from different ages of children, it is probable that any one of them could have passed through different stages of spelling in the order suggested here. That means that if we were to watch Brian over a period of about two years, we would see his spelling change so that it would resemble first Angela's, then Chris's, then Joyce's, and finally Lorraine's.

To give these spelling strategies names, we would call Brian's spelling *prephonemic.* We would call Angela's spelling *early phonemic.* Chris's spelling we call *letter name,* and Joyce's spelling we call *transitional.* Lorraine's spelling is, of course, correct.

Our purpose in this chapter will be to place these stages of spelling in developmental perspective and to explain how you may accurately

103

determine where a child is in his spelling development. Then we will describe the instructional goals that seem appropriate for a child at each stage of development and suggest several learning activities that have been found helpful at each stage.

**The Stages of Spelling Development**
*Prephonemic spelling*

Let us begin by fixing the stages of spelling development firmly in mind.

The characters in Figure 7 – 3 are examples of *prephonemic spelling.* They were written by Kurt at age five. At that time he formed letters accurately and wrote voluminously, but he had not yet discovered how spelling works. He had not discovered the phonetic principle, which is the notion that letters represent the speech sounds or phonemes in words. Hence, his letter strings *look* like writing but they do not *work* as writing works.

When children string letters together without attempting to represent speech sounds in any systematic way, they are spelling prephonemically. This is the sort of spelling Brian produced in Figure 7 – 1 and Figure 7 – 2.

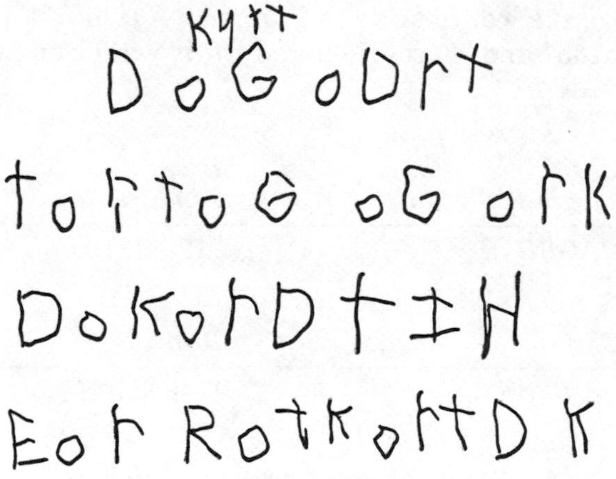

**FIGURE 7 – 3**
*Kurt* (left)
*Age 5*
*Prephonemic spelling*

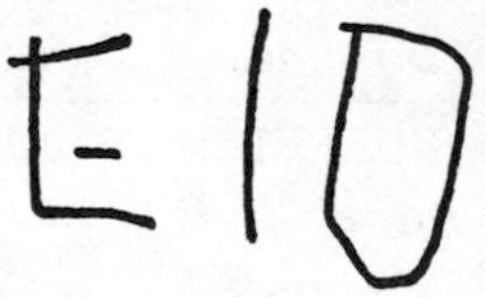

**FIGURE 7 – 4**
*Emily* (right)
*Age 4*
*"This could say 'Lauren'"*

Prephonemic spellers usually have not learned to read. But they appear to know a lot about written language. They know how letters are formed and that they are supposed to represent language is some way, as we see in the following anecdote.

Four-year-old Emily wrote what is shown in Figure 7 – 4 and said, "This *can* say Lauren — for make believe." (Lauren is her friend.) Then her mother wrote what is shown in Figure 7 – 5.

"*That* can't say Lauren," Emily objected.

"Why not?," asked her mother.

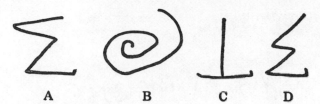

FIGURE 7–5
*Ruth*
*Age 35*
*"This couldn't"*

A    B    C    D

Pointing to the first letter, Emily said, "That's wrong." (Pointing to Figure C) "That's upside down." (Pointing to Figures A and D) "They're upside down."

Thus we see that Emily, a prephonemic speller, knows that letters can represent words, but only allowable letters can do this.

Figure 7–6 shows examples of early phonemic spelling. They are thus called because the children have attempted to represent phonemes in words with letters. These children have discovered the phonetic principle — they know basically how spelling works. But there is a curious limitation to early phonemic spelling. The children write down letters for only one or two sounds in a word, then stop. Thus, spelling in which letters are used to represent sounds, but only very sparsely, is called early phonemic spelling. Sometimes children in the early phonemic spelling stage will identify and spell one or two phonemes in a word, and then finish the word out with a random string of letters, as in Figure 7–7.

***Early phonemic spelling***

MBEWWMLnt

My Baby was with me last night.

**FIGURE 7–6**
*No name*
*Kindergarten*
*Early phonemic*
*spelling*

VL+ʌ DAL ísOM+hR

Valentine    Day    is almost    here.

ILngLeᴬDT⋊S

**FIGURE 7–7**
*Daryl*
*Grade 1*
*Daryl in October*

FIGURE 7 – 8
*Daryl*
*Grade 1*
*Daryl in*
*December*

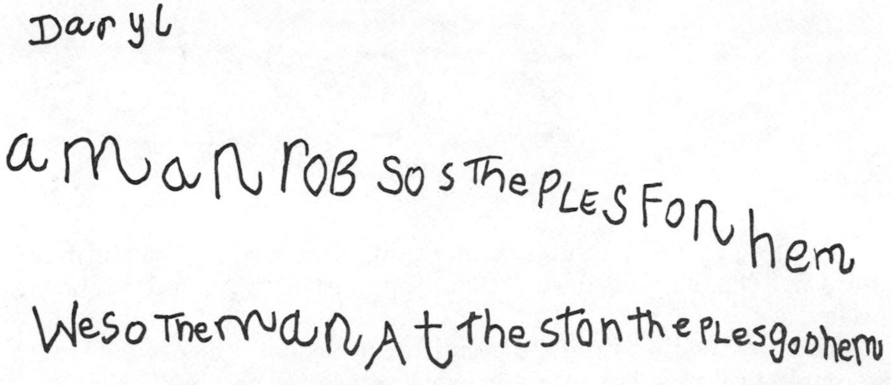

Daryl

a MaN roB so s The PLES For hem

Weso Ther Ma N A t the ston the PLes goo hem

The limitation seems to be related to the stability of the speller's concept of what a word is. The early phonemic speller cannot make words "hold still in his mind," while he examines them for phonemes and matches the phonemes with letters.

The transition from early phonemic spelling to the next stage, *letter-name spelling,* appears on the surface to be a matter of degree. A child represents more and more phonemes with letters until he is representing most of them. But the transition takes place rapidly. One month a first grader is producing early phonemic spelling, like Daryl's. Two months later he produces letter-name spellings (see Figure 7 – 8). The abruptness of this progress seems to be the result of an underlying factor; most likely the concept of word has stabilized between the early stage and the later one.

**Letter-name spelling**

Letter-name spelling is the practice of breaking a word into its phonemes, and representing the phonemes with letters of the alphabet (see Figure 7 – 9). The letters are chosen to represent phonemes on the basis of the similarity between the sound of the letter names and the respective phonemes.

Letter-name spellers often are not yet readers. That is, they may begin producing letter-name spelling before they are able to read. But the concept of word, and the ability to identify phonemes in words are important prerequisites for reading. Thus when a child begins producing letter-name spellings he usually begins to read soon after. For a time he will read words written in standard spelling and write words in letter-name spelling! This leads, not surprisingly, to confusion when a child reads his own writing.

Before many months have passed the experience of reading will present the letter-name spellers with differences between their way of spelling things and standard spelling. When their spelling begins to change as a result of this influence, they pass to the next stage.

**FIGURE 7 – 9**
*Daryl (no
relation)
Age 5
Letter-name
spelling*

He   had   a   blue
clth.   It   trd
in   to   a   brd.

Figure 7 – 10 shows *transitional spelling*. Words spelled by transitional spelling look like English words, though they are not spelled correctly. Transitional spellings employ many of the features of standard spelling — the silent letters for markers, scribal rules, and the rest — but employ them incorrectly. The conventional spellings for short vowels are normally employed at this stage, with occasional throwbacks to the letter-name strategies for spelling vowels. Words with irregular spelling patterns are usually misspelled by the children, and sometimes the misspellings have the effect of making the spelling of the word "look the way it *should.*"

**Transitional
spelling**

Can we go see the form
well we mite go later ohcaye
win will we go mom tsafter
noon ohcaye I will get redey
now no its not time yet ok
I will go play then ohcaye
can I go to Darlas house

**FIGURE 7 – 10**
*Susie
Grade 1
Transitional
spelling*

Transitional spellings will be mixed in with correctly spelled words whose forms the children have either accurately invented or memorized.

Children who produce transitional spellings often demonstrate that they have become aware of *features* of standard writing; particularly marking rules, scribal rules, phonological rules, and morpheme conservation rules. But they have not yet integrated all of these features into a systematic understanding of English spelling that works. In most cases, they will do so with practice.

Transitional spellers are readers. The source of the features, the generalizations about spelling that they are beginning to manipulate, is in the print they see around them. The path to correct spelling lies through more reading, more writing, and more attention to the way words are put together.

**Correct spelling**

Few of us spell everything correctly. All of us resort at one time or another to a dictionary for the spelling of a troublesome word. Still, most literate adults have an accumulated body of knowledge about English spelling that enables them to spell an immense quantity of words with hardly a second thought. We couldn't simply have memorized them all. Most of the words we write we were never directly taught. Many of them we have occasion to write no more often than once every two or three years — yet we still spell them correctly without hesitation.

**FIGURE 7 – 11**
*How can we read this?*

GLIGHLY DE BROMBLY SLOM GLARMED FROT DE FLOOZLE, ERMULLY, GLUGLISS, BOD GERFLIMANED DO LANG AY WHISS MOUT.

Moreover, we can write and read words nobody ever saw before (Figure 7 – 11). We couldn't do this unless our knowledge of spelling were based on generalizations or rules about the structure of words. We couldn't do it at all if what we had in our heads were simply a catalog of all the words we knew how to spell and read. The mature literate person's knowledge of spelling is a complex system of rules that relate phonemes to letters, and relate to phonemes a multitude of concerns involving the parts of speech of the words, the sound changes they go through, other words to which they are related, and even the old language — Latin, Greek, French, or Anglo-Saxon — from which they passed into English. Yet this knowledge exists only on a working level: the person may not be aware that he has it or is using it.[2]

You may wonder how it is that children make progress through the spelling stages if so many adults know so little about what they are doing! It does not seem that we could lead them to understand things that we are not conscious of ourselves. Clearly, children's learning of spelling concepts is largely self-directed. We teachers and the environment in general provide the wealth of information about written language through books, spelling lessons, reading instructions, and the like; but the children rather selectively attend to aspects of that information that they can use at any one time.

This does not mean that teaching has no role in children's learning about print, however. It is true that children can make progress in spelling if they are surrounded by print and encouraged to write. Their progress, nevertheless, can often be improved and confusion avoided if they are provided with encouragement, modeling, and instruction that is directed toward their current level of thinking about print.

If our teaching is to engage their thinking about spelling most directly, then we must have some means to determine where their thinking is. In the next section we will explain two procedures for assessing a child's level of spelling development. Then in the final section of this chapter, we will suggest instructional activities which are best suited to children at each level of spelling development.

In order to tell what children's spelling strategies are, we need to have them write words they have not been taught — words they have not memorized. That is because our object is to see the fruits of their spelling concepts, rather than to test their ability to memorize words. If children spell words correctly, there is no way to tell if they produced the spellings from their own concepts or carried them over from some other source — a memorized spelling or one copied from somewhere in the room where they were writing. So we need to set up circumstances where children will spell words incorrectly, because we may safely assume that incorrect spellings are neither copied nor memorized.

There are two ways to get children to spell words that they cannot always spell correctly. One is simply to invite children to write about some favorite topic, taking care to invite them to use whatever words they wish, spelling them as best they can. With some children this works easily. With others, using motivating topics like those suggested in the third section of this book will get them writing freely and producing creative spellings. But many children are too inhibited for either approach to yield freely spelled words. These children will write words they are completely sure of and few others. For them we can use a spelling test like the one Gentry used to sample their ideas about spelling. This structured prompting is just what some children require before they will take the risk of spelling words they are not sure of.

A recommended word list for such an assessment test is found in Figure 7 – 12.

**Assessing Children's Spelling Development**

**FIGURE 7 – 12**
*Experimental
spelling list*

1.  *late*       Kathy was late to school again today.
2.  *wind*       The wind was loud last night.
3.  *shed*       The wind blew down our shed.
4.  *geese*      The geese fly over Texas every fall.
5.  *jumped*     The frog jumped into the river.
6.  *yell*       We can yell all we want on the playground.
7.  *chirped*    The bird chirped when she saw a worm.
8.  *once*       Jim rode his bike into a creek once.
9.  *learned*    I learned to count in school.
10. *shove*      Don't shove your neighbor when you line up.
11. *trained*    I trained my dog to lie down and roll over.
12. *year*       Next year you'll have a new teacher.
13. *shock*      Electricity can shock you if you aren't careful.
14. *stained*    The ice cream spilled and stained my shirt.
15. *chick*      The egg cracked open and a baby chick climbed out.
16. *drive*      Jim's sister is learning how to drive.

When you administer the word list, it is best to follow these steps:

1.  Explain to the children that they are not expected to be sure how to spell many of the words. You want to see how they *think* the words are spelled. They should do their best, but they will not get a grade for their work.

2.  If they are stumped by a word, they should try to figure out how it begins, then try to figure out its middle, then its ending.

3.  Read the word, then the illustrative sentence, then read the word again twice. Give the word its normal pronunciation — don't exaggerate any of its parts.

Scoring the children's spellings is a matter of deciding which category the child's spelling of each word falls into. As you examine the way the children wrote each word, you —

* give the word a 0 if it is *prephonemic*;
* give the word a 1 if it is *early phonemic*;
* give the word a 2 if it is *letter name*;
* give the word a 3 if it is *transitional*;
* give it a 4 if it is *correct*.

You must assign each word a strategy according to the descriptions given in the previous section.

In Figure 7 – 13 we have scored a child's paper according to this system. If you are not sure how we categorized the spelling of each word, go back and review the early part of this chapter where the categories were described.

| | |
|---|---|
| Lat | 2 |
| Wnd | 2 |
| Sead | 3 |
| Gees | 3 |
| Gout | 2 |
| uL | 2 |
| cutp | 2 |
| Los | 2 |
| Lad | 2 |
| Suf | 2 |
| trad | 2 |
| ter | 2? 3? (The *y* spelling is learned.) Call it 2. |
| Sock | 3 |
| sad | 2 |
| cek | 2 |
| drif | 2 |

**FIGURE 7 – 13**
*Scoring a spell-
ing list*

There are two ways to tabulate the children's scores — you can find the average or the mode. The mode is the single score that occurs most frequently. To find the average, you add up the scores for the individual words and divide the sum by the number of words. The average for Figure 7 – 13, for example, is 2.2. The average, however, is subject to some distortion. If the child happened to know the spelling of several of the words, the accumulation of 4's could raise his average to make it appear by this way of reckoning that his strategy was more advanced than it really was. Thus it is safer always to calculate the *mode* as well as the average. In the example in Figure 7 – 13, the mode was 2. What this means is, most of the child's spellings fell into the letter-name stage of spelling. Since the average and the mode were in the same range, we may trust this conclusion.

Once we know the stage of spelling development in which a child is functioning, what can we do about it? Conceptual learning — and this includes learning how to spell — resists direct teaching. It is not very profitable merely to tell a speller that he is wrong when he makes a mistake. It is not much more effective to require him to memorize the

**Helping
Children
Make
Progress in
Spelling**

spellings of the words he will have to write. There are too many of them to memorize; and in any case, what we are after is that the students develop a set of concepts about spelling which will enable them to write thousands of words.

Conceptual learning has to run its own course, as children make discoveries, operate according to a particular hypothesis for a time, and then revise it as they find information that challenges the way they thought things were. But as teachers we *can* encourage this process along by offering helpful practice and steering children's attention to things that matter about the writing system.

In the following pages we will list goals around which to organize the spelling instruction of children at each stage of spelling, and illustrate activities to develop children's spelling ability.

*For the prephonemic speller*

Goals for prephonemic spellers are concerned with orienting them to the writing system. Books, magazines, and other written material should be a source of pleasure for the children. Parents and teachers both should read to these children. It is especially helpful to read certain books several times and then leave them around so the children can talk their way through them.

Parents can read the feature articles from the newspaper aloud to children and point to the caption words. They can also share comic strips that are easy to understand, and let children develop the habit of following them from day to day and Sunday to Sunday.

When parents take their children to a restaurant, they should read the placemat aloud to their children. They should read the menu, too; and point to the words as they tell the child the choices available. Parents can read cereal box cartoons and captions at the breakfast table.

Children should learn that writing communicates. Parents can point out to their children the messages communicated by other examples of writing around them. They can

- Read aloud the road signs the family passes that have words on them: "stop," "yield," "speed limit 55," "school zone," and so on.
- Read words that are flashed on the TV screen, such as show titles and cast of characters.
- Read labels on items around the house, such as toothpaste, cereal, spices (salt, pepper, mustard, catsup), and foodstuffs (flour, sugar, and so on).
- Write letters and other messages to, for, and with their children; for instance, parents can encourage children to dictate a message, write it down, and read it back. Then the parent can go over the message with the child and see if he thinks it is right. The beginning writer

will not know, of course; but by raising the question the parent suggests to the child that it is reasonable for him to concern himself with the print. Then the children can sign the dictations to make them theirs. . . . Ask children to label their art work, and then explain why they used the letters they did. . . . Label rooms or things around the house (or for teachers, around the classroom). Around the house these might be the bathroom, the television set, the refrigerator, the child's own room. At school these can be children's desks, lockers or clothes hooks, reading or science centers, pencil sharpeners, blackboards.

Early phonemic spellers have discovered that letters spell phonemes, but they cannot spell more than one or two phonemes per word.

*For the early phonemic speller*

Instructional goals for these children include the same general goals we have for the prephonemic spellers. We should continue to surround them with print: read to them, encourage them to identify particular books that they enjoy, that they can learn by heart and that they can read by reciting while they turn the pages. Also we should continue to have them experiment with writing. We give them plenty of opportunities to put down what they can by way of spelling out words.

We have some more specific goals for the early phonemic spellers, too. One is to encourage them to develop a stable concept of what a word is. The way to do that is to call the children's attention to words in print as we — or they — are saying words out loud. James Moffett has a procedure for this which he calls the Lap Method.[3] You hold a child on your lap, read to her a book with which she is very familiar, and point to each word in the text as you read it aloud. Gradually, you can get the child to try to point to words as you read them, and read words as you point to them. But the goal is to direct the child's attention to a written word at exactly the instant that the word is being read out loud. With this kind of support, the information that links a printed word with a spoken word is brought into focus for the child. Aspects of this information are things like the fact that a word in print is a configuration of letters bound by spaces on both ends, that they are arranged from left to right, that more than one syllable may be a single word, and that individual letters they recognize may resemble individual sounds they hear in words.

There are several successful variations of the Lap Method. One is done with a poem or a song that the child has memorized. The teacher and the child sit down with a written version of the poem or song, which is ideally four to six lines in length. They read each line chorally, as the teacher points to each word. Then the teacher points to a single word and asks the child what it is. The teacher points to the first word in the line; then the last; then one in the middle. It is not likely that the child will be able to recognize the words pointed to. Instead she will have to recite the line to herself and guess what each word must be by its order in the written line. This gets her thinking about words as units of writing, and gives her practice matching a word in her head with one in print.

There are commercially available read-along materials that children may use by themselves and gradually get the sense of words in print. Some of the best of these are Bill Martin's *Instant Readers*.[4]

Taking dictated experience stories, a part of the language-experience approach to reading and language arts instruction, also helps develop the concept of word in print. Dictated accounts are done either with individuals or in groups. After the children have undergone an interesting episode — perhaps an encounter with baby rabbits or a field trip to the post office — each child is invited to dictate one sentence to the teacher as part of a group composition. A number of reading activities usually follow the dictation: the group reads all the sentences chorally several times. Individuals volunteer to read words or sentences. The teacher also points to a word in the line and asks a child to read it. In cases where the child knows by heart what the line says but cannot recognize the word, he is likely to work his way through the line, matching memorized words with units of print until he makes a match with the word in question.

Many early phonemic spellers write their own names correctly, as well as the names of their friends, brothers, and sisters. Names can be used in learning activities to establish the concept of word. Write the child's name several times on a strip of paper without leaving any spaces between the names. Then ask the child to help you separate the names. The child spells her name first, pointing to each letter. When she comes to the end of one spelling, she cuts the name apart from the one that follows. When she has cut the names apart, she may paste them on another piece of paper, leaving spaces between them (see Figure 7 – 14).

A similar procedure involving whole sentences is suggested by Marie Clay.[5] Have the child dictate a sentence to you, write it down, and read it back to him. Then read the sentence with him, until he can read the sentence by himself. As you read the sentence each time, point to the words. When the child is able to read the sentence by himself (he is able to do this by memorizing, of course, not by actual reading), write the sentence a second time on a strip of paper. Now cut the words off the strip, one at a time, reading the sentence aloud minus the severed word each time. As a next step the child can match the cut apart words with those in the sentence that was left intact. A fairly easy task is for the child to arrange the cut apart words on top of the words to which they are matched. A more difficult exercise is to arrange the words into a sentence several inches below the sentence left intact.

Emily thought this activity up when she was not quite four. She puts a piece of thin paper on the cover of her favorite books and traces the titles. A sample of her work is found in Figure 7 – 15.

JULIEJULIEJULIEJULIE

JULIE JULIE JULIE JULIE

HAMD HAND
FHNDERS
THUMB

**FIGURE 7 – 14**
(left)
*Establishing the
concept of word*

**FIGURE 7 – 15**
(right)
*Tracing book
titles*

Another specific instructional goal we have for children who are early phonemic spellers is that they grow in their ability to segment spoken words into individual phonemes. The most natural practice is to continue to spell the parts of the words of which they are more certain. Thus their spellings may look like this at first: I W – T D – N – E P – – ("I walked down the path"). But in time, there will be fewer blanks left and more letters filled in as children gain practice in segmenting phonemes.

The final instructional goal we have for the early phonemic spellers is that they be more willing to take risks. We have seen abundant evidence that making errors is a necessary part of learning to spell. We want children to pay attention to the print around them and see how it is put together and how it works. But we want just as much for them to produce their own writing, in which they try out spelling the way they think it is. We want them to formulate ideas about written language and act on them; then they will know what to do with the information they gain from examining other people's written language.

Unless children take risks and unless they are willing to make errors, their progress as spellers will be slow and inhibited, and their delight in making their own messages in print will be small. Children who are willing to invent spelling for words usually become correct spellers in a reasonably short time — and they also become fluent writers in the process.

Whether or not a child is a risk-taker depends on a number of factors. His personality, the expectations of his parents, and the atmosphere of his classroom all contribute. There are several steps the teacher can take to help a child gain self-confidence and take risks:

1.  Provide many opportunities to write which will not be graded — at least not for spelling. If you have a spelling program and teach word lists and give tests on them, you need not also grade spelling on

other writing that the children do. Many kinds of writing need not be graded at all: For example, the child may put messages for the teacher in a message box or tack them on a bulletin board or write them to other children.

2.  Talk to the children and praise them for what they *know* about writing. If some children have discovered that writing goes left to right across a page, they may be congratulated for this discovery. If some have discovered that words have letters in them, and that the letters are mixed, this is something that the teacher can discuss with them. And if some have discovered that words are spelled by matching letters with individual sounds, this is a realization worthy of an adult's attention. Having an adult express interest in these issues as the children investigate them adds to the children's sense of accomplishment, and reassures them that their efforts are worthwhile.

3.  Parents and teachers should both understand the value of encouragement, practice, and freedom to make errors in learning to spell. If the teacher encourages invented spelling at school, but does not share her position with the parents, confusion may result. Parents may be alarmed that children bring home papers with uncorrected spelling errors, or that children enthusiastically produce writing with spelling errors at home. Unless the teacher enlists the parents' understanding and support, they are likely to say discouraging things to their children, with the best of intentions. They may even question whether the teacher is doing her job, mistakenly equating the teacher's encouragement of early writing and invented spelling with a lax attitude that leaves errors uncorrected.

*For the letter-name speller*    Children who produce letter-name spelling have developed a system of spelling that can be read by others who understand the system. Letter-name spelling represents the high-water mark of the children's intuitive spelling development, and their spellings during this period are their most original. From this point on children will become increasingly aware of the details of standard spelling, and their spelling will grow closer to that of adults.

By now their concept of a word in print is beginning to stabilize, but exercises to develop this concept still further will continue to be helpful — both for their spelling and for their reading. Their ability to separate individual phonemes out of words has become highly productive. What they do not yet know is all the business on the other side of the sound-to-letter representation issue. They are just beginning to explore the rules by which letters represent phonemes.

They can find the phonemes; but so far their ideas of how these phonemes should be spelled stick closely to the names of the letters. They use letter names as if they themselves were pieces of sound — building blocks out of which words can be constructed. They have not yet realized the amount of complexity that actually exists in rules for choosing letters to represent words.

If the disparity between their system and the complexity of standard spelling is pointed out to them too suddenly or too harshly, many children will lose confidence. If this happens, their progress into standard spelling will be delayed, because they will not experiment with new forms enthusiastically. The greatest amount of progress may be gained if children at this stage are encouraged to continue writing — indeed if they are given a steady agenda of interesting writing tasks. Their writing can be taken seriously for the sake of its message; the teacher and the parents can talk about what the child wrote and not just her spelling; focusing on the message is likely to be more motivating than dwelling on the spelling.

If the letter-name speller is exposed to a good supply of interesting print, this should provide him with data from which he can draw new conclusions about spelling at his own pace. We should continue to read to him. We should continue to help him find favorite books, read them to him frequently, and encourage him to read them to himself. The read-along books such as the *Instant Readers* can be highly beneficial at this stage both for reading and for writing. Language-experience teaching — dictated stories which are reread together — begins to bear even more fruit at this stage, both in the children's ease at finding words by the voice-to-print matching method, and in the number of words the children can learn to recognize after a dictated story. They will now recognize words in the story days after they were dictated, a feat they could not easily do before.

Having them build a word-bank — a collection of word cards for the words they recognized during the reading of the dictated story — is good practice. It's a good idea to check each child's word-bank occasionally, and see if she can still read all the words in her word-bank. Any words that she cannot read should be taken out, placed in a separate envelope, and reviewed at a later time. The children can be encouraged to use their word-bank cards when they are writing — these are always spelled correctly, so they constitute a source of correct spellings.

Teaching spelling by means of word lists begins to be helpful at this stage. Children need to have stores of correctly spelled words in memory. When children write freely, the correctly spelled words will not replace all or even most of the invented ones; the two types, rather, will stand side by side.

Gradually, however, children notice the disparity between their inventions and correct spellings, and then revise their spelling concepts accordingly. The revised spelling concepts will enable the children to approach more closely to standard spelling.

Learning correct spellings serves another purpose, too. It alleviates the burden of inventing *everything*, and often makes children's writing more fluent. As we have maintained throughout this book, invented spelling is worthwhile activity. Nevertheless, it is hard work. An indication of the intensity with which children work at invented spelling is given in this account by Graves.[6] Using a lapel microphone and videotape equipment, he recorded the oral "sounding" a child did simultaneously with each letter she wrote during invented spelling.

Jenny's message is "all of the reindeer loved them"

*Line 1:*   TRACK I:   luh, all, all, of, all of the, the,
(sounded)   the all of the reindeer

TRACK II: L  OLL       AVE       THE
(written)

*Line 2:*   TRACK I:   rein *ruh*, rein loved them, all, of, them,
(sounded)   the *muh muh*

TRACK II: R  IENDEER          LOVE  E    M
(written)

Children can collect words they frequently need in their writing and list them in a spelling dictionary they make themselves. Using a small spiral notebook, arranged alphabetically, they can write all of their words that begin with the letter A on one page, with B on the next, and so on. This practice, again, offers a source of correctly spelled words as grist for the mill of spelling concept formation. It also reduces some of the burden of invention and aids fluent writing.

Care must be taken, however, not to limit the children's writing to the words on the spelling lists or in the spelling dictionaries. It would be sad indeed if a preoccupation with these correctly spelled words undermined their confidence in their ability to think out spellings for themselves. Their willingness to try spelling on their own is necessary for them to move beyond memorization and learn the system of English spelling.

*For transitional spellers*

Children who are transitional spellers are adept at breaking out phonemes for words and finding letters to spell them. They are moving beyond the intuitive one-sound one-letter spelling of the previous stage. They have begun to take note of the way standard spelling works and are trying to gain control over the patterns they perceive in standard spelling.

As we observed in Chapter Six, the patterns of standard spelling are many and complex. It takes time, curiosity, and much exploration for a child to master these patterns. These children need to be led gradually to learn the patterns at work in standard spelling. It is best if they learn these in the context of meaningful writing, though isolated activities are sometimes helpful.

Inductive approaches often work well for helping children learn spelling patterns. In these, children compare the spellings of several words in light of their pronunciation, meaning, part of speech, and origin. Then they are led to formulate their own generalities about the patterns that appear to be at work.

*Word Sorts* are teacher-made or home-made activities that help children notice and form concepts about spelling patterns. Word sorts are a categorizing exercise in which children are led to group words together that share a common feature. This exercise gets them thinking about spelling features of words, and it works with words the children know.

The procedure works as follows. The teacher or the children write down a collection of words on small pieces of tagboard. If the teacher is using the Language-Experience approach, the words used are those in the children's word-banks. If he is not using the approach, then he or the children can jot down fifty words or so from the children's sight words on word cards. It's important for all of the participants in an activity to know the pronunciation and meanings of every word used.

With an individual or small group of children, the teacher starts off the activity by dividing the cards among the participants. Then he puts a card in the center of the table. He asks the children to read it and to put any words they have in hand that *begin with the same sound* on the table below the guide word (sometimes the teacher uses a picture of an object for a guide word, so the children may not get by with only a visual match between the first letters of the guide word and the words in their hands). The teacher makes sure that the participating children have several cards in hand that match the guide word, as well as some that do not.

Besides working with beginning sounds, the activity can be centered on long and short vowel sounds, other vowel sounds such as diphthongs and R-controlled vowels, grammatical endings such as *–ed* or *–s*, words that end in a *v* sound, words that undergo phonological changes, words with similar prefixes and suffixes, compound words, and many other features. The activity can be directed toward any word feature — including similarities of meaning and nuance — that the teacher intends. In fact, word sort activities often bring to light interesting word features of which the students and the teacher may have been unaware.

Word sorts have much potential for helping children to construct concepts about spelling patterns and to enable them to display the concepts they already hold. Additional reading about this activity can be found through the reference section at the end of this chapter.[7,8,9]

Children at this stage of spelling profit from games and exercises that play on the spelling patterns of words. There are many games which play on children's recognition of allowable sequences of letters — letter sequences that typically spell words. Boggle, Perquackey, and Spill 'n Spell are games of this type. In all three the players roll out letter cubes and try to identify English words within a specified time limit out of the letters that surface. Word hunts, Hangman, and Password are more games which regard children's efforts to think of spelling patterns in English. All are worthwhile both in the classroom and at home.

## Conclusion

Making progress in spelling is like making progress in playing chess. Both require enthusiastic commitment not only of the memory, but of the intellect as well. It is unnatural to think of spelling this way. After all, spelling and multiplication tables are two subjects that are still learned by rote at school.

A certain amount of memory work in spelling is necessary, it seems, to spell the truly exceptional words accurately. However, the active study of words, with a mind for learning how they came to be spelled the way they are and how they resemble and differ from other words, seems to be just as necessary for accurate spelling.

Those who undertake word study soon find more patterns, more clues for predicting the spellings of words, than they might have expected. Even when some words fail to fit patterns, they become more memorable as exceptions if the normal patterns are well fixed in mind. The memory thrives on associations; reasoning and reflecting on spellings thus makes memorization easier.

The teaching of spelling in school should therefore include plenty of discussion and exploration of words — including the patterns present in their spelling, the part of speech they can be, and the meanings they can have. In the home, games that play on spelling patterns and word meanings should be encouraged, as should frequent trips to the dictionary.

## References

1.  J. Richard Gentry and Edmund H. Henderson. "Three Steps to Teaching Beginning Readers to Spell," in Edmund H. Henderson and James W. Beers (eds.), *Developmental and Cognitive Aspects of Learning to Spell*. Newark, Del.: International Reading Association, 1980.

2.  Noam Chomsky and Morris Halle. *The Sound Pattern of English*. New York: Harper & Row, 1968.

3.  James Moffett and Betty Wagner. *Student-Centered Language Arts and Reading*. Boston: Houghton Mifflin, 1978.

4.  Bill Martin. *Instant Readers* (various titles). New York: Holt, Rinehart and Winston, 1970.

5.  Marie Clay. *The Early Detection of Reading Difficulties*. 2d ed. Exeter, N.H.: Heinemann Educational Books, 1979.

6.  Donald Graves. "The Growth and Development of First-Grade Writers." Paper presented at Canadian Council of Teachers of English Annual Meeting. Ottawa: May, 1979.

7.  Charles Temple and Jean Wallace Gillet. "Developing Word Knowledge: A Cognitive View." *Reading World*, December 1978.

8.  Jean Wallace Gillet and M. Jane Kita. "Words, Kids, and Categories," in Edmund H. Henderson and James W. Beers (eds.), *Developmental and Cognitive Aspects of Learning to Spell*. Newark, Del.: International Reading Association, 1980.

9.  Elizabeth Sulzby. "Word Concept Development Activities" in Edmund H. Henderson and James W. Beers (eds.), *Developmental and Cognitive Aspects of Learning to Spell*. Newark, Del.: International Reading Association, 1980.

# Exercises for part two

1. Figures 1 and 2 are transliterations of spellings by beginning first
   graders:
   a. See if you can decipher them.
   b. Make a list of letter-name spellings that appear in them.
   c. What exceptions to the letter-name principle do you find?
   d. Where do you suppose the correct spellings came from?
2. Adults have lived with writing for so long they often confuse the
   letters used to write a word with the speech sounds, or phonemes,
   it contains.

FIGURE 1

Donald hats me

Donald liks plag sokr

Donald olwas bregs a snak

FIGURE 2

Las nit I pold out mi lustuth
ad pot et ondr mi pelr ad wen
I wok I fid a 2 dilr bel.

a. In the following list of words, see if you can identify the phonemes and count their number. The word "late," for example, has *l, ā,* and *t* — a total of three.

b. Write the words the way a young inventive speller would. Pay special attention to the letter-name treatment of consonant digraphs, short vowels, N's and M's before consonants, TR's and DR's, and unaccented syllables with N, M, L, or R.

| | |
|---|---|
| wind | whether |
| wrap | cheap |
| shed | think |
| letter | whittle |
| driven | laid |
| straight | spread |
| chicken | school |
| champ | |

3. The *Oxford English Dictionary* gives the origins of English words and the various spellings each has had throughout its history. Many words formerly had more "phonetic" spellings than they have now. In the *Oxford English Dictionary* trace the changes in the spellings of the following words: "some," "come," "of," "shove," "which," "what," "lick," and "duck." Try to determine when the spelling of each word was closest to its pronunciation, and when the two diverged. Why do you suppose the spelling and pronunciation drew apart?

4. In Figures 3 and 4, two children's responses to our test spelling list are reproduced. Using the method described in Chapter Seven, decide which stage of spelling development each child is working in.

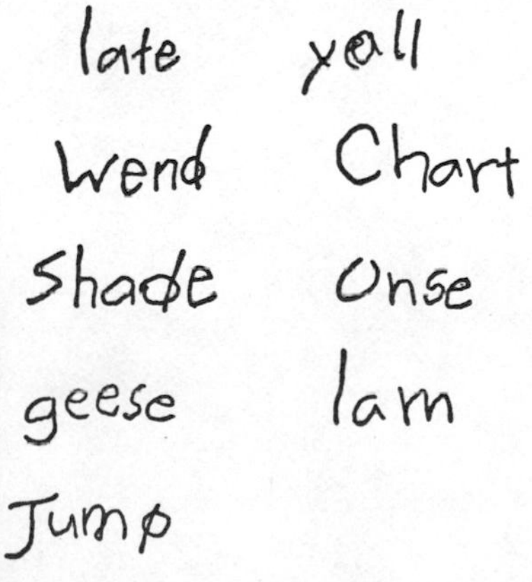

late        yoll

wend       Chart

Shade      Onse

geese      lam

Jump

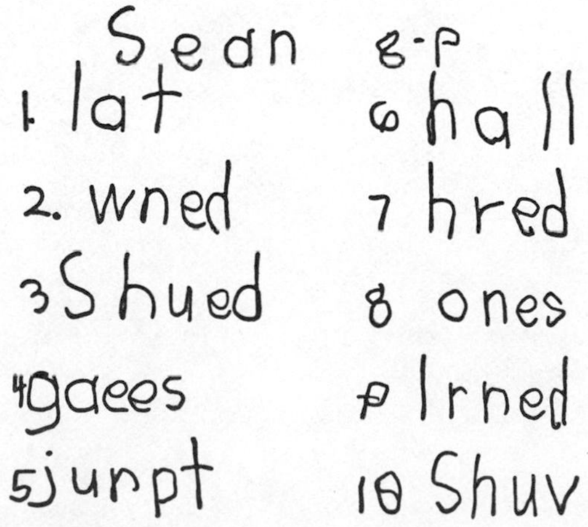

Sean        8-P

1 lat        6 hall

2. wned     7 hred

3 Shued     8 ones

4 gaees     9 lrned

5 jurpt     10 Shuv

**FIGURE 3**
(left)

**FIGURE 4**
(right)

# III

# The Beginnings of Composition

Three-year-old Emily was intently watching her mother write. Suddenly a pencil flew across the desk and her mother sighed over another rough draft that refused to work. "Oh, Mom," said Emily, "writing's such a cinch. All ya gotta' do is get the letters."

For Emily, and many other nursery and kindergarten children, that is what writing is all about for a while, "getting the letters." They have been exploring with pencil and paper, learning for themselves the distinctive features of alphabetic characters, and sorting out the relationship between the way words sound and their representation in print. "Getting the letters" and arranging them in some meaningful order are, in the early stages of development, prerequisites to becoming a writer.

In Chapters Two through Seven we have explored these developmental processes in depth. Now in the chapters that comprise this section, we will explore children's emerging compositions. We will examine the emerging patterns in the way children frame their messages — in other words, their compositions. We will look at children's movement from writing that sounds like talk to writing that sounds like written language — writing that achieves some of the purposes for which adults use it: telling a story, describing something, explaining the steps in a process, or waging an argument.

# 8

# The Functions and Emerging Forms in Children's Composition

**Reviewing What Children Know**

Those who undertake to teach children soon learn "to put first things first." You don't teach children to multiply before they can add. Nor do you teach them to add before they can count. In teaching young children to write, most teachers follow a similar common sense order of learning. Children are not expected to write before they can spell words. They are not taught to spell before they have sufficient handwriting skill to form the letters properly. They usually are not taught either one before they can read.

As we have attempted to demonstrate in the first two sections of this book, children who grow up in literate cultures often figure out for themselves more about writing than common sense would give them credit for. Strangely enough, the children themselves often do not realize how much they may know about it. The following dialogue between a teacher-researcher and a group of early first graders demonstrates this point.

*T – R:*    Boys and girls, today instead of reading together we're going to be doing some of our own writing. When your group comes out into the hall today, please bring pencils with you. I have paper, so don't worry about that.

*Children:*  What are we doing?

*T – R:*    We're going to be doing some writing.

*Jonathan:*  But we can't write yet.

*T – R:*    What do you mean, Jonathan?

*Jonathan:*  Well, we don't know how to spell.

*T – R:*      Oh, that's all right. I'll show you how to get around that problem. We're going to write some of our own thoughts today. What do you think of that?

*Jonathan:*      Oh.

That day the children were anxious to try to write. The spelling constraint that worried Jonathan was removed with a short discussion of invented spelling. The children were told to try and spell words they didn't know by saying the word very slowly and using the letters they could hear most clearly. The assignment seemed of interest to them: the children were asked to describe just one person or pet from their family. Figures 8 – 1 to 8 – 4 show some of the papers that resulted from the teacher-researcher's request. You'll note the invented spellings, which required little coaxing, and you'll probably appreciate the freshness and honesty that is so vividly expressed in their first compositions.

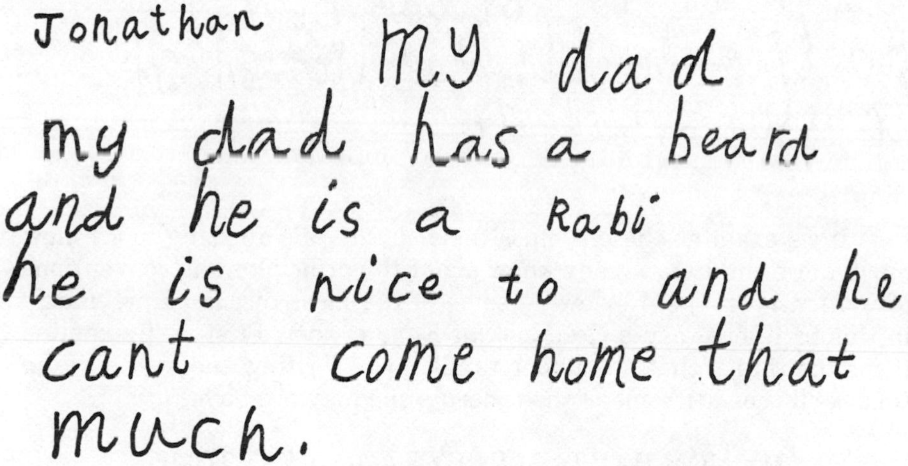

Jonathan

my dad
my dad has a beard
and he is a Rabi
he is nice to and he
cant   come home that
much.

**FIGURE 8 – 1**
*Jonathan*
*Grade 1*

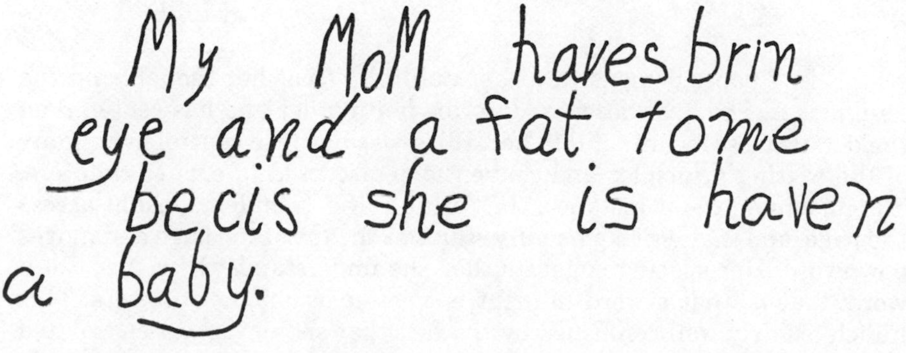

My MoM haves brin
eye and a fat tome
becis she is haven
a baby.

**FIGURE 8 – 2**
*Elise*
*Grade 1*

**FIGURE 8–3**
*Heather*
*Grade 1*

My dog is love ll she is Blak
Heather

**FIGURE 8–4**
*Ronnen*
*Grade 1*

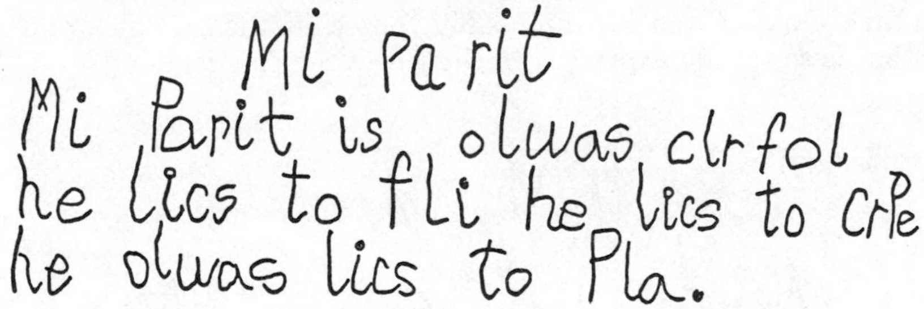

Mi Parit
Mi Parit is olwas clrfol
he lics to fli he lics to crPe
he olwas lics to Pla.

If we examine these compositions closely, it's amazing to see how much these children already know about the principles and conventions of written language. Reviewing some of the ideas discussed previously in this text, let's take a close look at Elise's paper. First we'll examine it for the things that she understands about writing and spelling and then we'll consider some of the concepts she may not have.

MY MOM HAVES BRIN EYE AND A FAT TOME
BECIS SHE IS HAVEN A BABY.

ELISE

Elise's paper demonstrates her ability to focus her thoughts on the assignment. She has chosen to describe her mother and has centered on the details most meaningful to her. Elise also has firm control over many of the writing principles and conventions discussed in earlier chapters. She understands, for instance, that print moves from left to right across the page, and that writing usually starts at the top of the page and moves downward. Her spacing suggests that she understands the concept of a word; that is, that a word in print is a letter or cluster of letters. This hunch is fairly well confirmed by the fact that she never writes isolated syllables as if they were words. Other conventions associated with the printed material she reads are also evident in her capitalization and punctuation attempts. In regard to spelling, Elise has spelled over half the words in her piece correctly, and those she hasn't spelled right are spelled phonetically (e.g., brin, tome, becis, haven). She is in the transitional stage of spelling, though she has begun to acquire conventional spellings for several words (e.g., eye, she, and my).

Elise's use of the word "haves" tells us something about her knowledge of English word formation. To form the third person singular of many verbs we often just add an "s" (e.g., I jump, she jumps). As Elise writes the third person singular of the verb "have" she overgeneralizes and produces "haves." Note also that she has used an "s" to end that word even though the ending sound of "haves" is *z*. This spelling honors morphemic or grammatical information instead of sticking slavishly to sound-symbol correspondences.

Recapitulating what Elise knows, we see that:

1.    Elise can focus her thinking and move from thought to print.
2.    To a limited extent, Elise understands how to describe someone.
3.    She knows the direction in which print usually goes.
4.    She appears to understand the concept of a word in print.
5.    She has internalized some of the mechanical conventions used in print, such as the use of capitals and periods.
6.    She appears to be in the transitional stage of spelling.
7.    She's begun to acquire some conventional spellings.

Why highlight what Elise knows about writing? The reason is simple. When children begin to talk we're so glad to hear from them that *how* they say *what* they say doesn't really matter. This isn't so with our school culture; often teachers find it difficult to see beyond children's mistakes. To add insult to injury, when mistakes are spotted they're often red-tagged and handed back. Imagine if we were to do this to children as they were learning to talk! Initial writing attempts need the same accepting atmosphere as initial attempts at speaking. It's as simple as that. If we honor what Elise knows, she may well gain confidence and fluency in writing.

Returning to Elise's paper, let's take a look at what she may not know:

1.    Does she know the word "eye" should be plural?
2.    Her first use of "have" is incorrect. Why?
3.    She has spelled many words incorrectly.

The best way to resolve some of these questions would be to ask Elise to read her paper aloud. We did, and this is what she read: "My mom has brown eyes and a fat tummy [*pause*] because she is havin' a baby."

Of the three mistakes noted, Elise's reading of the paper corrected the first two. The third problem can't be taken too seriously since she's only a first grader and already approaching the transitional spelling stage.

Can Elise write? Jonathan, our original skeptic, was amazed that he could. Elise was equally overjoyed. Building on the excitement children feel gives us a base on which to help them grow. We teachers should make sure that our evaluative comments focus on the positive aspects of children's writing. We can share instructive insights with children without damaging their desire to compose, if we focus on the positive.

Before moving on to the second part of this chapter, choose one of the other compositions shared here and analyze it for what the child knows and doesn't know. First, consider everything your chosen youngster demonstrates he knows about writing. Next, consider where he needs help, and what might be done, if anything, to help him.

## Composition: What Is It?

In analyzing the samples just now, you may have paid close attention to the issues of spelling and graphic principles, the topics of our previous chapters. In those chapters we treated at length the principles and conventions of written language as a graphic display and of invented spelling. What we need to discuss now are the writers' *messages* themselves: what the writer says and how he puts it together. "Putting together" is simple English for "composition," a term which comes to us from Latin. Composition is the topic of the rest of this, and the next two chapters.

To think of composition as "putting together" suggests ideas and their relationships to each other or their structures. That description fits fairly well, for a composition is a product, an artifact, a paper lying on the table in front of us. To describe composition as an activity, however — to talk of how we compose — we must consider some elements in addition to ideas and structures.

We must consider the writer's self and his purposes for writing. Furthermore, we must consider the reader, his relationship to the writer, and his need for information. How many different kinds of compositions can you think of? There are:

| | |
|---|---|
| poems | traffic tickets |
| jokes | short stories |
| obituaries | graffiti |

| | |
|---|---|
| songs | menus |
| state constitutions | love letters |
| examination papers | bills |
| editorials | textbooks |
| novels | notes passed in class |
| the Ten Commandments | declarations of war |
| plays | and countless others. |

Each type has an *author*. Each one has some *topic*. Each one has some *purpose* for his writing. According to the purpose, the author's organization of his ideas will take some *form*. Each piece has an *audience* — a reader.

Before you read on, go back and consider the types of composition we listed and any you listed. Who is likely to be the author of each type? What is likely to be the topic? What is the purpose? Who is intended to be the reader? The distinctive character of each of the types of composition may largely be defined by these questions. In some, the writer is very much present in the work. We know who she is, and we sense her feelings, opinions, and beliefs. In others, the author is far in the background: who can picture the actual author of a state law? In some, the audience is a specific person, but not one well known to the writer. In still others, the audience is anyone who cares to stop and read.

A mature writer considers, consciously or unconsciously, the issues of self, topic, purpose, form, and reader as she writes one or another type of composition. How does she get to be a mature writer, though? There is much developmental change from the young scribbler to the adult novelist, pen pal, or editor. In our focus on young children, we will observe only the first steps in this development. Yet even in children's early writing, we can clearly see the issues of self, reader, topic, and purpose taking shape.

**The Purpose and Function of Children's Writing: Some Useful Categories**

The sort of writing in Figure 8 – 5 seems to come naturally to young writers. The author is very much in the center. The reader could be anyone who is interested in the author. The purpose is pure *expression*. We may say that JoBeth has written in the *expressive voice*, about which we will say more later.

Figure 8 – 6 shows a piece of writing with a clearly different purpose or function.

Following in the footsteps of James Britton, a long-term observer of children's writing, we will call this function *transactional*.[1] A piece of writing with a transactional function may be said to be written in the transactional voice.

**FIGURE 8-5**
*JoBeth*
*Grade 1*

Jo Beth

I Love The ABcs

I Love The 123

BUT most of All

I Love music

**FIGURE 8-6**
*Missy*
*Grade 2*

Missy

firstyou get on your bicyle andput your left hand on one bar. And you put your right hand on the other bar. Then put your left foot on one pedle. And yourother foot on the other pedle. And then you put your but on the seat and you know how to ride a bike.

In the transactional voice the writer is concerned with getting something done in the real world — she may wish to persuade, describe, or give directions. She may be thought to assume that the reader is interested in her message because of its objective attributes — not because of the reader's interest in the writer herself. She may also assume that the reader can engage her ideas for their truth value or usefulness: the reader may say, that's right or wrong, worthwhile or not worthwhile.

Note that it doesn't matter who the writer is in Missy's piece in order for the piece to achieve its purpose. Moreover, the truth of the statements can be verified by a simple test: We can get on a bike and see if by following her directions we can ride the thing.

A third category of the functions of writing has been termed *poetic*. Poetic writing is not limited to poetry. It refers to any written work whose function is to stand as a product of creativity in itself — as a work of art or as a verbal object to be admired. As with the transactional voice, when a writer uses the poetic voice we are not usually concerned with *who* he is. A story is a story, regardless of the teller. Note, however, that the reader does not respond to this kind of writing in the same way he does to writing in the transactional voice. It is not appropriate to criticize a story as to whether it is true or not; but rather according to whether it is whole, complete, or "storylike." In other words, does it have all the elements a good story should have?

Consider this story Jessica dictated at age four:

The rabbit was at his house and his mother told him to go to the well and fetch some water. But Bunny didn't go to the well because she was very curious. She went to the woods and picked some raspberries. So she said to herself, "Why don't I go and find Daddy? Have lunch in town and ride home with him. That will be more fun."

She rided out with Daddy but then a great THUMP THUMP filled up the whole air. It was a real big air-walking giant. She really was frightened. She ran to the house and said, "Mamma, help!" And she hid them both. And they lived happily ever after.

Jessica
Age 4:8

This piece is not designed to express Jessie's wants, likes, and dislikes — at least not directly. The story does not stand or fall on the reader's knowledge of and interest in Jessica. Nor is its truth or falsehood meant to be testable in the real world. It is not literally true, but that is irrelevant. The function of this piece is to stand as a work of delight — much like a picture to be hung on the wall.

The three major categories of writing that we have discussed have been succinctly outlined recently and are listed below.[2]

1.  *The expressive voice.* This is language which is close to the self, used to reveal the nature of the person, to verbalize his consciousness, and to exhibit his close relation to the reader. Expressive language is a free flow of ideas and feelings.
2.  *The transactional voice.* This is language concerned with getting things done. It involves giving information or instructions, and attempting to persuade and advise others.
3.  *The poetic voice.* Poetic language is a verbal construct, fashioned in a particular way to make a pattern. Language is used in the poetic voice as an art medium.

Some early writing of young children falls into the transactional voice. We will recognize it as language meant to get something done. Examples of such transactional writing would be, for example, directions for the care of a plant or pet, or instructions for a game in the science center. Some writing falls into the poetic category: its pattern as a simple story or poem will usually be recognizable. A great deal more of early writing will fall into the expressive voice: we can identify this as written language that is very close to the child's casual speech.

Which voice do you think most young children use first in their writing? How are the voices of written discourse found in developmental perspective? Most children begin with the expressive voice and move out gradually in two directions toward transactional writing on one end and poetic writing on the other.

Transactional ⟵ Expressive ⟶ Poetic

As we shall see, however, a child's writing may fall in transitional points between expressive and transactional and expressive and poetic. Before we explore these, however, let us begin with expressive writing and see how it works, and how a child moves out from it.

**The expressive voice**

Usually expressive language sounds a lot like talk. In fact, dialogue in the writing is a frequent feature of children's early prose. Sometimes the other speaker is the writer's intended audience. Sometimes it is some other character. Figures 8–7 and 8–8 are two typical examples.

Though it shows up frequently in early prose, dialogue does not prove to be an especially easy medium to maintain in writing. Many children never use it in their early work because it is difficult to handle on paper. Consequently, monologue, speech for oneself that does not require a response from a listener, is another language source used by children. Researcher Britton feels monologue is a natural lead-in to writing, and for this reason he encourages teachers to amplify children's

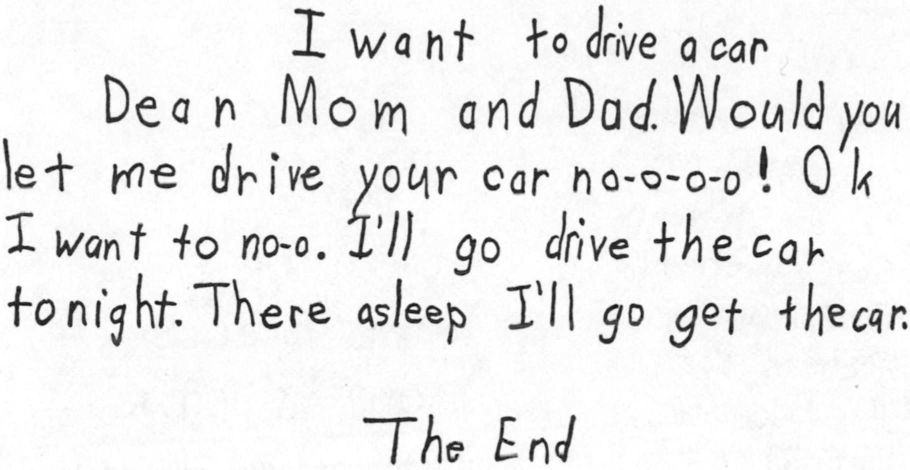

FIGURE 8–7
*John*
*Grade 2*

I want to drive a car
    Dear Mom and Dad. Would you
let me drive your car no-o-o-o! Ok
I want to no-o. I'll go drive the car
tonight. There asleep I'll go get the car.

        The End

FIGURE 8–8
*Susie*
*Grade 1*

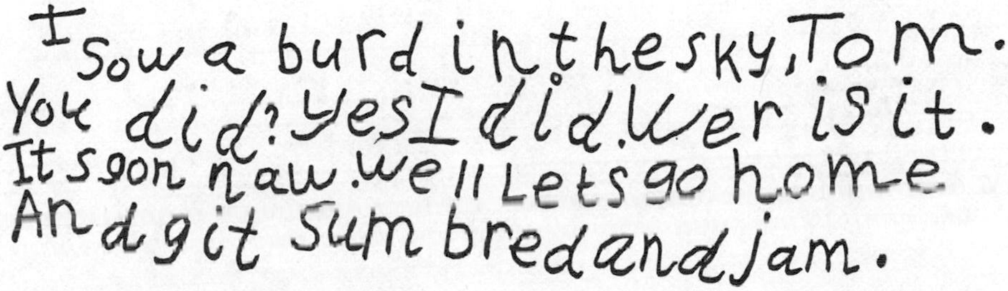

I sow a burd in the sky, Tom.
You did? Yes I did. Wer is it.
It sgon naw. We ll Lets go home
And git sum bred and jam.

contributions to conversation by questioning: "Yes, and then what happened?," "Was there anything else you saw?," and so on.[3] The composition in Figure 8–9 is an example of monologue.

JoBeth, a first grader, entered this piece in a diary that she and the rest of her classmates were keeping at school. A diary or journal is an excellent way to encourage children to create fluent expressive writing, monologues in particular.

Movement out from expressive language is slow. Children, and adults for that matter, approach the transactional and poetic categories only as they begin to think about the things their audience (the people who read their work) may need to know, and as they begin to consider the content and structural requirements of the various forms of discourse. Britton points out that young children will not be able to comply fully with all the demands readers of transactional or poetic writing make on the writer. It is by *attempting* to meet such demands that children gradually acquire the differentiated forms.[4]

FIGURE 8-9
*JoBeth*
*Grade 1*

Sant paTriks day is comeing in to weeks. my Teachr hasant GoT a chance To PuT up The Pichers for it. I Like it Becose We Get to edT Goas and Turky BuT The BesT ParT is. you GeT TO GeT FaT.

A

Boy is this boring. S.t. Paterics day is in two Months if you Thank thats not Boring Tell Me What is.

B

No Geting To eat turcky. No Pillgrims. No indeins No ine thang. Like I say if you Dont thank thats Not Boring Whdt is

C

Much of children's writing falls between the three categories of transactional, expressive, and poetic. This can be intentional, as in the case
of many great writers. (Would you categorize the story of "The Boy Who,
Cried Wolf" as poetic or transactional?) Sometimes through a lack of
skill or maturity a child's writing will start off in one category and end
in another. How would you categorize Debbie's piece in Figure 8 – 10?

    Debbie wrote this in response to the following assignment: "Think
of something you want to do and of someone who will not let you do it.
Then write a letter to that person and try to *persuade* him or her to let
you do it."

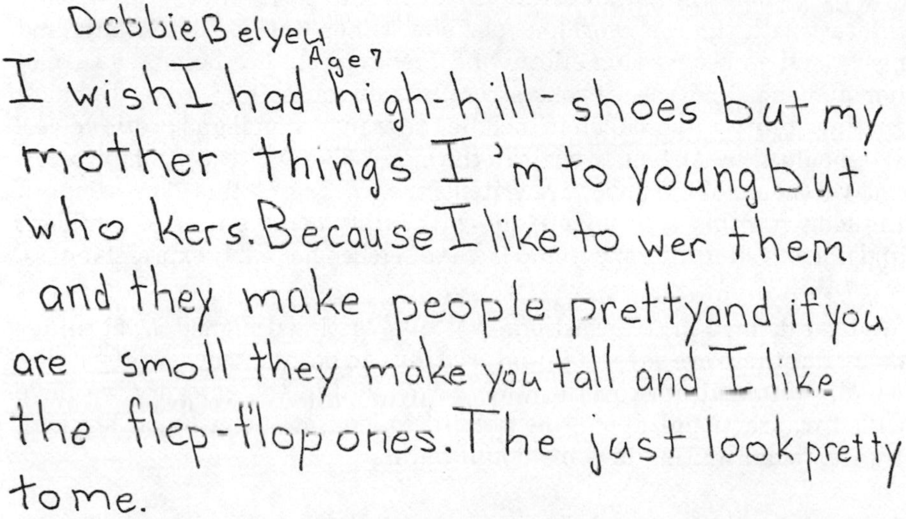

*Transitional
categories*

*Debbie Belyeu*
*Age 7*

I wish I had high-hill- shoes but my
mother things I'm to young but
who kers. Because I like to wer them
and they make people pretty and if you
are smoll they make you tall and I like
the flep-flop ones. The just look pretty
to me.

*FIGURE 8 – 10*
*Debbie*
*Grade 2*

    The teacher's intent was clearly to get the children to write some-
thing transactional. Did she succeed? Debbie's is a bouncy, personal, and
somewhat rambling statement. It is very close to the way we might expect
her speech to sound in its spontaneity and flow. She sounds as if she is
talking to herself or a peer, though, rather than sincerely trying to persuade her mother. To use this piece seems expressive with just a leaning
toward transactional. It is in between the two; thus we may call it
*transitional.*

Transitional writing should be welcomed. Children's early writing attempts do not always meet the requirements of prose that is to be considered "literature" (poetic) or prose that is meant to get something done
(transactional). But their writing in the transitional categories indicates
development along the right lines.

*Welcoming
transitional
writing*

Teachers usually request some form of transactional or poetic prose in their assignments. It is important to realize, however, that the urge to be expressive will often overshadow the requirements of any formal assignments contrived by teachers. Whether children are writing directions for washing the blackboard (transactional) or creating a story (poetic), their work may suddenly break down into a very personal piece that articulates some deeply felt emotion or new awareness.

In giving assignments a teacher needs to keep in mind and help the children keep in mind the basic questions that give shape to any writing: "What is the purpose of the writing?" and "Who will be reading it?" while carefully honoring expressive qualities.

As Debbie, the author of the "high-hill" composition, sees her writing interact with the real world, as she shares her work with teachers and peers, and as her writing efforts and reading help her become aware of her audience and the various structures discourse may take, Debbie's writing ability will broaden to include the transactional and poetic voices. We should allow Debbie to write in the expressive and transitional voices, and we should offer supportive criticism, encouraging this expression. In the long run this will pay off; she will surely become a more confident and fluent writer than she would if we squelched her early expressiveness.

## The transactional voice

We have defined the transactional voice as writing designed to get things done. But there are several things writing can do, and teachers of writing usually differentiate several other forms within the category we have called transactional. It will be helpful to look at the common forms of transactional writing in some detail here.

## Exposition

Exposition explains a subject. It is used to tell what a thing is, how it functions, its history, how its parts are related to each other, and/or how it is related to other things. Aliki Brandenberg's discussion of how dinosaur bones turned into fossils is an adult example of one type of exposition.[5]

> When the dinosaurs died, they were covered with sand and mud. They were buried for millions of years.
> The sand and mud turned into rocks, and the dinosaurs' bones became fossils.

Simple directions are expository as well, and most classrooms abound with hundreds of examples. Just open any mathematics workbook and undoubtedly an example will pop out at you.

Most young children are capable of writing expository prose. Consider Figure 8 – 11, which shows an informative piece by JoBeth, a first grader whose work we met earlier in this chapter.

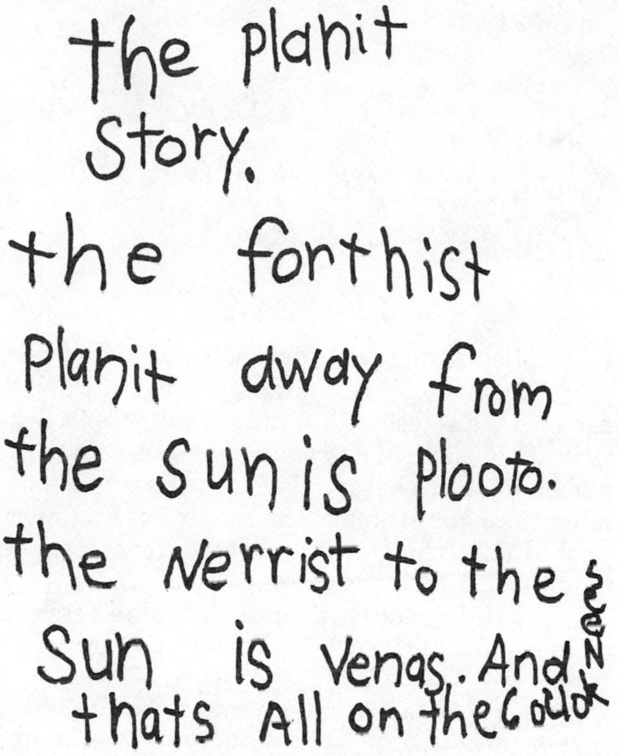

FIGURE 8 – 11
*JoBeth*
*Grade 1*

the planit
Story.
the forthist
planit away from
the sun is plooto.
the Nerrist to the
sun is venas. And
thats All on the 6 o'clock

The last sentence says, "And that's all on the 6 o'clock seen [scene]."
Although she calls this piece the planet *story*, she is obviously aware that
she is informing and not storytelling. Her "sign-off" is proof of that.

Expository prose can be used to give directions. Young writers can
do this, too. Figures 8 – 12 and 8 – 13 are the responses of a group of first
and second graders to the assignment: "Tell us how to float on your back."

FIGURE 8 – 12
*John*
*Grade 2*

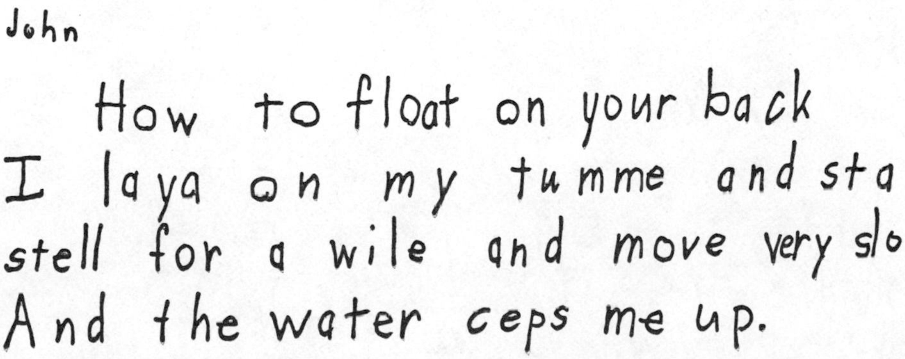

John

How to float on your back
I laya on my tumme and sta
stell for a wile and move very slo
And the water ceps me up.

**FIGURE 8–13**
*Rachel*
*Grade 2*

Rachel

You Prtend theat You are
Laying on a bad and you
Jost lay back.

*Description*

Description is discourse that helps us visualize. It focuses upon the appearance of an object. "In description, we see vividly and concretely; we perceive the object with a kind of fullness for which exposition does not strive."[6] Readers of descriptive prose expect the writer to display a subject's unique or characteristic appearance. When writing describes a familiar face, for example, the reader expects information about style and color of hair, color of eyes, skin tone, general expression, and so on, rather than a list of facial subparts.

A paragraph from Jean Henri Fabre's essay about the praying mantis is a fine adult example of descriptive prose.[7]

> Apart from her lethal implement [the forelegs], the mantis has nothing to inspire dread. She is not without a certain beauty, in fact, with her slender figure, her elegant bust, her pale-green coloring and her long gauze wings. No ferocious mandibles, opening like shears; on the contrary, a dainty pointed muzzle that seems made for billing and cooing. Thanks to a flexible neck, quite independent of the thorax, the head is able to move freely, to turn to right or left, to bend, to lift itself. Alone among insects, the mantis directs her gaze; she inspects and examines; she almost has a physiognomy.

Children are capable of writing descriptive prose. First-grade students wrote descriptions of people they know or pets they have. Notice in Figure 8–14 how Angie has sensed the requirements of description,

**FIGURE 8–14**
*Angie*
*Grade 1*

Angie
My Dog
He is Big
And He Hes bran Eyes
He is wit And Balk

and how she focuses on her subject's individual, rather than general characteristics.

Argumentation, or persuasion, offers evidence in support of a statement. Sometimes it is concerned with establishing a statement's truth value: for example, *There are more women than men in the United States*. At other times argumentation is concerned with matters of "what ought to be": for example, *Children should obey their parents*.

*Argumentation*

Advertisements are attempts to persuade and offer evidence in support of a statement. Count how many arguments are listed in the following ad to persuade you to go to Hawaii.

> You can search every corner of the earth. And you'll never find more spectacular golf than right in your own backyard. So come home to Princeville, Kauai. It's more than 27 holes of the world's best golf. It's limitless tennis. Deep sea fishing. Sailing. Windsurfing. Or snorkeling in crystal clear waters. It's romantic Hawaiian sunsets. Glorious sunny mornings. Bright, blue skies. And fresh sea air. At night, it's cocktails, gourmet dining and king-size accommodations (with full kitchens, lanais and daily maid service). Princeville, U.S.A. So nice to come home to.

Both the structure and content of an argument are crucial; as children, to the amazement of their parents, know all too well. Figures 8–15 and 8–16 are examples of children's arguments.

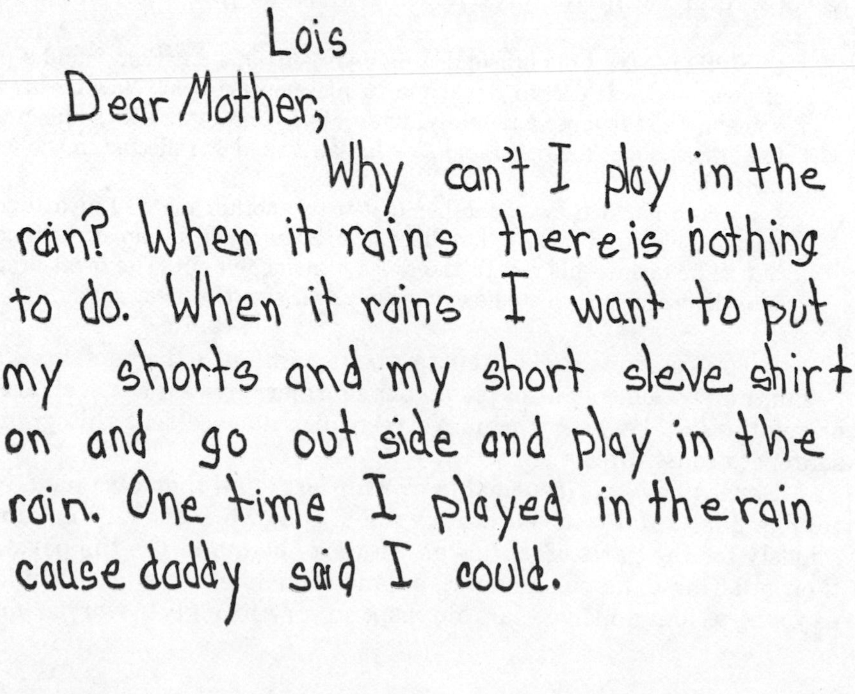

Lois

Dear Mother,

Why can't I play in the rain? When it rains there is nothing to do. When it rains I want to put my shorts and my short sleve shirt on and go out side and play in the rain. One time I played in the rain cause daddy said I could.

**FIGURE 8–15**
*Lois*
*Grade 2*

FIGURE 8-16
*No name*
*Grade 2*

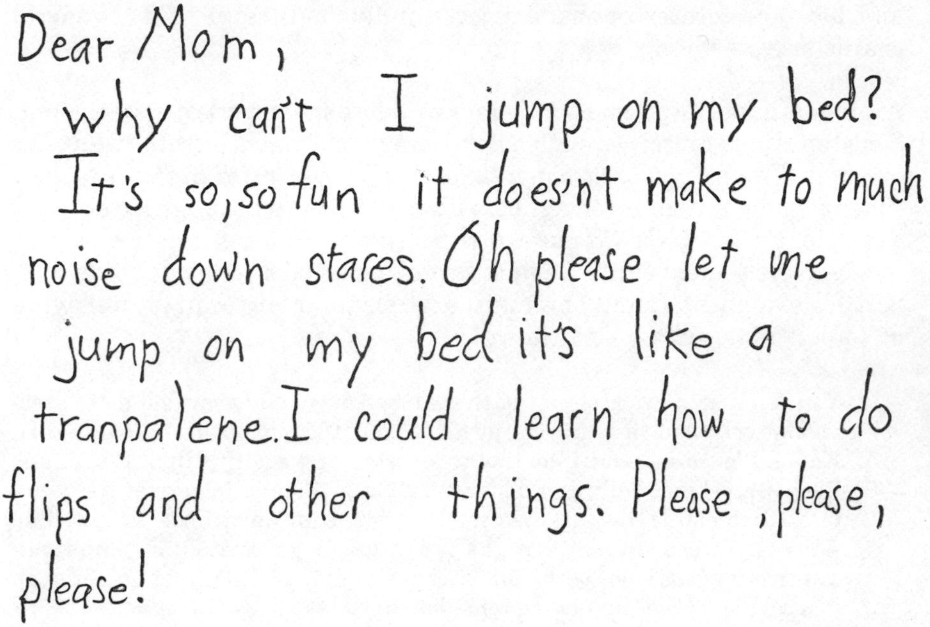

Dear Mom,
why can't I jump on my bed?
It's so, so fun it does'nt make to much
noise down stares. Oh please let me
jump on my bed it's like a
tranpalene. I could learn how to do
flips and other things. Please, please,
please!

**The poetic voice**

Writing that is done in the poetic voice is meant to stand as a verbal object — something to be admired as a whole. Though the name "poetic" suggests that this mode is limited to poetry, it includes stories, plays, songs, and the like. Writing in the poetic voice is usually structured in one of several distinctive ways. Consider the following lines, for example:

> Once, there was a big brown dog named Sam. One day Sam found a piece of meat and was carrying it home in his mouth to eat. Now on his way home, he had to cross a plank lying across a running brook. As he crossed the brook, he looked down and saw his own shadow reflected in the water beneath.
> He thought it was another dog with another piece of meat and he made up his mind to have that piece also. So he made a snap at the shadow, but as he opened his mouth the piece of meat fell out. The meat dropped into the water and floated away. Sam never saw the meat again.[8]

If you compare the sentences about Sam with the sentences that began this section, you discover that the former have a distinct structure, or relationship between them. We recognize at once that this group of sentences constitutes a story.

Stories have an identifiable overall form and they also have identifiable parts. Many scholars have noted that we seem to look subconsciously for the parts of stories as we read them and use the parts and their ordering to help us understand and remember the stories. Children as young as four and five years old respond very strongly to story elements and story structures in stories that are read to them.[9] As we shall see, identifiable elements of story structure turn up in stories that young children write.

Let us now lay out a simple scheme for examining story structures. This approach is sometimes called a *story grammar* because it portrays elements of a story and their relationships much in the same way that a sentence grammar shows sentence elements and their relationships.

A simple story grammar would have the following elements: a setting, an initiating event, an internal response, a goal, an attempt, a consequence, and a reaction.[10] Let us define these elements now and illustrate them, using the story of the unfortunate dog, Sam.

*Story grammar: the organization of story information*

1. *a setting* — the main character is introduced in some place at some time:

   > *Once there was a big brown dog named Sam. One day, Sam found a piece of meat and was carrying it home in his mouth to eat. Now on his way home, he had to cross a brook.*

2. *an initiating event* — there is an occurrence, or an idea strikes someone and sets events in motion in the story, or causes some important response in the main character.

   > *He looked down and saw his shadow reflected in the water beneath.*

3a. *an internal response* (event) — following the initiating event, the main character has an emotional response:

   > *He thought it was another dog with another piece of meat.*

3b. *an internal response* (state) — following the initiating event, the main character has an idea and sets a *goal.*

   > *and he made up his mind to have that piece also.*

4. *an attempt* — the character makes some overt action to achieve the goal:

   > *So he made a snap at the shadow,*

5. *a consequence* — some action or new situation results from the character's success or failure to achieve the goal:

   > *but as he opened his mouth, the piece of meat fell out. The meat dropped into the water and floated away.*

6. *a reaction* — there is some emotion, some idea, or some further action that may either express the character's feelings about whether or not he achieved his goal, or relate his success or failure to some broader set of concerns.

   > *Sam never saw the meat again.*

Children often write stories which demonstrate the same sense of organization that we find in stories written by adults. Figure 8 – 17 is a sample written by Cheryl, a second grader.

**FIGURE 8 – 17**
*Cheryl*
*Grade 2*

When I Were a Tomato
Once I walked to a wishing well.
I through a penny in it, and I said
"I wish I were a tomato." And then
all of a sudden I became a tomato.
Someone saw me laying on the
road by the wishing well. And she
picked me up and I could tell it
was a girl because her hands were
very soft. I thought she was nice,
but she ate me. And that was
the end of my wish and me.

Often, teachers or parents will ask a child to write a story without quite realizing the difficulty of the assignment. What are some good elements of the story in Figure 8 – 17 that you would call a child's or a class' attention to?

**Conclusion**

When rhetoricians set about identifying different *forms of compositions*, their lists range from half a dozen to more than a dozen. In this chapter we described only four basic forms of composition: narrative, descriptive, expository, and argumentative. These could easily have been subdivided to yield several more forms, had it suited our purposes. These forms, in turn, spring from three rhetorical *voices*: the expressive, the poetic, and the transactional (the expressive voice seems to correspond to its own rhetorical form of expressive writing). These can be displayed in diagram form (see Figure 8 – 18).

Children write most naturally in the expressive voice. As we shall see, their attempts to write in either the poetic or transactional voice (and the corresponding rhetorical forms) are not at first successful.

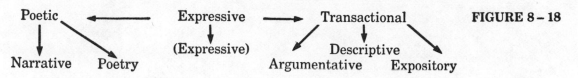

**FIGURE 8 – 18**

**References**

1. J. Britton. *Language and Learning.* Harmondsworth, England: Penguin Books, 1970.
2. L. Sealey, N. Sealey, and M. Millmore. *Children's Writing: An approach for the primary grades.* Newark, Del.: International Reading Association, 1979.
3. Britton, *Language and Learning.*
4. Britton, *Language and Learning.*
5. A. Brandenberg. *My Visit to the Dinosaurs.* New York: Crowell, 1969.
6. R. Weaver. *A Rhetoric and Composition Handbook.* New York: Morrow, 1974.
7. E. Teale, ed. *The Insect World of J. Henri Fabre.* New York: Dodd Mead, 1949.
8. S. McConaughy. "Using Story Structure in the Classroom." *Language Arts* 57 (1980): 157 – 165.
9. N. Stein and C. Glenn. "An Analysis of Story Comprehension in Elementary School Children," in R. Freedle (ed.), *Multi-Disciplinary Approaches to Discourse Comprehension.* Hillsdale, N. J.: Ablex, Inc., 1977.
10. J. Mandler and N. Johnson. "Remembrance of Things Parsed: Story Structure and Recall." *Cognitive Psychology* 9 (1977): 111 – 151.

# 9

# *Writing in the Poetic Voice*

We know, and Annabrook knows, that the events described in Figure 9 – 1 are not literally true. She has created a story, and in so doing she has used language in quite a different way from the manner in which we normally use it. Her words have not been used to set up some contentions for us to argue with nor has she described a thing or event that she and we can see before us in the real world. She certainly does not teach us anything. However, by combining words and ideas to make a verbal creation to be taken whole and admired, she has created a work of pleasure, a work of art.

We must be careful to let Annabrook see that we appreciate her story as a work of art and not as a piece with some literal businesslike function. She has written in the poetic voice, but it will take time for her work to be properly understood as such. She must learn to observe certain conventions that are often beyond the psychological scope of young writers. For example, as in all poetic writing, the writer must keep herself in the background, a difficult task for first and second graders. This is not an occasion to tell us what *she* likes or is excited about; rather, she must create some images and actions for us with her words that will delight and excite us, her audience. Since Annabrook has written a story (a story is just one type of poetic writing), certain other conventions must eventually be observed. The storyteller should present information that fits the categories we expect to find in stories: the setting, the initiating event, the internal response, attempts, outcomes, consequences, and reactions. (These elements were discussed in the previous chapter.) Details must also be presented in a certain order. The steps required to produce a story are restrictive, rather like opening a combination lock: one must produce the right elements in the right sequence.

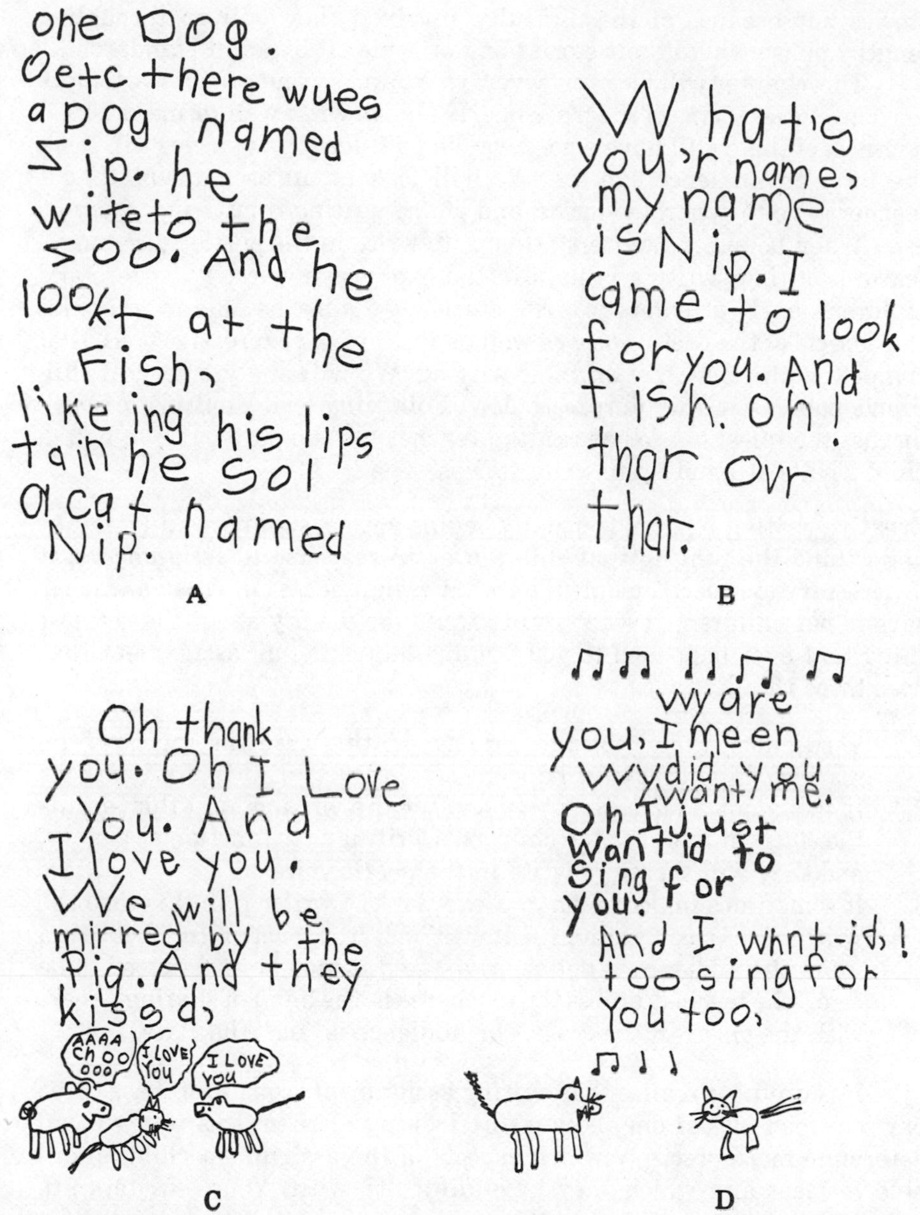

FIGURE 9–1
*Annabrook*
*Grade 1*

ohe Dog.
Oetc there wues
a Dog named
Sip. he
witeto the
soo. And he
lookt at the
Fish,
like ing his lips
tain he Sol
a cat named
Nip.

**A**

What's
you'r name,
my name
is Nip. I
came to look
for you. And
fish. oh!
thar ovr
thar.

**B**

Oh thank
you. Oh I Love
You. And
I love you.
We will be
mirred by the
Pig. And they
kissd,

**C**

wy are
you, I me en
wy did you
want me.
Oh I just
wantid to
sing for
you. for
And I whnt-id!
too sing for
You too,

**D**

Stories are hard to write because the allowable combinations of elements are so restrictive. Nevertheless, stories are the form of writing that children encounter most often in the reading they do and that is done to them. Stories are a form of writing that is assigned very frequently in school: the "story starter" may be the most common writing assignment children get. The upshot is that youngsters will often try to write stories but because of the difficulty involved they will go through a lengthy phase where their stories do not come off by adult standards.

This chapter will focus on several first and second graders' attempts to write stories. Some of them are nearly able to write well-formed stories; but most of them still have a good way to go before their stories will have the form an audience expects. We will look at an assignment that a teacher gave to generate stories, and at the writing that ensued from it.

When beginning writers attempt to write in the poetic voice, many features of their writing remain in the expressive voice. To understand children's early attempts to write stories, we must be able to recognize the aspects of the poetic voice as well as those of the expressive voice that compete with each other in their writing. We will analyze several children's papers for this purpose below. Following that analysis, we will discuss the question: What can the teacher (or the parent) do to help a child who is attempting to write stories?

**Assignments and What They Are For**

Creative writing in schools usually begins with assignments. In order to understand the writing that children do in response to assignments, it is necessary to reflect a moment on what assignments *do*. When a teacher says to her children, "I want you to write me a story about the scariest thing that ever happened to you," she is launching an assignment that does three things:

1. It specifies a *topic* for the writing; in this case the topic is "the scariest thing that ever happened."
2. It spells out a *purpose* or *function* for the writing, and this entails the *voice*; in this case the children's writing is to function as a story, and they will therefore write in the poetic voice.
3. It sometimes indicates an *audience* for the writing; in this case the writing was clearly stated — it was "me," the teacher. In school even when the audience is not clearly stated it may be understood to be "me," the teacher, unless the teacher is in the habit of sharing papers with the class. In that case, the audience is "us," the class.

It is useful to realize that writing assignments consist of these three parts instead of just one, because by looking at them this way we can determine more precisely which aspects of the assignment children are able to meet and which they have difficulty with. Young writers are especially uneven in the way they respond to the three elements of a typical assignment.

Let us look now at an assignment that was given to a second-grade class.

If you had the power to become any vegetable, which would you like to be? Pretend you have suddenly become that vegetable and you are off on an adventure. Can you make up a story about what happens to you?

We can see at once what the three elements of this assignment are. The topic is what would happen to you if you turned into a vegetable. The function is to be a story. The audience is not specified, but the children could safely assume it was the teacher; or, if the teacher was in the habit of reading the children's creative writings aloud, the audience might have been considered to be the whole class.

Now let us examine the first batch of stories that were turned in for this assignment by the second-grade class (Figures 9–2 to 9–7).

**FIGURE 9–2**
*Jennifer*
*Grade 2*

The Qcomebr Gril

I like a Qcomebr because I am
a Qcomebr do you on yi I am a
Qcomebr on we do not on yi you are
a Qcomebr

The End

**FIGURE 9–3**
*Paul*
*Grade 2*

The Hulk

A Carit gros and gror Out of the grand
then it comes out of the seed. Then
I am thaken to the store.

**FIGURE 9–4**
*Naloya*
*Grade 2*

I am a tomatoe. I like tomatoes they are my favrt kind of vestavle. I dream about my favrit vestavle.

**FIGURE 9–5**
*Stacy*
*Grade 2*

THE ADVENTURE of BLACK EYED PEAS

If I were a black-eyed pea I wouldn't like it. Because I will get aten by someone. Be in their stomach wouldn't be very fun would you like to be in somebody's stomach? My answar is no I wouldn't like that one bit. That's what I think .

The papers are alike in that they don't look very much like stories. To review our three elements of the assignment, though, let us consider how these children met the *topic*, the *function*, and the *audience* requirements.

The children all stuck to the topic. All of them limited their papers to a discussion of one vegetable or another. Not all of the children imagined they had *become* a vegetable, though.

the Carrot Stick

the Carrot stick, is healthy
for you. and it make you
storg and healthy
it make your bons, storg.
and it is good to eat
and it is healthy.
Say the Carrot stick.

**FIGURE 9-6**
*Tera*
*Grade 2*

The store about
a Carrots.
Carrots. are good
for peole. Don't
you think. I eat Carrots
for Snaks. Thay are
good. I wete Swiming
Wehe I got out. I ate
Sume Corrots .Thay
wrer good. Corvot.
I eat Corrots every
day.

**FIGURE 9-7**
*Denny*
*Grade 2*

None of these children observed the *function* of writing a story. One of them called his piece a story, but neither that one or any of the others wrote a story or wrote in the poetic voice. If these children did not write in the poetic voice, what voice did they use? Mostly the expressive. From our discussion in Chapter Eight you should remember that the expressive voice is language close to the self; personal, spontaneous, and loosely organized. The feelings and views of the writer are central in the expressive voice. Expressive voice is like casual speech, so we can expect to see characteristics of spoken language very much in evidence in expressive writing.

Sure enough, two of these children used dialogue, a pattern of spoken language, to structure their pieces. In speech, dialogue simplifies the task of talking, because the speaker needs only to produce short bits of language before he gets a response from the listener. The response indicates whether he is accurately meeting the listener's need for information, and gives the speaker something further to comment upon in his next bit of speech. We usually think of writing as monologue; that is, an extended utterance by one person that goes a long time without a response. Jennifer and Stacy, however, seem to have found it easier to use dialogue in their writing: they seem to desire to have an interaction with an audience, rather than to bear the responsibility of filling up all of the airtime by themselves. Dialogue as a structure of young children's writing is a fairly common characteristic of expressive writing.

Another sign of expressive writing in these papers is the focus on the self. Of course, the assignment invited that focus by asking the children to put themselves in the position of a vegetable, and to make up an adventure. Jennifer and Paul put their stories in the first person, as did Naloya, Stacy, and Denny. Only Tera did not. Jennifer not only wrote in the first person, but also told us that she likes cucumbers. Naloya told us she likes tomatoes, and Denny told us he eats carrots every day. Statements of this sort were not called for by the assignment, but the children's need to express their own preferences and experiences led them to put these statements in anyway.

Expressive writing is spontaneous and loosely organized. The same is true of many of these papers. Jennifer's "I like cucumbers because I am a cucumber do you know why I am a cucumber . . ." is an example. Naloya's, too, takes us from being a tomato to liking tomatoes, to dreaming about them — an unpredictable unfolding of ideas. The title of Denny's piece leads us to expect a story but the paper goes on to make a point about carrots being good for people, then states that Denny likes them, then lists his personal experiences with carrots. Tera's paper tells us several factual points about carrots and then abruptly closes with ". . . say[s] the carrot stick." The closing seems to be an attempt to make the work a fictional piece, and the shift from factual to fictional would lead us to call her piece expressive.

There is a term for the sort of organization, or nonorganization, that occurred in the other papers. Susan Sowers, researcher at the University of New Hampshire, calls them *inventories*.[1] Inventories are collections of statements about a particular topic which are not otherwise related to each other; that is, there is no logical flow from one statement to another. When a child writes an inventory, it is as if he had located a file in his head on the topic of his writing, dumped out its contents, and written them up in the order they fell out. Sowers identifies two kinds of inventories: the "love/like" inventory and the "knowledge-based" inventory. The love/like inventory is a list of statements of the form, "I love (or like) so and so." Note Naloya's piece again in Figure 9 – 4. Except for the sentence, "I am a tomato," which was prompted by the assignment, all of Naloya's sentences are variations of the statement, "I like tomatoes." This is a love/like inventory.

Knowledge-based inventories are collections of loosely related sentences that center on what the writer *knows* about his topic. Denny's is a knowledge-based inventory about carrots (Figure 9 – 7); he has mixed general information with personal experiences. Eventually he will be able to structure the piece so that the personal experiences serve as supporting evidence for the general information. But for now the statements stand bunched together and unrelated — an inventory of what Denny knows about carrots.

In terms of the continuum between the expressive voice and the poetic, all six of these compositions were largely written in the expressive voice. There may be several reasons why. The assignment itself is a difficult one: it is hard to envision a vegetable having an adventure. But assuming that the assignment is possible, it seems that these children may not be able to express themselves in the poetic voice. How they might be led to do so is the topic of the final pages of this chapter. In the meantime, let us consider another group of papers, responses to the same assignment, that came closer to the customary form of stories.

## Between the Expressive and the Poetic: Writing in the Transitional Voice

The expressive, transactional, and poetic voices are not totally discrete categories. There is much gray area in between, and for years children's and young people's writing will fall into the transitional area to one side or other of the expressive voice (see Figure 9 – 8). Transitional writing between the expressive voice and the poetic voice is more stylized and structured than the writing samples we saw earlier in this chapter. The "vegetable assignment" drew many compositions that were written in the transitional voice. Before you read several of them in the next group of

**FIGURE 9 – 8**
*Writing may combine elements of more than one voice*

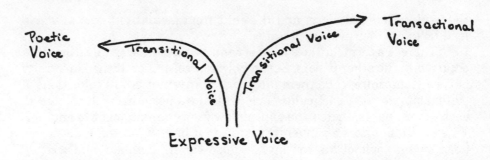

samples (Figures 9 – 9 to 9 – 16), it will be helpful if you ask the following questions with regard to each paper:

1.  What things about this paper keep it from being purely expressive; what elements of a story does it contain?
2.  What things about this paper keep it from being purely poetic; what elements of story does it lack?

**FIGURE 9 – 9**
*Tina*
*Grade 2*

> Me corrot
> It started off me
> being a little bitty
> seed then a girl maned
> Julie bouth me she
> barred me and I grew
> and grew and grew then
> I was a corrot. then she
> picked me. But now to-
> night she is going to eat
> me and I am so, so sad
> so good by farwell!

**FIGURE 9 – 10**
*David*
*Grade 2*

I had a pikkle. it ran
one day Four roches
came and saw it.
they strted to run.
the pikklle saw
them coming at him
he ran to they
were caghching up
with him. then he
jumped up anded
tricked them he was
safe the end.

**FIGURE 9 – 11**
*James*
*Grade 2*

My goodness! some one
opened my package and
i fell out. Splash! were
am I. I must beat a
sewer. The next day,
the little seed couldn't
move. Something had
attached it to the water.
I look orange like he
said. I a carrot! he shouted.

One week later. Someone
found the carrot. So he got
a stick and cut the roots
washed it and ate it gulp!

FIGURE 9-12
*Tara*
*Grade 2*

The Adventure of the
Cabbage Head.
Ones open a time ther
eas a cabbage head
He wanted a house of
his own.

So he set off th enext
mornig and he's far of
in the wood. He ran
into a gardena carrot
was in the garden. I asked
the carrot whir I was
he would not talk so I
went on. I met a lettuce
and an ear of corn.

FIGURE 9-13
*Danny*
*Grade 2*

I am a carrte
Holle my name is carrte
an I'm going to tall you
a stovy ones the wus a
boy an he plate. my.
and let my grow and
into I got big. and got
my ot and he aet my.

FIGURE 9–14
*Elise*
*Grade 2*

Peas, like me.

First peas start out like little tiny seeds and we get put in all kind of package and sent to all kinds of stores. I went to Walkers with my friends. A week after I was sleeping and some body picket up the bag. I knew some one was going to buy us and I spred the words. When she spush some of us. I was the forst one to be planted. Thay fed us and gave us some water. thay pick me. That night thay ate me and my family.

In what ways were these pieces more poetic than expressive? Many of them contain elements of stories, which were lacking from the samples that we studied in the first part of this chapter. Recall our discussion of story grammar in Chapter Eight. There we found that stories are often said to have the following elements: a setting, an initiating event, an internal response, a goal, an attempt, an outcome, a consequence, and a reaction.

**FIGURE 9 – 15**
*Frank*
*Grade 2*

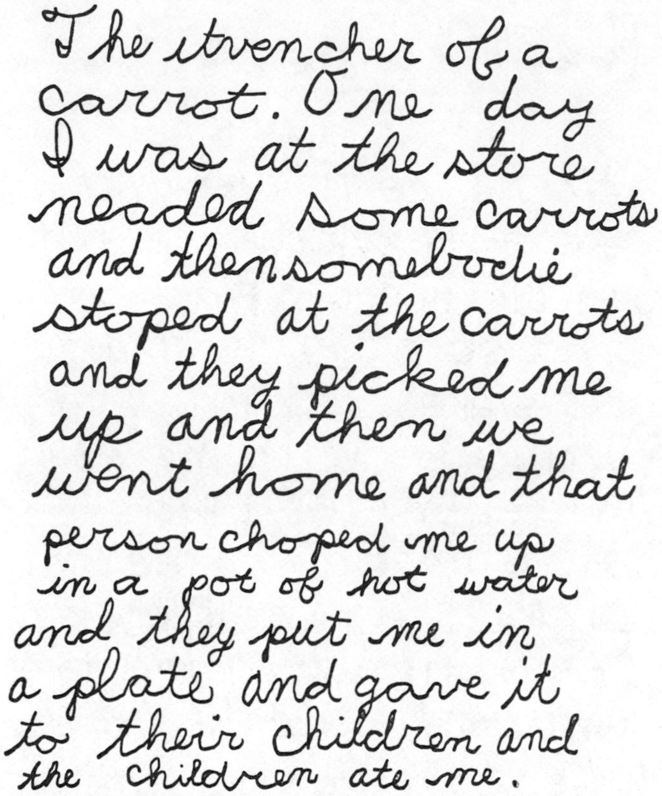

The itrencher of a carrot. One day I was at the store neaded some carrots and then somebodie stoped at the carrots and they picked me up and then we went home and that person choped me up in a pot of hot water and they put me in a plate and gave it to their children and the children ate me.

**FIGURE 9 – 16**
*Christy*
*Grade 2*

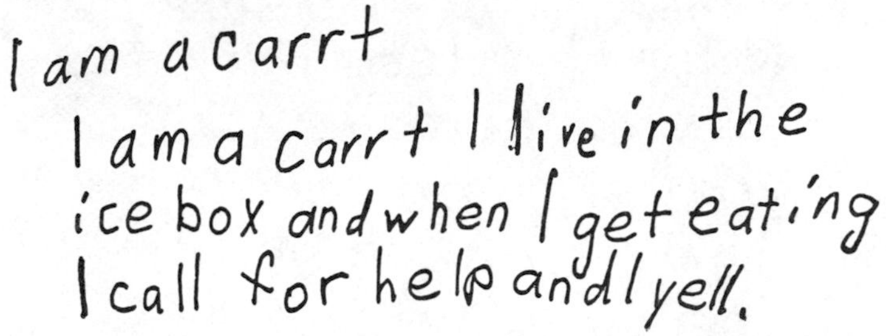

I am a carrt

I am a carrt I live in the ice box and when I get eating I call for help and I yell.

In addition to including needed elements, stories must present their elements in a certain order. Setting must come first, then initiating event, then internal response, then the others. To put it more simply, stories must have a beginning, a middle, and an end. Put this way, the order of the elements in a story are easy to look for, so we can analyze the present compositions in this way first.

As we look over these stories, they seem to be divisible into two main plots. The first plot goes something like this:

| Beginning | Middle | End |
|---|---|---|
| They found me at the store | They took me home | They ate me |

Frank's account follows this plan. So does Christy's. The second plot is similar:

| Beginning | Middle | End |
|---|---|---|
| They planted me (I'm a seed) | They harvested me | They ate me |

This is the plot that Elise followed, and also Danny, Tina, and James. Whichever plot they developed — either of these or some other — the children who wrote these accounts had a fairly definite sequence that included beginning, middle, and end. (Compare these with the accounts that opened the chapter.)

When we examine the story elements that these accounts contain and do not contain, we begin to see some striking differences between them and adult stories and many things that both have in common.

As for adult qualities in the children's accounts, we note that many of them start with *settings,* stated in varying degrees of clarity. "Once upon a time there was a cabbage head," writes Tara. This is the story language for the setting of a tale. "Hello my name is carrte," says Danny's paper, and then it proceeds, "ones the wus a boy and he plate [planted] my . . ." "One day I was at the store," begins Frank's paper. "I am a crrt. I live in the ice box . . .," writes Christy. All of these openings could be considered as settings. But none of the first six papers we considered at the beginning of this chapter had lines that would qualify as settings.

How about initiating events? "It started off me being a little seed and then a girl named Julie bought me . . . ," begins Tina's paper. "Julie bought me" is an initiating event, the event that gets the action going in the story. ". . . Then somebody stopped at the carrots and they picked me up . . . ," is the initiating event in Frank's story. Tara writes, ". . . He wanted a house of his own . . . " Hers is not an action but an idea that strikes someone; nevertheless, it is still an initiating event. "Someone opened my package and I fell out" is James's initiating event, one of the more active variety. With respect to the inclusion of initiating events, then, these accounts resemble well-formed stories.

When we look for *internal responses,* we discover a striking difference between these accounts and adult stories: there aren't any internal responses in the children's accounts. The internal response usually has two important functions: It shows us how the protagonist felt about things that happened at the beginning of the story, and it shows the protagonist setting a *goal* that gives a motive for the rest of the events of the story. The children's lack of internal responses in their written stories is a serious shortcoming, especially the absence of a goal. Without a goal, the events in their story tumble down a sliding board toward a very predictable conclusion. In a more mature story we might expect the vegetable to resolve *not* to be eaten. This would set up a goal, and arouse some interesting conflict that would leave the reader in some suspense until the end of the story. Not so with these accounts: ". . . He planeted me and let me grow and into I got big. and got me out and he ate me up." Again: no internal response and no goal.

Turning now to the *attempt,* we find that this element does not fully materialize in the children's accounts either. The attempt is a protagonist's effort to achieve his goal. These accounts have plenty of efforts in them, but few of them are carried out by the protagonist (the vegetable). Moreover, the protagonist has no goal.

We do find *outcomes* — the vegetable is eaten. But there is no *reaction,* and really no *consequence* either; there is no sense in these accounts of choices having been made, or of events, consequences, and reactions flowing from those choices.

Why are so many of these elements missing? Part of the reason is undoubtedly the nature of the assignment. It is hard to imagine a vegetable setting goals, making attempts, and having ruminative inner reflections. The nature of the protagonist in this assignment undoubtedly makes it hard to make a well-formed story. Nevertheless, other researchers have found the same result when studying children's stories; that is, many children leave out the same elements.[2]

There is a pattern to the elements the children leave out; no internal response, no goal, no reaction. Accounts by our children have plenty of overt action, but they are lacking in psychological developments. Similarly, children in other studies have shown the following tendencies:

1.   First graders stress the *settings,* the *initiating events,* and the *consequences* of a story.
2.   As they get older, children tend to include more details of *attempts* and *outcomes.*
3.   Most children leave out *internal responses* and *goals* of stories.[3]

The pattern here is the same that we found. Children treat the overt action elements of their stories, and leave out the covert psychological dimension.

This is very different from the sort of stories adults write. Adults are interested in goals, in cause and effect, in consequences of actions, and of morals. Adults tend to remember the psychological or moral aspects of stories as much or more than the events that occur in them. This contrast can be illustrated if we compare an hour of Saturday morning children's programming with an hour of adult drama, such as *Masterpiece Theatre* on the Public Broadcasting System. The children's shows are practically all action and sound effects — few words and almost no psychological dimension are present. The adult shows, on the other hand, stress characterization and internal drama in place of action. Children are bored with adult shows and adults are nonplussed by the children's shows.

But we must not overstate this point. The difference between children's stories and adults' stories is one of degree. Some of the accounts in the group we have been discussing have elements of the psychological in them. Elise's account contains something of an internal response that adds real depth to the work. Let us look at it again:

> PEAS, LIKE ME.
> FIRST PEAS START OUT LIKE LITTLE TINY SEEDS, AND WE GET PUT IN ALL KINDS OF PACKAGE AND SENT TO ALL KINDS OF STORES. I WENT TO WALKER'S WITH MY FRIENDS. A WEEK AFTER I WAS SLEEPING AND SOMEBODY PICKET UP THE BAG. I KNEW SOMEONE WAS GOING TO BUY US AND I SPRED THE WORS. WHEN SHE SPUSH SOME OF US. I WAS THE FORST TO GET PLANTED. THAY FED US AND GAVE US SOME WATER THAY PICK ME. THAT NIGHT THAY ATE ME AND MY FAMILY.
>
> ELISE

The line "I knew someone was going to buy us and I spread the words" is a psychological reaction that transforms her piece. Try reading her composition without this line; it is not nearly so good.

A few of the children in this group worked a psychological dimension into their papers indirectly. Christy (Figure 9 – 16) does not tell us directly that her goal was to not be eaten, but she does suggest it in the line, "I call for help and I yell." Tina does likewise when she writes, "But now tonight there goigo to eat me and I am so, so sad so good by farewell!"

So far we've only talked about written text. But quite often young children draw when they write. Occasionally their drawings are peripheral to the text; that is, their pictures don't add to the reader's understanding. But sometimes a child's picture is intricately bound up with his text and contains some of the psychological elements we've been talking about. Look at Leon's picture in Figure 9 –17 in combination with the account he wrote, "The Cevets went to the fluer and the fermer saw him He rant to the grtn and he got back." We can make a chart of the kinds of information that he communicated by the text and by the picture.

**FIGURE 9 – 17**
*Leon*
*Grade 2*

The C evets went to the flver and the fermer saw him. He rant to the grtn and he got back.

| *Leon's story in terms of story information categories* | Story–information categories | Source of information | |
|---|---|---|---|
| | | *Text* | *Picture* |
| | Setting | | X |
| | Initiating Event | X "The cevets went to the fluer" | |
| | Outcome | X "and the fermer saw him" | |
| | Goal | (implied from the attempt below) | |
| | Attempt | X "He rant to the grtn" | |
| | Outcome | X "and he got back," | X |
| | Reaction | | X Smile on carrot's face |

This is an interesting discovery. It seems that Leon communicated at least some of the psychological material in his story by means of his picture. The smile on the carrot's face may well show its relief and glee upon getting "back to base" safely. This would qualify as a *reaction*, in story grammar terms: "an emotion . . . that . . . expresses the character's feelings about . . . achieving his goal."

Leon seems to have found it easier to convey an emotion by means of a picture than in words. On reflection, this seems consistent with children's verbal communication. Children seem to reserve words for expressing ideas about actions or particular things, and convey feelings and emotions through nonverbal means — tone of voice (whining, shouting, or giggling) or body language. Verbalizing psychological material does not come easily; it may be easier to *draw* it instead.

Sheldon's account also conveyed more story information in the picture than in the writing (see Figure 9 – 18). The writing is almost expository: "Carrots are good for your eyes." But the picture introduces "Suprcarit," an orange version of Superman, who takes to the air with a hearty, "Up, up and away!" while a chorus of astonished little birds cheep, "Oh my God, oh my God!"

**Writing in the Poetic Voice: Teaching Implications**

By adjusting the assignments we give children, teachers can make it easier for them to write in the poetic voice. One such adjustment is to choose a protagonist who has a characteristic way of behaving. If we want to see more story elements developed in children's work, we can ask children to write a story about a mean bully, about a hungry wolf, about a little bird who has lost its mother. Each of these characters brings an implied goal along with it: the bully to bother someone, the wolf to eat, and the bird to find its mother.

This limits the choices facing the children as they write about these characters. Limiting the choices is good for the development of story structure, but it may restrict some children's exercise of imagination to the point where they find it harder to write. The teacher must decide how much specification to give these aspects of the assignment based on what he knows about each of his children. That is, a child whose writing is fluent and expressive may be ready for a more limiting assignment, while a less fluent writer may need an interesting but more open one.

Here is another suggestion for coaxing children to employ more story structure. In assigning story topics to beginning writers, we can suggest not only a setting (including a protagonist) but also an initiating event *and* an internal response (including the goal). For example, the vegetable assignment could be lengthened to this:

> After you have decided which vegetable you'd like to be, pretend that you are growing in the garden and you hear the farmer say, "Tomorrow I'm going to pick that vegetable and eat it."
> "Oh, no!" you say. I've got to get away!"
> Then what happened?

With the assignment stated in this way, it is no longer a foregone conclusion that the vegetable will be eaten. Many interesting twists are

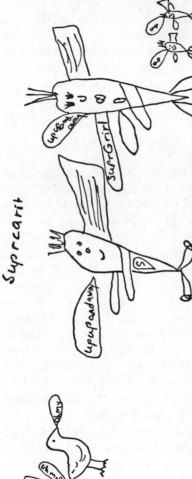

**FIGURE 9 – 18**
*Sheldon*
*Grade 2*

164

imaginable — each possibly involving an attempt and an outcome — before the story is completed.

We can call children's attention to story structure and story elements by means of discussion, too. The class can make up a story as a group, and the teacher can introduce certain elements and ask the children to note the effect these new elements have on the rest of the story. For example, if the vegetable assignment were being used as the basis for a group story-inventing session, the teacher can interpose suggestions such as: "Let's say the tomato decided she didn't want to be eaten. What would happen then?" Or: "Just before the people threw the tomato into the stew pot, she did something to get away. Class, what could she do? What would happen then?" In this way children come to appreciate the wrinkles that make stories more interesting, and they get ideas about the ways they can be worked into stories. The drawback to this procedure is that the story becomes somewhat more the teacher's creation; somewhat less the students: the teacher is advised to proceed carefully, and be sensitive to his children.

Critically reading and discussing professionally written stories is another important way for children to become more alert to story structure. The teacher can read just a few passages from a story and then stop. "What do you think will happen now?" she may ask. "Why do you think so?" Questions which ask children to make *predictions* about what will happen in the story are very useful to get children to pay attention to details. A teacher who is skilled in this process will ask all of the children in her group either to make their own specific predictions or to choose a prediction that another child has made before she will read more material. This procedure has been called the Directed Listening – Thinking Activity and is described in Stauffer.[4]

The Directed Listening – Thinking Activity asks children to predict future developments in a story on the basis of their understanding of story structure — though the elements of story structure are not necessarily mentioned by name. This practice could be expected to help children write better formed stories when it becomes their turn to write.

Another way to help children write stories is to encourage them to draw the picture *before* they write the story. The act of drawing may serve the writing process in several ways. First, drawing may serve a rehearsal function. As children are manipulating their crayons or pencils, they may be organizing their thoughts, planning and replanning what they're going to say. Also, a drawing can serve as a type of memory bank that children can easily refer to as they write. The actual mechanics of forming letters and spelling words takes considerable attention away from the thinking processes needed to generate a good piece. Having a picture available reduces the necessity of holding one's ideas in memory. Unfortunately, the need to draw is often underestimated or misunderstood in school.

Some of the children whose work we reviewed in this chapter drew pictures which were more expressive than their writing. In their pictures they often included some of the psychological material of their stories (the sort of material that children rarely express in writing). Teachers would therefore do well to encourage children to draw a picture soon after the assignment has been given. Then the children should be led to discuss their picture as it relates to the story they are about to write, and only then write the story. This should result in more fluent story writing.

Finally, we must emphasize that it is unrealistic to expect all first-grade children or many second-grade children to write stories. Stories are harder to write than other prose, for adults as well as children. They are not the most suitable fare for children to develop their writing skills on. Description, exposition, and persuasion are easier formal prose styles for beginning writers. But sheer expressive writing will come more naturally to children even than these. Children should be encouraged to write a lot, and in the first years most of this writing will naturally be expressive.

## Conclusion

Stories turn out to be complicated things when we break them down into the parts that make them up. It is, therefore, not surprising that they should be difficult for children (and many grown-ups) to write. Because so much of the literature that surrounds children is in story form, it is understandable that they and their parents and teachers might equate writing largely with writing stories. But the greater complication of stories compared to, say, expressive writing or even directions still makes stories a hard form to control.

Helping children structure their stories seems to help. For instance, unless the story characters set goals in opposition to the way events seem to be pushing them, then the cause-and-effect relations of the real world, rather than story logic, tend to dominate. In children's stories, carrots get eaten. We can help by asking what the carrot would do if it did *not* want to get eaten.

## References

1.  S. Sowers. "Young Writers' Preference for Non-Narrative Modes of Composition." Paper presented at the Fourth Annual Boston University Conference on Language Development, Boston, 1979.
2.  N. Stein and C. Glenn. "An Analysis of Story Comprehension in Elementary School Children," in R. Freedle (ed.), *Multi-Disciplinary Approaches to Discourse Comprehension*. Hillsdale, N. J.: Ablex, 1977.
3.  Sowers, "Young Writers' Preference."
4.  R. Stauffer. *The Language-experience Approach to the Teaching of Reading. Second Edition* New York: Harper & Row, 1980.

# 10

# Approaching the Transactional Voice

Alex's mother gave the authors a message she found under his pillow (see Figure 10 – 1). It's to the Tooth Fairy ("T. fary"). He lost one tooth and now a second has come out. He is asking the Tooth Fairy to please find the first tooth, but also to recognize that "this one has silver in it."

Writing can be used for different purposes. Sometimes we use it to express whatever thoughts and feelings happen to be crossing our minds. Sometimes we use it to tell a story. And sometimes we use it to get something done, as Alex has in his note to the Tooth Fairy. Writing used in this last sense is called *transactional* writing, or writing in the *trans-*

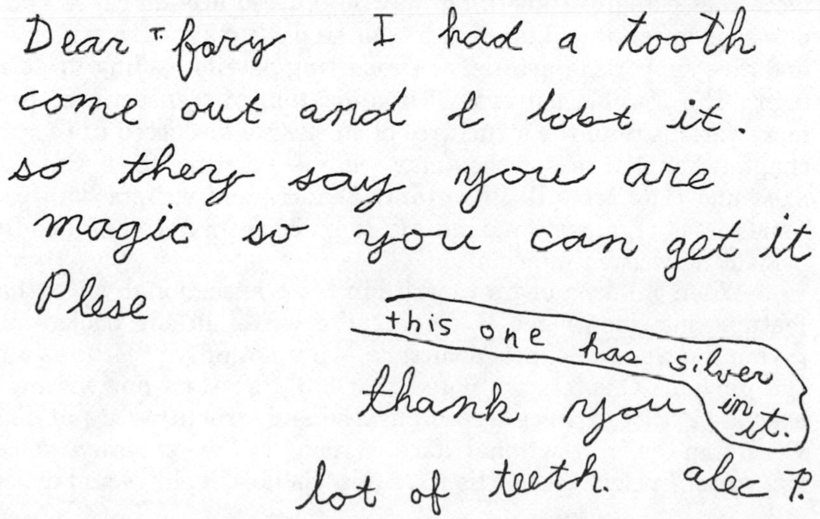

Dear T. fary    I had a tooth
come out and I lost it.
so they say you are
magic so you can get it
Plese

this one has silver in it.
thank you
lot of teeth.    alec P.

**FIGURE 10 – 1**
*Alex*
*Grade 2*

*actional voice*, because it serves as a transaction between the writer and the person or persons he is writing for.

In this chapter we shall examine the attempts of some first- and second-grade children to write in the transactional voice. There are two distinct types of transactional writing that we will observe. Sometimes transactional writing consists of imparting or sharing information, or explaining something. We lump these functions together and call them *expository* writing. In this chapter we will look at two sets of papers that contain expository writing. Sometimes transactional writing consists of an attempt to persuade someone to do something or to believe something. This sort of transactional writing is called *argumentative* writing. We will explore argumentative writing in this chapter also.

Expository and argumentative writing have at least two things in common: the writer stays in the background, and the topic of the writing is in clear focus. It is assumed that the thing that is being described, explained, or argued is more important than the person doing the writing. For example, when we read a newspaper story about a train wreck, we do not expect to read a personal account about the reporter's trip to the scene, what the wreckage reminded her of, and so on. When we read a set of instructions for assembling a bicycle, we do not expect to hear the writer's views on bicycle riding, or what happened when he tried to assemble one himself. In both cases we expect the topic to come across to us directly, and we do not expect the writer to enter the picture.

Transactional writing also has a definite pattern of organization. This is not to say that all transactional writing has the same pattern, or even that all writing of a certain type of transactional writing does either. Every piece of transactional writing, though, normally has *some* pattern, some structure around which the information is organized. An expository piece that explains something may be ordered around cause and effect, or a sequential unfolding of events or steps. It may present a main point and give supporting details, or supporting details leading up to a main point. The possible patterns of organization in transactional prose are more various than the structures of stories we discussed in the previous chapter. For that reason they may seem less distinct to us. But they still exist and they are still important. Readers and writers both count on some sort of organizational pattern to guide them in comprehending and presenting written information.

When children begin to write in the transactional voice, these two features just mentioned — keeping the writer in the background and giving the work a definite structure — are not fully present as a rule. In the previous chapters we noted that children start out writing in the *expressive voice*, a voice whose purpose and structures are at odds with writing in the transactional voice. Writing in the expressive voice keeps the writer in clear focus. His likes and dislikes, feelings and experiences dominate the work. The writer assumes that the reader will be interested in him as a person, so this focus on the self is thus justified. Expressive writing is very loosely structured, because it is patterned after casual speech. It can shift from one aspect of a topic to another with the only connecting link being the writer's experiences and feelings. Expressive writing sometimes takes the form of a dialogue in print, where the other party actually enters the work and talks back to the writer. Writing in the expressive voice differs from writing in the transactional voice mainly in these two particulars: in the expressive voice the writer remains in full view and the writing is patterned more in the manner of conversational speech than in the orderly styles of the transactional voice.

Because children's early writing starts out in the expressive voice, their first efforts to write in the transactional voice will not fully live up to the characteristics of that mode. Their writing is apt to be somewhat expressive and somewhat transactional. This in-between writing, it will be recalled from our previous discussion, is sometimes called *transitional*, with reference to the transition from the expressive to the transactional voice. Almost all of the papers we will examine in this chapter are transitional. In order to understand them, we have to consider the elements of transactional writing — be they expository or argumentative — that have emerged in them, at the same time noting the aspects of the expressive voice that linger on.

**Assignments for Expository Writing**

We have come to think of the movement from expressive writing to transactional to be developmental; that is, of two children the more mature will write in the transactional voice, while the less mature writes in the expressive voice. But judgments of more mature or less mature writing are very tricky. It is not enough to observe what voice the child writes in; we must also note what his purpose for writing was. Expressive writing is acceptable and desirable in many circumstances, such as writing letters or making journal entries. It is only inappropriate when circumstances call for some other purpose for writing, such as reporting an event for a newspaper, or explaining a procedure to an unknown audience.

When we give children writing assignments, we can often influence the purpose for which they write. Thus we can give them valuable practice in exercising the different voices of writing and also gain an opportunity to see to what extent they are able to use the different voices. But even when children are writing for an assignment, we must be careful in making judgments, because children may not interpret an assignment the same way we as teachers do.

It is important to examine assignments to see what they require. In the previous chapter we noted that an assignment usually specifies three things:

1.   a *topic* — what the writing is to be about;
2.   a *purpose* or *function* — what the writer should do about the topic (e.g., explain it, give directions, describe it, tell a story about it, or argue for it);
3.   an *audience* — to whom the writer should assume the work is addressed.

We should examine our assignments to see how clearly they specify topic, purpose, and audience before we evaluate the writing that results from them. Sometimes children do not adequately honor one or more of the elements of the assignment because the assignment was not sufficiently explicit. Other times they do not honor all of the elements of an assignment because they are developmentally unable to. It is important to know the difference.

As an extended example, let us consider an assignment that was given to a group of second graders.

*The "expert": an expository assignment*

"How many of you feel you're an expert in something?" asked the teacher. All of the children raise their hands. "Let's talk about who's an expert in what." A class discussion follows. "I have a roll of adding paper tape in my lap. Johnny, you said you know all about sharks. Do you know this much?" The teacher pulls tape to about 6 inches in length.

"No, I know more than that," said Johnny.

The teacher, pulling tape, asks, "Do you know this much?"

Johnny says, "More."

The teacher continues pulling the tape until Johnny says, "stop" and gives him the paper.

Later the teacher says, "Now all of you have your own paper. Today each of us is going to write about something that's very familiar, something we feel we know a lot about. Everyone has chosen his own topic, so every person's paper will be different from his neighbor's. As you write, remember you're the expert and we your audience probably know very little about your subject. Keep this in mind as you write, and try to explain exactly what you mean — exactly what you know. If you need more paper you can just tape some extra onto what you've taken. If you've asked for too much, you can just tear the extra off. Feel free to draw if you'd like."

This assignment makes the *topic* very clear: Each student is to write about something in which she or he is an "expert." The *purpose* of the writing is a bit ambiguous: Are the children to tell us *about* something, or are they to tell us *how to do* something? That is, should a child describe the excitement of participating in a particular sport, or should he tell us how to play the game? The writer will have to decide. As for the *audience*, who it is made up of has been made clear: it is "us," the teacher and other students in the class.

As you read the papers in Figures 10 – 2 to 10 – 9, ask yourself these questions:

1. Which of the writers stuck to the topic?
2. How did each writer interpret the purpose?
3. Which of the writers consistently addressed whichever purpose was chosen?
4. Which of the writers seemed to keep in mind the same audience all the way through?

The children stuck fairly well to the topic of this assignment. All of the children wrote about something they considered themselves an expert about. Nevertheless, they interpreted the "something" in different ways: Brian wrote about a sport; Rachel, Marc, and Bryan wrote about hobbies. These are alike in that they are activities in which the children participate: they might lend themselves to papers which explain how to *do* the activity. Susan, Mara, Ian, and Paul wrote about things they *know* about. These approaches lend themselves to papers which provide facts about the topic. Thus there were potential differences in the way the children approached their topic: One group could have described a procedure, and the other group could have presented facts. Nevertheless, all of the children presented facts.

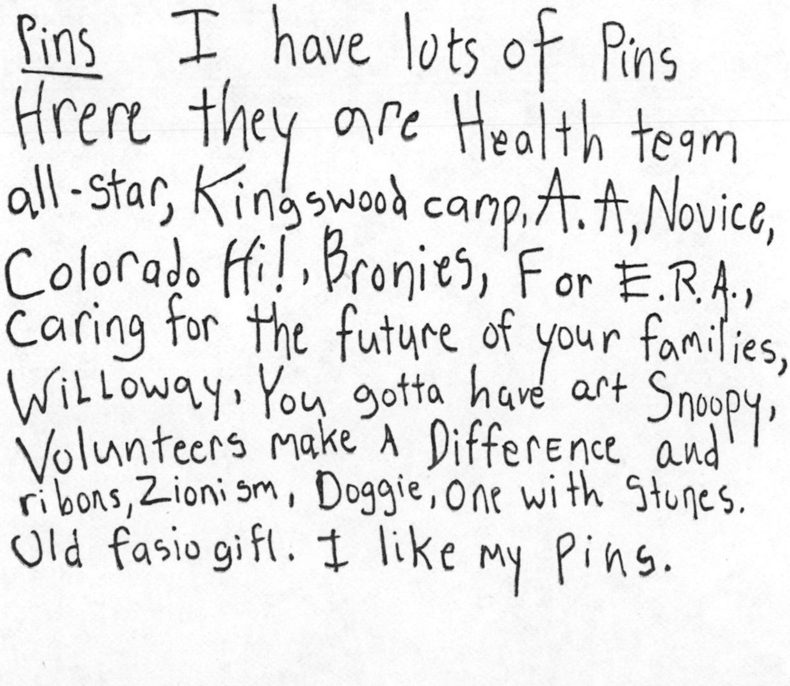
Pins I have lots of Pins Hrere they are Health team all-star, Kingswood camp, A.A, Novice, Colorado Hi!, Bronies, For E.R.A., Caring for the future of your families, Willoway, You gotta have art Snoopy, Volunteers make A Difference and ribons, Zionism, Doggie, One with Stones. Old fasio gifl. I like my Pins.

**FIGURE 10 – 2**
*Rachel*
*Grade 2*

FIGURE 10-3
Marc
Grade 1

Art Art is fun. You can learn a lot of things from it. And most of all you have to have alot of pacontes. And I like to make things in Art and one day in art we made paper masa. In school the art teacher is Mrs. Grill She is very nice. I like it because I am very creative and That is why I like to do Art. And I'm a very, very, very good Artist. And I love makeing things with clay, and I like makeing things with paper And I like making things made from paper masa, but, most of all I like makeing faces of people, cartons, Comics,

FIGURE 10-4
Bryan
Grade 2

Building Models. It's like a jigsaw puzzle at first and now it is so simple I could finish it in a half an hour matoring what kind it is I could finish a snap together modle in 10 minits and I could finish a hard glue together in a half an hour and let its dry and put it on my shelf and show it to my freinds I have im motle I glue together and and 7 snap togethers in and oher I get time I qaint them I have 18 cars 1 helcoplor and 5 air plane and the ones tat are titetey together I play with and have fun and with my brother with my air planes and I always win. I never lose.

FIGURE 10-5
Brian
Grade 2

Hockey. I know how to play forword and defents and goley. I know how to shoot the pyk. I know how to play write wing and left wing. I know how to play

172

left defents and write defents. Hocky is very very very fun. I yshuly play defense.

**FIGURE 10-6**
*Susan*
*Grade 1*

## Mice

One thing about mice is that a cat will get Rid of mice, mice love cheese most of all. they live in holes in the wall. People don't like mice so they put traps in the house. If it dosent work get a cat. some Mice are in some Books in the library. Mice are good. Mice and cats don't get alon to well.

**FIGURE 10-7**
*Paul*
*Grade 2*

## Space

The sun was made by gases and dust forming a big cloud. one day the cloud started to burn and the dust and gasses get tighter turned in to a ball of fire. This is watt the sun is today. in about 5,000,0000,000, years it will run out of gas to burn. then it will burn up. earth and mars then it will get white and very smal. A teaspoon of it would way about a ton. then it would turn in to a hole. The sun is a medcim size star. there is no air in space so jets can't fly, but rokets can. When people make rokets they can't make it go so far. the have only gone to the moon.

**FIGURE 10-8**
*Ian*
*Grade 1*

Siuprman. Siuprman kan See thru
anenthig Be Cas he has a X rai
vitin and he is the Stnogest
in the wirild and he kan fili
and he is fatr than a ScPetcy
dulat and he is Abul to Lep
tal buldeg in a Sege ldod and

**FIGURE 10-9**
*Mara*
*Grade 1*

Baby
thy mack in thar pans
and criy all the time they
Sleip in a crip and thr up
all niht and slep in the day
they crey if they don have fiod
whan they want it they srem in
my eras but ther is sum tigfunny Bucus
When my mom picshim uP he
stops and sum time when my mom
pits him down he sceme he only nos
tow wrds he stac uP til midniht
But sum times hes Jesfin.

How well did the children achieve the *purpose* of explaining? What sort of purpose did the children take the assignment to be requesting? All of the students addressed what would be considered an expository purpose; there were no stories, and no purely expressive pieces handed in. Within the expository purpose, as we already noted, none of the children elected to give directions for a procedure — although we might have expected some to from the assignment.

How consistently did the children stick to their purposes? This varied, with strong shades of expressive writing entering into most of the papers.

Brian (Figure 10 – 5) for example, has interpreted the "expert" assignment in a personal way, and we see he has written an inventory of all the positions he can play and things he can do. In total his paper explains his broad hockey expertise, and indirectly his reader learns a little about the game.

But Brian, the writer, is in center stage in this piece, giving an account of his own experiences and feelings. "Hockey is very very very fun for me." Brian's piece is organized around all of the things he knows how to do. We would call this organization a knowledge-based inventory — more of a list than a structure. This is a feature of expressive writing. Rachel (Figure 10 – 2) chose to write a paper about collecting pins. She, like Brian, has also written an inventory, in this case an inventory of the pins she has collected.

Both Brian and Rachel have achieved many aspects of expository writing. Their pieces are both factual; there is no story involved. The pattern that both of them have managed fits the "inventory" we described earlier: Rachel's is an inventory of the pins she has collected, while Brian's is a list of all the things he knows how to do in hockey. Note that neither one explained how to do these things; they both simply listed things. They did not stay completely within the inventory pattern, however. Both told how they felt about their hobby: an expressive thing to do.

From Marc's paper (Figure 10 – 3) we learn something about art. But just as in Brian's paper, we also learn a great deal about Marc, the writer. The "very, very, very good artist," who feels "very creative" and "who loves making things with clay" and "likes making faces of people, cartoons, and comics" is full of pleasurable feelings he wants to share. He also has the beginnings of conventional expository organization emerging in his paper. He has given us a main idea ("art is fun") and provided supporting statements for it ("You learn a lot of things . . . "and "you have to have a lot of practice"). He lists several important things, and then tells us the most important: "I love ——; I like——; but most of all, I like ——." But his focus is still personal, still expressive.

Bryan (Figure 10 – 4) is as wrapped up with building models as Marc is with art.

From the papers we have examined so far it might appear that all these children need to do in order to write better papers is focus a little less on *themselves*. But this is certainly not the case. In exposition, it is not enough for children to keep themselves out of the writing. Limiting the topic is also a consideration.

### Mice

1. One thing about mice is that a cat will get rid of mice.
2. Mice love cheese most of all.
3. They live in holes in the wall.
4. People don't like mice so they put traps in the house.
5. If it doesnt work get a cat.
6. Mice are in some Books in the library.
7. Mice are good.
8. Mice and cats don't get along to well.

Susan
Grade 1

Susan's composition is less expressive than Bryan's, Brian's, or Marc's. She seems to have taken a step forward *by attempting to focus on her topic* and limiting her personal intrusion into the paper. Yet we sense she's not nearly so comfortable with her theme as the previous writers were with theirs. Susan seems to be searching for things to say. Her jump from catching mice to "Mice are in some Books in the library" and "Mice are good" is a disconcerting leap for her reader.

Her paper might have a more natural focus if she were writing about some personal interest, as the writers did who preceded her. If we may presume she has moved beyond the focus on her own likes and dislikes, she has yet to replace it with any other strong center. Of course, Susan is only a first grader! Her piece is an inventory. Eventually, for her writing to have a concentrated punch to it, she must learn to limit her topic around one aspect of the facts she is presenting and integrate the points she makes about her topic into some kind of organization. However, we should not pressure her to do so in first grade.

### Baby

1. thy mack in thar pans and
2. cri all the time
3. they sleip in a crip
4. and thr up all night and slep in the day
5. they crey if they don have fiod
6. when they want it they screm in my eras
7. but ther is sum tig funny
8. bacus when my mom pics him up
9. he stops and sum time when my mom
10. pits him down he sceme

11. he only nos tow wrds
12. he stac up til midniht
13. But sum times hes Jes fin

Mara
Grade 1

Mara is writing from personal experience, while trying to keep herself in the background. Mara knows a lot about babies because her mother has recently had one. She manages to begin her paper with a detached "expert" voice. Presenting information as "one who knows" she writes, "Thy mack in thar pans and cri all the time." But Mara's voice changes in the second half of her paper (line 7); now it's more personal and expressive, ". . . when my mom pics him up he stops." Suddenly, "he" substitutes for "they," the specific for the general. Now we leave the detached realm of factual description and enter Mara's world. Mara's composition is a good transitional piece between the expressive and transactional voice. It shows development upon the right lines.

Sometimes a child's topic is so removed from personal experience that it's not very difficult for him to sustain an objective point of view. Ian's description of Superman (Figure 10 – 8) is objective, but this doesn't mean that he is a more sophisticated writer than Mara or the other children. He's learned about Superman indirectly, so he doesn't have the problem of stepping back. Moreover, he has heard the familiar catalogue of Superman's powers again and again. Nevertheless, one can't help but be awed by his extraordinary invented spelling effort. He has forged through his words the way Superman slashes through steel!

Paul's paper, "Space," (Figure 10 – 7) is the last piece we'll discuss. It needs a few adjustments, but Paul's is a fine piece of exposition. He restricts his subject to the sun's evolution and change. He carries his idea through from the time it was "made by gases and dust" until the time when it will "turn in to a hole."

A few children in second grade will write expository papers like Paul's, but not many. Paul's paper satisfies an adult reader's expectation of what expository writing should look like. But teachers should be aware that children must move gradually away from writing that puts themselves first, toward writing that succeeds in giving an organized accounting of a subject and satisfies most of the reader's need to know.

What is it about the audience that has such an effect on the writing? These children wrote their pieces in school, for their peers. It seems that this audience invoked personal expression, because the writer was justified in assuming that the audience was as interested in herself as in her topic.

When children are writing in school, the writer-audience relationship is not unknown; the child's audience is Miss Jones and the class.

Consequently, teachers should assume that expository papers written in school will often be more expressive than transactional. They will often take the form of elementary personal essays, where the child, not the subject, is center stage. The writer will not always be left in the background in deference to his paper's topic.

*Another*
*expository*
*assignment:*
*how to ride*
*a bicycle*

We might be tempted to conclude from this discussion of first and second graders' expository writing that this age group cannot handle that form of discourse very well. But first let us look at another expository assignment that was given to another group of second graders.

This time the assignment more clearly specified the purpose the teacher was after. Here is the assignment:

> "I'll bet you all know how to ride a bicycle," said the teacher. Most of the students said they did. Many started to describe the procedure to her.
> "Well, some people over in Victoria [that is where two of the authors work] want us to write down how to ride a bicycle for them."
> "Teacher?" said David.
> "Yes?"
> "Don't they know how to ride bicycles in Victoria?"

As you read the papers the children wrote (Figures 10 – 10 to 10 – 13), decide:

1.    which children stuck to the topic?
2.    which children honored the purpose of giving directions?
3.    which children kept their audience consistently in mind?

We can see that virtually all of the children stuck to the topic. They all focused on bicycles and how they are ridden.

As for the discourse mode, they stayed within the expository form on this assignment far better than in the previous one. In all of them the writer kept in the background; the focus was on the task of riding a bicycle, not on the person who could do it. There were no personal statements: we did not see "I like to ride my bicycle," or "riding a bicycle is fun" or even "I'm very, very, very good at riding a bicycle."

Why did the writers keep themselves in the background of their compositions this time? We suspect it was largely because of the audience. First, they were aware that the papers were being written for strangers — for people they would never see. They may have known that the readers would have been more interested in bike riding than in the writers themselves. Or they may have been shy about sharing a lot of personal material with people they didn't know and couldn't see. However, it could also have been because the topic clearly called for them to explain how to ride a bicycle, not to talk about bicycle riding. The wording of the assignment,

bicycle
first you must take your left leg and put it on the pedal.and then you take your right leg. and put on the pedal, and push the pedal with your right leg. and hold on to the bars. and when you want to turn you take your bars and either push the right or left, and never ride, without holding onto your bars.

**FIGURE 10–10**
*Andy* (left)
*Grade 2*

first thing you do is to pettle. than you

balance yourself so you

won't fall off your bike than you steer so You won't run into Something. and thats all you have to know.

**FIGURE 10–11**
*Russell* (right)
*Grade 2*

Deskib abuot a bike
You got to geep your bales and pedol and keep the wheel stat and turn going around a turn.

**FIGURE 10–12**
*John*
*Grade 2*

All you have to do is peted the bike and the wheels will turn around and around. And when you want to stop pull back ward on the petels.

**FIGURE 10–13**
*Lois*
*Grade 2*

that is, made it clearly inappropriate for a child to list all of his experiences and feelings related to bicycles.

Note how well organized most of these papers were. The children kept closely to a sequential, step-by-step pattern for presenting their ideas. By David's question, we may gather that the children understood that their task was to tell their readers how to ride a bicycle. They succeeded very well in thinking through what steps would be helpful to share, and in what order.

The contrast between these papers and the "expert" assignment that preceded them is striking. Most of the children responding to the expert assignment put themselves prominently into their papers, but these children did not. Moreover, several of the children writing about the expert assignment chose to write about processes (building model airplanes, playing hockey, doing art, and collecting pins), but none of them explained how to perform those processes. In contrast, all of the children responding to the bicycle assignment explained how to ride a bicycle.

It is not always necessary or desirable to give children explicit assignments for the writing they do. But when the teacher does want to make assignments with the intention of having the children practice writing in a particular discourse mode, the assignment must be worded very carefully. The teacher should discuss the assignment with the children to determine what they understand the assignment to mean. As we have seen, the difference between children's responses to two assignments that purport to generate the same kind of writing may be great indeed. It would be unfortunate if a teacher were to give an assignment of the expert variety and conclude from the children's responses that they *couldn't* write expository prose.

Who the children perceive their audience to be can have an important effect on their writing, too. Transactional writing is reserved for getting things done in the real world. It is certainly more natural for children to produce transactional writing when they have real purposes for a real world audience.

**An argumentative assignment**

Argumentative writing may include works that attempt to convince a reader of a certain point of view. In children's writing, however, argumentative writing probably more often takes the form of an attempt to persuade someone else to do something (i.e., give the writer something, allow him to do something, do him a favor, and so forth).

Argumentative or persuasive writing is an appropriate form for children to practice, because in this form the topic and the audience are inherently made clear. The topic is *what we want;* the audience is the person or persons *from whom we want it.* The discourse mode of argumentative writing may pose difficulties, however, that have little to do with writing. Persuasion requires that a person know how to structure an argument according to his social standing vis-à-vis his audience. For example, we can say some things to our close friends by way of persuasion for which we would be sent to our room if we addressed them to our mother or thrown in jail if we addressed them to the President of the United States. The following is an argumentative assignment that was given to a second-grade class:

> Think of something that you would like to do, but for one reason or another cannot do. Write a letter to persuade the person who is preventing you from doing what you'd like, to change his or her mind.

This assignment was followed by class discussion, and then the children wrote. Several of their papers are reprinted here, but before we look at them, let us decide what to look for.

This assignment points to a definite topic, but it leaves the writer latitude to specify exactly what the topic will be. The assignment leaves it to the writer to decide who his audience is, but it does make it clear that he must decide (compare this with an assignment to write a story or a description in regard to how clearly the audience is placed in focus by the assignment).

The discourse mode is suggested also. The purpose, at least, is clear: The writer is to persuade someone to let him do something. But it is up to the writer to decide how the persuading is to be done and how to organize his points. It is also for the writer to note that he may wish to structure his arguments differently, to use more or less politeness, depending on his audience. Consider now Figures 10 – 14 to 10 – 20. How did the children treat each of the elements of topic, purpose, and audience?

First of all, how many of these children thought of a topic and stuck to it? All of them, really: Johnny chose to write an inventory of all the things he wanted to be allowed to do, rather than to pick one and arrange an argument for it. All of the others stated their request and then sought to drive it home somehow. Johnny may have found it easier to make an

**FIGURE 10–14**
*Corey*
*Grade 2*

Corey F.

Dear Mrs. Vargas　why won't you let us　talk in the　cafatearia? We have　a　right to!　after all you talk in　the　longe. any way.

**FIGURE 10–15**
*Johnny*
*Grade 2*

dear mom and dad,

I want to ride my bike on the dirt road. Let me play with frogs. I want to run splash in the mud.

love,

Johnny

**FIGURE 10–16**
*Jeanette*
*Grade 2*

Dear Debbie,
One day Debbie. Pow! Write in the ciser. O.K. Why is it allways we have to play baby. We never ride bikes.

**FIGURE 10–17**
*Annie*
*Grade 2*

Dear Dad,
Why can't I get a hourse? I would keep my room clean. I'd tak care of it. I'd be extra good I never would fight. pleas! pleas! I would let my sisters ride it.

Sincerly,
Annie

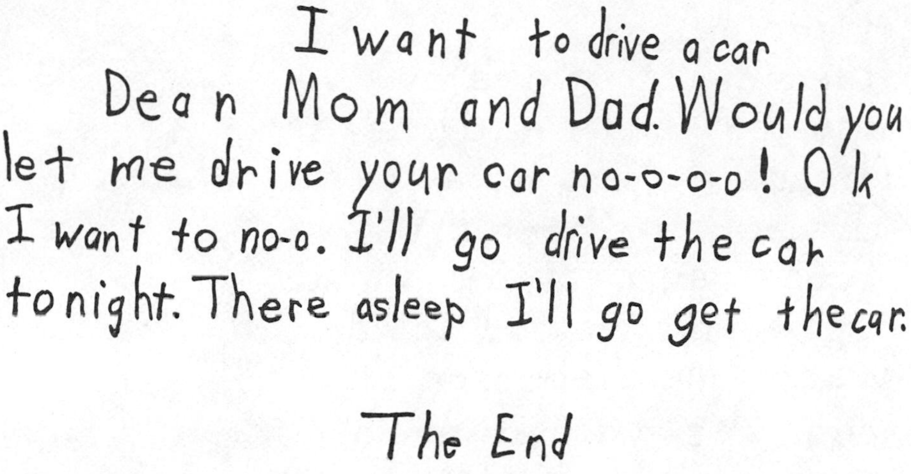

I want to drive a car
Dean Mom and Dad. Would you let me drive your car no-o-o-o! Ok I want to no-o. I'll go drive the car tonight. There asleep I'll go get the car.

The End

**FIGURE 10–18**
*John*
*Grade 2*

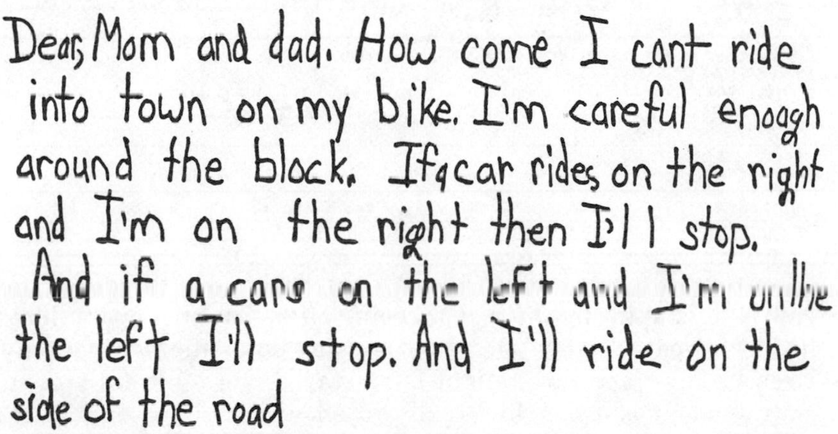

Dear, Mom and dad. How come I cant ride into town on my bike. I'm careful enough around the block. If a car rides on the right and I'm on the right then I'll stop.
And if a car on the left and I'm on the the left I'll stop. And I'll ride on the side of the road

**FIGURE 10–19**
*Andy*
*Grade 2*

inventory of requests rather than to structure an argument for one request.

How many of them kept their audience constantly in mind? All but two. John and Alexis did not actually address their compositions to their parents, the supposed audience. But in John's case that is surely because his request to be allowed to drive the family car was fanciful anyway. His work turned into a story toward the end.

In John's work (Figure 10 – 18) the device of dialogue showed up as a method of structuring a composition. This is a manifestation of expressive writing, which we discussed in Chapter Seven. John's writing did not come off as a persuasive piece. Perhaps if the topic had been derived from a need that was real to him rather than imagined, his paper would have shown a more definite structure.

**FIGURE 10–20**
*Alexis*
*Grade 2*

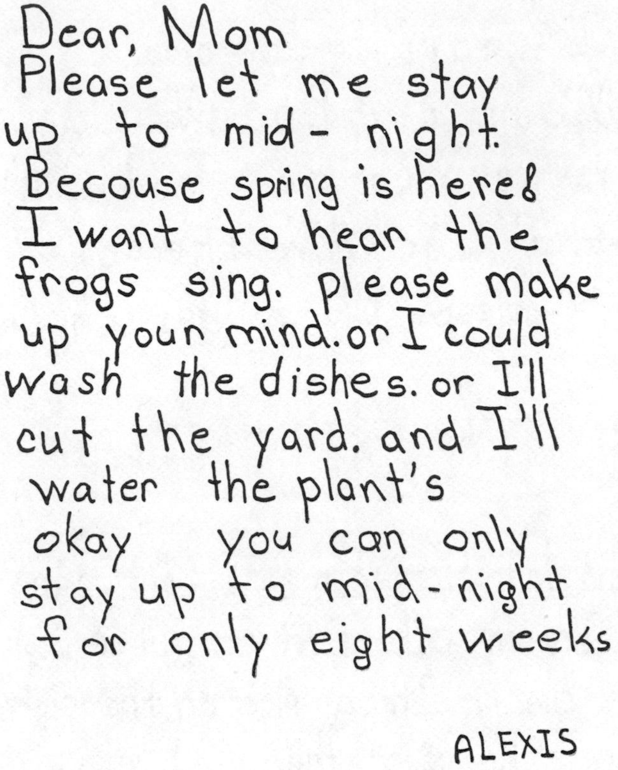

Dear, Mom
Please let me stay
up to mid - night.
Becouse spring is here8
I want to hear the
frogs sing. please make
up your mind.or I could
wash the dishes. or I'll
cut the yard. and I'll
water the plant's
okay    you can only
stay up to mid-night
for only eight weeks

ALEXIS

Alexis's paper (Figure 10 – 20) resorted to a bit of dialogue at the end. After making his pitch about being allowed to stay up until midnight he has his parents say, "O.k., you can stay up to midnight for only eight weeks." This paper, too, might have stayed more faithfully in the persuasive mode had the child really intended for his parents to read the letter and make a determination because of it.

The children stayed within the argumentative mode of discourse, with the two exceptions we have just mentioned. Their papers generally began with the request and then listed support for it. The arguments they put forward took various forms. Annie's paper (Figure 10 – 17) for example, was a "tit-for-tat" argument. She would keep her room clean, be extra good, wouldn't fight, and even let her sister ride it if only her parents would get her a horse. Alexis (Figure 10 – 20) uses this line of argument too, promising to wash the dishes, cut the yard, and water the plants. Alexis also uses the tack of explaining his request: because spring is here! and he wants to hear the frogs sing.

Corey (Figure 10 – 14) uses a "fair is fair" approach. If the lunchroom manager gets to talk in the lounge (her rest area away from work) then by rights the children should be allowed to talk in the lunchroom (their rest area away from work).

Jeanette (Figure 10 – 16) uses the "get tough" approach: "One day Debbie, Pow! Write in the ciser!"

Andy (Figure 10 – 19) uses perhaps the most sophisticated approach of all. In his piece about bicycle riding on the street he *anticipated his parents' objections*. He put himself in their place and realized that their objection to his riding his bike on the street was a concern for his safety. Then he set out to convince them that he knew how to be safe. This is a sophisticated approach, and it is also pitched at an effective level of politeness for parents. It would not necessarily be a good argument approach for someone else; say, a friend of Andy's.

Johnny (Figure 10 – 15) provides no support for his requests, but rather adds other requests to the list and makes an inventory.

The children in this group were able to rise to the challenge of writing an argumentative or persuasive piece fairly well. A couple of them could have used some encouragement when the assignment was given in order to approach it in more realistic terms. This would be easier if the assignment had arisen from a real need, and the letters could actually have been mailed. For the group as a whole the children raised a remarkable variety of persuasive tactics, from "tit-for-tat" to "fair-is-fair" to threats to anticipating and allaying objections. The teacher could capitalize on this variety by sharing the papers and discussing the approaches the children took to arguing their cases. He could ask: "How could we make an argument like Alexis used to ask for permission to talk in the lunchroom?" "How could we make an argument like Annie used to talk Debbie into riding bikes?"

Another issue to which the teacher could call attention is the difference in the way arguments would be couched for different audiences. Jeanette could be asked how she would have worded her argument if she had been addressing her mother. Alexis could be asked how he might have worded his argument differently if he were addressing it to his big brother or to the babysitter. These questions get at an important but often overlooked aspect of language learning. That is, we use different language forms and degrees of formality and directness with different audiences.

## Conclusion

Young children write slowly. To write successfully in the transactional voice requires a writer to maintain her topic, her purpose, and her audience in mind during repeated trips to the pencil sharpener and conversations with neighbors. It is not surprising that early attempts to write in this voice are highly personal, or that they tend to feature inventories of ideas rather than integrated arguments. It is good practice for children to be given transactional (and poetic) assignments. But, at least in the early years, we should not be disappointed if they revert to expressive writing. The goal in these formative years is fluency, with a bit of variety in writing tasks thrown in for good measure.

# 11
# Writing: The Child and the Teacher

In previous chapters we have discussed children's composition in terms of voices, modes, and compositional forms. Our attention has been focused on the papers children write, and we have sought to describe those elements that made the composition of those papers either narrative, expository, or persuasive. Our work will not be complete, however, until we examine the activity that children go through in order to produce a composition, and the things teachers do to help children compose successfully. This chapter begins with a description of what children do when they write: the process of composition. Once we have highlighted the steps children take to produce a written work, we will then turn our attention to the things teachers must do to support children's writing at each step.

**The Process of Writing**

Few of us understand that writing is as much backward motion as it is forward thrust. Traditionally, when we think of writing in the classroom, we visualize a cycle which has a forward five-stop lever. There's a talking stop, a writing stop, a collecting, a correcting, and a handing-back or pinning-up stop. First we talk about or present a topic to write about. Then young authors get out their writing materials and go to work, as best they can. Papers are collected, often sooner than expected; they are corrected primarily for spelling and punctuation, and then handed back or placed on the bulletin board for show.

Donald Murray has written a description of the process professional writers appear to use.[1] His description seems viable for school writing, too. Murray's model shows writing to be a process of continuous thinking, experimenting, and reviewing. In order to help children write, we must have a clear view of what is involved in that activity.

186

The activity of writing a paper involves three stages. There is a stage for *rehearsing*, for *drafting*, and for *revising*. During all three stages the writer's activity is dominated by some combination of four forces: the writer is *collecting, connecting, writing,* and *reading*. The forces of collecting, connecting, writing, and reading are normally at work, though to varying degrees, during all three of the stages of rehearsing, drafting, and revising. Let us describe the stages first; then we will give examples of the forces at work in writing.

*The stages of writing*

Rehearsing is the stage in which writers discover what they have to say. In the rehearsing stage, the writer considers the widest range of ideas that might possibly be written about. Sometimes teachers encourage rehearsing by means of brainstorming sessions, in which children think up and write down as many details as they can about a person, a place, or an event which is meaningful to them. Sometimes teachers promote free writing during the rehearsal stage. Free writing is timed writing in which the writer puts down absolutely anything that occurs to him, without stopping and without making any corrections, for a specified period of time: usually five or ten minutes.[2] Both methods are intended to bring out into the open a range of particular ideas and details a writer can subsequently employ in his deliberate writing. There are other activities used during the rehearsal stage that we will describe later.

*Rehearsing*

The second of the stages in the process of writing is drafting. The term "drafting" is chosen because this sort of writing is a tentative activity. When we speak of a "first draft" or a "second draft," we imply that a piece of work is undergoing change, that other drafts may follow. Drafting involves writing the work out. It is during the drafting stage that the writer experiences clearly what he has to say. Drafting enables the writer to put his thoughts outside of himself and to consider them as if they belonged to someone else. The writer may thus have a dialogue with himself through the drafting process. He may appraise the work with some detachment, considering it as something that may stand on its own before a reader, in Murray's terms.[3]

*Drafting*

Revision is the final stage, although we should remember that revision can lead to further rehearsal and further drafts. The writer examines his piece and clarifies for himself what the writing *should* say. When necessary, the writer prunes words or adds them, all in an effort to make the meaning that is in the piece speak more clearly. Sometimes revising is a matter of "patching up" phrases or sentences in order to make them smoother or clearer. Sometimes, however, the writer discovers whole new possibilities that should be developed in the work. In the latter event, revision can mean changes to larger parts of a work, and sometimes to

*Revising*

the whole work. In Murray's words, "the writing stands apart from the writer, and the writer interacts with it, first to find out what it has to say, and then to help the writing say it more clearly and gracefully."[4]

With Murray's three stages of the writing process in mind, let us consider for a moment a pair of examples of children's papers and reflect on the circumstances by which they came about. Afterward we'll discuss the four forces that operate during the writing episode.

Chris's paper (Figure 11 – 1) is a product of the traditional approach to writing, the forward five-stop lever model. His teacher, obviously liking his paper very much, placed a star at the top and wrote, "Nice." Chris's composition is beautiful, there's no denying it. However, since he was not given the time to interact with his piece, Chris missed an important experience in learning how to revise. Chris needs some time to discover how his paper shifts in focus, or to explore ways in which to make "The Wilderness" a little clearer for his reading audience. It is true he may have made only one change given the opportunity to revise, but at least he would have been one step closer to becoming his own critic. Ultimately, that is a primary goal for all writing teachers: to enable children to become their own critics and editors.

Tony's paper (Figure 11–2) is also a product of the traditional classroom writing episode. Tony had no opportunity to play around with his thoughts; no time for serious rehearsal. Furthermore, he was not given time to revise; his paper was just handed back. Tony's teacher, like Chris's, approved of his paper — or did she? She put a smiling face in his upper right-hand corner; but then, at the bottom, she wrote, "Could you write more, Tony?" In spite of his teacher's purple comment, there was no follow-up. "The Jig" went home, along with all his other language assignments.

## The Forces at Work during the Writing Process

Returning to the description of the writing process, the forces at work during the whole writing process are: *collecting, connecting, writing,* and *reading. Collecting* represents humanity's drive to gather information. What we gather becomes the raw materials of our intellectual life. The amount we collect becomes so immense and diverse, however, that it demands *connecting.* We need to make order out of chaos, to "build chains of information which lead to meaning."[4] The serious writer fears that the collecting apparatus will be controlled by the connecting one. That is, if we see, hear, or read something new and can't connect it to our existing knowledge structure, we are prone either to toss it out as unimportant or irrelevant, or distort it to make it conform to what is familiar to us. The teacher therefore has to "encourage the gathering of contradictory and unpredictable information which will force the writer to adapt old meanings and construct new ones."[5]

christopher

The wilderress. The wilderness is full with things like trees and animals and flowers and weeds and logs with frogs and squrrels and raccoons fish deer and rivers to get across and logtomakedamsan a bridge to get across sometimes when it is to wide to ge across to and goto the campand set up the tent and afterword we'll make a fire and roast

A

marsh mellows thenin the moring we go toa new camp sight and collect rocks and go swiming and find logs in the water to ride on and jump offof and start off swiming and look at the bottom of the lakeand see if I can find another onix like rock. Then I and Ralph will great lunch and after that we'll walk around the camp sight.

B

The Jig
by Tony Schiff

It is fun to Jig
with a pig.

189

*Writing* and *reading* are the other two forces in the writing process. *Writing* stems from our basic human drive to express ourselves. People have a primal need to speak; to comment upon their experience both for others and for themselves. Children want to write, because writing is an outlet for this drive for self expression. The force of writing is an important one in the whole process of composing. This seems like an odd statement, but there are, as we have seen, other forces at work in this process besides writing only.

We have also a drive to read what we write. To a large extent, the drive to read works in opposition to the drive to write; reading is accompanied by criticism, and our powers of criticism inhibit our powers of expression.

In Murray's model of the writing process, the forces of collecting and connecting are paired with each other, and are to a large extent locked in opposition to each other. The same is true of writing and reading. Each of the forces, however, relates not only to its pair, but to each of the other forces as well, as Figure 11 – 3 signifies. For example, as we collect, we often record our collections by writing them down. Then as we read them, we find connections that had not originally occurred to us. These new connections, in turn, lead us to more writing, which is then read. However, the new connections may alternatively point up to us some inadequacy in our thoughts and lead us to do more collecting.

During *rehearsing* Murray suggests that two of the forces be given a slight advantage. Which two do you feel should be the strongest? Do we want to feel inhibited as we think about what meaning our paper may find? Murray feels we shouldn't, and therefore he would want our collecting force to be more powerful during rehearsal than our need to connect or order. Also, he wants the writing force to be stronger than the

**FIGURE 11 – 3**
*Interaction of
forces in the
writing process*

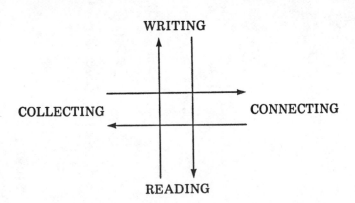

reading force during this time. That is, if we read back our collections too critically we may eliminate sooner than we should. On the other hand, Murray suggests when revising the opposite should be true. "We load the dice in favor of reading and connecting. We become more critical, more orderly." Our revising continues in this way until the scale balance tips. "When the advantage becomes again writing and collecting, then revising becomes rehearsing" and the beat goes on. We can't help but see, with Murray's lucid and colorful description, that writing is indeed a dynamic process. As teachers it's very important for us to recognize the tremendous amount of thinking that occurs during rehearsal and revision, the stages traditionally given the least teaching emphasis. Clearly, this lack of emphasis must change.

**Atmosphere, Assignment, and Response: The Teacher's Role in the Writing Process**

It is now time to discuss the teacher's role in all this. In light of the previous writing process discussion, what are the classroom characteristics and activities that are most helpful to children in their growth toward literacy? We will explore the issues of atmosphere, assignments, and response in an effort to forge an answer.

*An atmosphere for writing*

Every classroom has both a physical and an intellectual atmosphere. Some basic features of the physical atmosphere are crucial to children's well-being, for example, lighting and ventilation; provided these necessities are met, the intellectual atmosphere, however, is far more important. A healthy intellectual atmosphere is one where writing is received with enthusiasm and respect, where praise is judiciously bestowed, where children are helped to discover their next goal, and where a purposeful audience exists for each student's writing. In a healthy intellectual atmosphere young authors feel they can take risks and make mistakes without fear of censure. Ideally, children come to know that trying new forms and experimenting are an important part of the writing process. Most nonessential physical constraints can be overcome in the classroom. Extraordinary writing centers, dazzling with prepared booklets, notebooks, borrowed typewriters, paints, crayons, and paste, are fine — but hardly necessary. (All too often they are more show than we care to believe.) But intellectual constraints, those which take discovery out of the writing classroom and replace it with formulas for sentence patterns, rules for punctuation, and demands for correct spelling are more difficult for children to overcome. Such concerns have their place, too. But those teachers who are most sensitive to their children's writing development make sure that a preoccupation with correctness does not take the place of the intellectual "romping room" that effective composition demands.

**Suitable assignments for writing**

Just as the atmosphere in a classroom affects children during every stage of the composing process, the assignments we give, and the topics children choose, affect the writing process also.

A person's choice of topic can either set the writing stage or destroy it. Generally, when we are writing about things that matter personally and in areas in which we're knowledgeable, the rehearsing and drafting stages are welcomed as a chance to express how we feel and say what we know. In this situation revision also becomes more meaningful because now we. have the chance to try and get closer to our thoughts, closer to what we really mean. On the other hand, when we're forced to write about issues that inspire no images or ones that strike no emotion — revision becomes a nonissue: we have nothing in mind that we're trying to capture.

**Appropriate responses to children's writing**

An important part of the composing process is receiving some response to one's writing. Writing is, after all, an attempt to trigger some kind of mental experience in a reader. Writers, like target shooters, gain refinement in their strategies as they see where their efforts go. And that is a matter of response. In this chapter we will be concerned with *who* makes the response, *when* it is most useful, and in *what forms* it should be made. Responses to what has been written and the discussions that ensue provide the classroom dynamics for children's writing development. Unfortunately, in many classrooms response is limited to bright stickers and colorfully penned "Great" signs. If we're after writing development, this type of response will have to yield to a more sensitive and knowledgeable commentary from the teacher.

In the remainder of this chapter, we will discuss the composing process in light of the important areas of the writing teacher's responsibility: atmosphere, assignment, and response. We will suggest detailed guidelines for the teacher to consider while school children are rehearsing, drafting, and revising: guidelines that we hope will be sensitive to the child, the teacher, and to the whole dynamic process of growth.

**Rehearsing**

Eight guidelines will be suggested for rehearsing, a time when children are discovering what they have to say.

1. *Be aware that children operate differently, and that there are many avenues available to help them realize what they want to say.* Individual children have different styles of thinking and prefer different arrangements in which to get their ideas going. Some youngsters only realize what they have to say as they begin to draw. Others respond well to paired interviews; where they discuss their proposed paper with a friend, making short notes as they go along. On the other hand, a few children may want to sit alone at their desks thinking and making notes. Some-

times children enjoy classroom brainstorming to make their thoughts flow.

2. *Reserve sufficient time for children to reflect before writing.* During rehearsal children are discovering what they have to say, but discovery is not always instantaneous. They need time to orient themselves to their topic, their purpose, and their audience. Wondering what to say is a question all too familiar to many of us. We must realize that if a child says she needs to sharpen her pencil, or another feels the bathroom urge even though you've just returned from a classroom lavatory visit, it may be that the rehearsal function is operating. Perhaps it would be a good idea to discuss assignments with children the day before you want them to write.

3. *Provide an emotional environment conducive to thinking by eliminating as many constraints as possible.* During rehearsal we don't want children to feel inhibited, so we must encourage them to ignore mechanical constraints. Spelling should never be an issue, nor handwriting, nor ugly scratches and erasures during the note-taking process. To encourage thinking out, rather than writing out, consider using small paper, perhaps index cards for initial sketches or lists.

4. *Provide a writing stimulus that is meaningful and an audience that is real.* That is, create a social atmosphere that requires the written word. Class newspapers, literary magazines, published original books, areas in the room for hanging works in progress as well as finished products, classroom mailboxes and group sharing are but a few suggestions that give social meaning to writing. Every writing attempt should ideally have social meaning: It should serve some purpose in the affairs of the writer and his audience. Of course writing for oneself has social meaning also. Diaries and journals are important writing experiences as well. Motivation is an important part of writing. Whether writing is assigned or unassigned, children have to feel the need to write and also know that their writing matters. They don't want to write dead letters: papers that go nowhere and have no function.[6]

5. *Make oral language a part of every writing cycle as well as a fundamental element in your classroom as a whole.* Large group and small group language experiences provide a fine base upon which the personalized activity of writing can be constructed. Oral language must be part and parcel of the writing classroom's atmosphere because there is a strong relationship between oral language and thought. A child's thinking can affect what she says, and what is said can affect her thinking. For those who teach the young this has great significance. The more ideas we explore orally, the more we provide children with potential concepts to use in their thinking.

An anecdote may bring our point home. Recently a young child, wanting to write about her doll, brought it from her room downstairs to her mother. "I want to write about my doll, but I don't know what to say," Amy said.

Her mother asked, "You've picked that doll over all your other dolls to write about, Amy. Why?"

"Oh," Amy said, smiling, "I pretend every room upstairs is a different house, and my doll and I go visiting."

"Well," her mother said, "why not write about that?"

Amy needed someone to talk to that day. Sharing helped her to think about possible ideas to include in her composition. Relating her experiences helped her find the language patterns she would use in her composition (see Figure 11 – 4).

Sharing literature also plays an important function in children's writing. In the Epilogue to this book you will read how Amy's experience with literature profoundly affected her as a writer.

*6. Rehearsal is easier when children are personally involved with their topic.* Choosing a topic is sometimes directed by the teacher and sometimes open to the children. When open to the children, rehearsal is

**FIGURE 11 – 4**
*Amy*
*Grade 2*

It is fun to play
with uthr toys
But I like my
Dull the moste
Beaces I bretend I am
in fantace land.
I breand that evry
bedrum in my house
is a u prtmiet.
Me and my dull
go to uthn pepleix
u prtmiet me and
my doll are very
good frans.

made easier if they are writing about something that's important to them. Donald Graves, who has worked extensively with young authors, suggests children bring something from home to write about, something that's particularly meaningful.[7] Before they begin writing, he recommends they talk about their object with another child in an interview fashion. Remember how fruitful Amy's discussion was with her mother?

When topics are chosen by the teacher, they should be broad enough to allow for child input. For instance, the expository assignment in the last chapter lent itself to individualization quite nicely. If you recall, each child was asked to write within his or her own field of expertise. Some wrote about the city, others chose different topics such as sharks, babies, or hockey.

7. *Limiting one's topic is as important as choosing a topic.* To encourage a meaningful rehearsal period it's important that children decide upon their topic and then gradually limit it. Julie, a second grader, was asked recently to write her autobiography. When she got home from school, she set right to work but soon she was downstairs in tears. She didn't have the slightest idea how to go about this large task. Should she list every place she had lived, describe how she'd physically grown over the years, tell about her family, what —? Her mother suggested that she pick just one area of her life and center her whole composition around that. Julie, an animal lover, decided that throughout her eight years she had had many pets. During rehearsal, she made a list of all the pets she had ever owned. Moving into her draft was easy from there; the tears were gone and she went along quite nicely. Experienced writers know how important it is to limit one's topic, but children must be taught. It not only makes good writing sense, it makes good psychological sense as well.

8. *The forces of collecting and writing should dominate rehearsal, critical responses being limited at first.* During rehearsal children are either taking short notes while thinking alone, or being interviewed, or they are drawing their ideas out on paper. Critical responses should be kept to a minimum here. As we pointed out earlier, Murray suggested that the forces of *collecting* and *writing* should overpower the need to connect or read during this early stage. Rehearsal is a time for getting kernel ideas out in the open. Once there, they can be played with: rearranged and reconsidered for inclusion in the first rough draft. Our only suggestion at this point would be to consider helping children limit huge topics that may be too broad to handle. The example of Julie's autobiography assignment demonstrated that having oversized topics may be upsetting to children. We may help spare them some frustration and help them delve more deeply into one aspect of a topic if we lead them to narrow the focus. Using the autobiography assignment again as an example, children may first list all the things in their lives that they

could possibly explore: their moves, their houses, their family, their pets, hobbies, friends, and so on. Then, using Murray's strategy, they could pick and consider (through a second brainstorming session) the area that most surprises or interests them.

*Drafting*

While drafting, children are attempting to find out what they have to say by bringing together their various thoughts collected during rehearsal. We suggest the following guideline for teachers during this stage.

1. *Consider the first draft of every paper a rough draft.* (It may be the only draft, but that's not important here.) Encourage the children to skip lines so they will have space for revision later. Also, consider using yellow legal pads or scratch paper for first drafts. Tactics like this clue children in to the tentative nature of their first thoughts. Just as during rehearsal, all mechanical and grammatical constraints must be removed. Now is the time for writing out, not a time for worrying about minor problems. Professional writers don't allow themselves the luxury of revision while drafting. Remember Ian's Superman paper (Figure 10 – 8)? Imagine if he had been worried about how to spell "Superman" or "x-ray vision" as he wrote his composition. Ideas come first. Cleaning them up comes later.

2. *During the drafting phase the teacher should be available to provide assistance.* When children begin drafting, many of them are afraid that their ideas aren't good enough. If this problem persists, sometimes the answer can be found in more rehearsal or rehearsal of a different type. Sometimes all a child needs is the teacher nearby for a moment.

3. *While children are drafting, it's often a good idea for the teacher to write something as well.* This provides visible evidence that writing is something that adults value and take seriously. Children will take more interest in writing if they see that it is important to adults, too. In these days of television and telephones, it has become a rare event for the child to see an adult engaged in extended writing. Even the small amount of modeling that the teacher provides by writing in front of the class often exceeds what the children are likely to see outside of the classroom.

4. *Consider having the children write two or more alternative openings for a paper.*[7] This is a good strategy because: (a) it removes the pressure children feel when they first sit down to write a whole paper — that is, it gives them a smaller immediate task; and (b) it reinforces the valuable idea that writing is at every stage a matter of making choices. In regard to our first point, sometimes it's hard to get writing going. The thought of producing a whole composition is often frightening to young children.

In regard to our second point, using multiple leads allows children to see from the beginning that choice is a part of the writing process. We believe it also helps the pressure issue. At first, we have observed some children resist the three-level request, but it's not long before they con-

sider this strategy very helpful. What's more, they seem to take particular
pride in demonstrating to others how easy it is to choose the best one.
They often cavort around the room begging others to try their hand at
making the "best" choice. Figure 11 – 5 is an example of a second grader's

Lead #1

~~Ø~~ Wow   more and   more mahic
I Love   mahic.

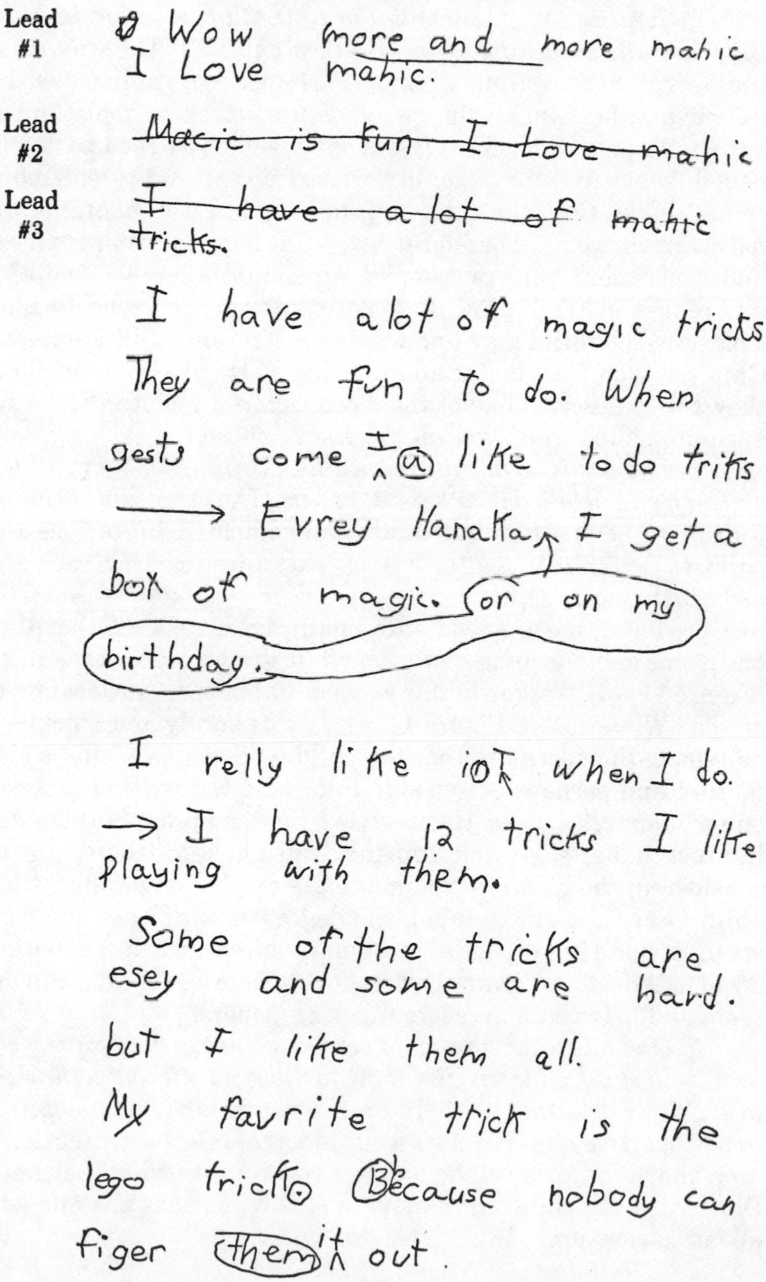

Lead #2

~~Macic is fun I love mahic~~

Lead #3

~~I~~ ~~have a lot of~~ mahic
~~tricks.~~

I have a lot of magic tricts
They are fun to do. When
gests come $\overset{I}{\wedge}$@ like to do triks
⟶ Evrey Hanaka↑ I get a
box of   magic. or on my
birthday.

I relly like io↑ when I do.
→ I have 12 tricks I like
playing with them.
Some of the tricks are
esey and some are hard.
but I like them all.
My favrite trick is the
lego trick⊙ Because nobody can
figer ~~them~~it out.

**FIGURE 11 – 5**
*Amy*
*Grade 2*

rough draft which includes her three leads. Which lead would you have picked? Which one did she?

This practice of writing from alternative leads is best held off until second grade. The sheer quantity of writing practice it requires is too much for many first-grade children.

5. *Realize that the amount of time it takes to produce a draft will vary with the chosen topic and between children.* The way we write fluctuates with each writing attempt. Perhaps today, at home with our topic, we move rather quickly; last week, while attacking something new, even our snail's pace seemed too fast. Today we hardly read back a line as our pencil flies across the page; last week we read and reread more than we should have. Children's drafting habits, like the habits of all writers, naturally fluctuate. Therefore, if we want our youngsters to try new forms and experiment with new topics we should allow for and expect great differences in their drafting time. Children who tend to like to write expository material may find writing a story quite different and difficult. Children who feel comfortable writing narratives may wallow about as they try to describe one of their characters in depth. Be aware of their variance as topic and writing forms are chosen.

6. *The desire to be critical as a first draft is written will vary among children and between their several papers.* The process of rehearsal enables a draft to be written, but drafts are composed in various ways. Some children pour out line after line of text, never looking back and spelling as best they can. Others write a word or two, stop, reread what they've just produced, move ahead once again, then back another time, on and on in this same fashion. Amy, the first grader who wrote about her doll (Figure 11 – 4), worked in this way on that paper. Christopher, the author of "The Wilderness" (Figure 11 – 1), wrote surely and quickly. We might be tempted to speculate that the child who writes easily is simply more mature and perhaps better able to handle the writing process than the one who moves slowly. However, we have no proof of this. Many things interact that affect revision during drafting: knowledge of the topic being considered, the desire to communicate on this day and in this way, the ability to hold ideas in mind, the degree of one's ease and conventional spelling, one's knowledge of grammar, and so on. Consequently, the quality of first drafts will vary tremendously between children in every classroom and between a given youngster's papers.

7. *One role teachers should consider during the drafting stage would be to help children internalize how to move on without telling them where to go.* While drafting, teachers should be available but essentially operate in a supportive role. We don't want to force children's attention on a small area and perhaps cause them to lose control over what they have in mind. Don't rush the child who's moving slowly, nor ask the one who's racing ahead to slow up.

On the other hand, when children ask for your help, you must be available. If they're having a writing block the best way to handle their dilemma is through questioning. Read what they've written and model the questioning behavior you'd like them to internalize. Ask questions that will lead them to think about their organization — Where have they been and where would they like to go? In their opinion, where should they logically go? The internalization of questioning behavior is what teachers should be after. We want the cues for their next line to be located in what they have just said.[6]

8. *Children often like to share parts of their working draft with other children. This should be encouraged because friends can provide helpful feedback.* Frequently, identifying areas where young authors don't see they have a problem, children's peers provide a nonthreatening and helpful audience. Young readers might ask, "Who's the *they* you're talking about, Johnny?" or "Don't these two ideas go together?" Also, as they're writing kids can laugh together over a piece that's going well and provide the motivation necessary to move on and finish.

*Revising*

Of the three stages, revising is the one where the most development toward language awareness takes place and where the potential rests for learning how to connect one's thoughts and choose words effectively. Revision is the stage which enables young children to become young writers in the truest sense of the word. During revision writers, their teachers, and perhaps their peers are interacting with what's been said.

The atmosphere during revision should be characterized by excitement, not nervous tension. Revision should always be a positive experience, never a punitive one. In order to create such an atmosphere here are six suggestions.

1. *Display rough drafts of papers you've written demonstrating to the children that rethinking is a natural part of the writing process.*

2. *Obtain permission from each child to display her drafts and finished products.* Helpful criticism from our peers is necessary to our making progress as writers. We need to know if the images and ideas that our writing evokes in our readers are close to what we had in mind when we wrote. But criticism must not be forced on children. They need to see it as a valuable experience as writers, and a responsible task as readers.

3. *Teach children proofreading shortcuts used by experienced editors.* If children know about these symbols, they're more likely to realize revision is indeed expected. Large dictionaries list both the symbols and their meaning under Proofreader's Marks.

4. *Model questioning techniques for children that you would like them to emulate.* For instance, you might ask a child if an overworked word like "said" conveys exactly what she means. Would "screamed" or "whispered" be better? Or perhaps two short sentences would be clearer

as one. If a sentence seems out of place, let the youngster know that the flow of her ideas is confusing. Ask your students to clarify what they mean out loud, and then encourage them to go back to their papers privately.

5. *Allow sufficient time for revision.*

6. *As the school year progresses, compare revised sentences, paragraphs, or complete compositions with the whole class often.* This type of behavior demonstrates that revisions can produce positive results. Also, as a whole class, share chains of revisions so children don't get the misconception that one's first attempt to clarify is always one's last.

Here are some further suggestions for teachers to support the revision process.

7. *When children are writing about topics that interest them and for purposes about which they are concerned, revision becomes a crucial part of the writing process.* Without revision children lose the opportunity to understand the concept of audience awareness and the chance to experience the wonderful feeling of *finally* saying (after a number of tries) exactly what they mean. When revising, our purpose is to help our paper say what we mean. Sometimes, when we understand our topic well or feel strongly about what we're thinking, it is hard to put ourselves in the place of an uninformed audience. Even experienced writers have this problem; thus, they seek out criticism and rewrite their drafts any number of times. Criticism and revision become both important and real issues: important because children have an idea in mind of what they want to get across; and real because their mental involvement with their subject will tend to mask their ability to write clearly. Consequently, when assignments are relevant and interesting to children, criticism and revision together become a necessary and important part of the writing process.

8. *If assignments have social meaning; that is, if they're attached to some purpose beyond the experience of writing per se, revising for mechanical and grammatical errors becomes a valid issue.* When children are forever writing for their teacher, for an audience that they know understands them, an audience that they realize knows what they mean in spite of all their mechanical, grammatical, and spelling errors, then why should they revise? Revision takes place, but only because the teacher demands it, not because it's necessary. However, when children's audiences expand beyond the teacher and into the classroom library, school newspaper, literary magazine, library bulletin board, office showcase, as well as to unknown people in the community and beyond, then the reason for revision shifts. It is no longer done for a relatively unimportant teacher's grade, but for the purpose of communicating more clearly. Children will learn, through experience, that readers appreciate and better understand writers who make their compositions readable.

9. *Every paper need not be revised.* Experienced writers don't attempt to rewrite every rough draft. For the professional writer, revision may or may not occur; it can depend on a variety of factors: the degree of personal involvement with what's been said, how sure the writer is of a paper's meaning, or perhaps the relative comfort she feels with a paper's point of view. That is, revision for the professional is usually a matter of choice.

To some extent, revision should also be a matter of choice for children. If revision represents an attempt to get closer to what one means, some papers, depending on their origin and personal involvement, will naturally "mean" more than others.

The elements of composition typically stressed by the teacher while the children revise will influence what they focus on in revising their writing, even when the teacher is not present. As educators, we want children to focus on their ideas first. Initially we don't want an over-emphasis on technical elements such as grammar, capitalization, and punctuation because such concentration may overshadow the most important aspect of writing: the quality of ideas and expression. Professional writers equate revision with the heart of the writing act, a process whereby the writer discovers what she is trying to say. If children are taught that revision means getting the technical features straight; that is, if revision in our classrooms is equated with recopying, what will children have learned about the writing process and how will they develop in their ability to move from inner thought to print?

10. *A major responsibility in teaching writing is helping students learn to evaluate their own work.* A few pointers may help you and your children considerably. First, ask students to wait a day or two before reacting to their compositions. When very young people are writing from their knowledge-base or personal experience, strong emotional involvement leaves little room for revision. Ask a young child to reconsider a rough draft he's just spent a half-hour penning, and you're in for trouble — perhaps self-defeating trouble. All authors, not just youngsters, need time. It's difficult to sense problems moments after completing a draft.

Second, teachers should feel responsible for modeling self-evaluation strategies. Though children may be able to sense problems with their papers, even to the point of pinning an area down, it's quite possible that they don't understand what's wrong. Effective questioning by the teacher helps children become aware of the elements of good writing. If sentences aren't ordered logically, it's the teacher's responsibility to help the child see the need for logical development. If a sentence isn't clear, teachers must help youngsters become aware of it. Slowly your class should be able to develop a composing skill chart to be used individually or with a friend to help the editing process. A composing chart might include such questions as: "Did I say what I wanted to say?" "Does each sentence

lead to the next sentence?" or "Will everyone reading my paper understand what I'm talking about?" Questions like these, first modeled by the
teacher and then written on charts, will be valuable self-evaluation tools.
Charts can also be made for mechanical skills. A few questions that might
be included are: "Does each sentence have a capital and an end punctuation mark?" "Did I capitalize all the words that should be capitalized?"
or "Have I underlined the words I don't know how to spell?"

Third, encourage students to read their own writing aloud before
beginning revision. Many minor problems such as faulty subject verb
agreement or sentence fragments can be spotted simply by listening to
one's own writing. Be aware, however, that young children may not see
the difference between what they've written and what they read back.
Consequently, it's helpful for a teacher or a friend to listen to them reread
their papers whenever possible.

11. *Peer evaluation is another source of feedback, but first and second
graders need to move into evaluating each other's papers gradually.* Peer
evaluation, a process where children work together to improve their
writing, requires a special classroom atmosphere. Students must develop feelings of mutual trust and cooperation. If the teacher is sin-
cere about developing a writing classroom, chances are quite good that
early in the school year peer feedback will be a viable alternative to
teacher feedback.

Just as with individual evaluation, peer evaluation strategies must
be modeled first. The best way to start is by setting up a writing workshop.
Your objective in these workshops should be to teach children how to
focus their attention on a particular issue. If, for example, you would like
your students to begin helping each other with a particular mechanical
skill, choose a paper you've received which has both strengths and weak-
nesses. With the author's permission, make a transparency or a ditto
master and work as a whole class looking for correct and incorrect instances of the skill you've chosen. It's wise, after conducting a classroom
workshop, to have another overhead or ditto handy. Break your children
up into small groups and ask them to work together, looking for correct
and incorrect instances of the same skill. Keep an accurate record of all
your workshops, and when you feel comfortable enough with your class,
let your children begin helping each other. For a detailed account of an
editing workshop, see Cramer.[8]

12. *Interaction, not reaction, is the key to good teacher feedback.*
Responding honestly and intelligently to children's writing is the most
important thing a teacher can do to effect growth in their awareness of
the writing process. Worthwhile response necessarily means *interaction*
with what's been written however, not *reaction* by way of a grade or
sticker.

What does interaction mean? Let's observe Amy and her second-

Whon day a little
girl named Emily
and her sisster Julie
war planting a tree
and it grew so fast
you could barly see it.
But nothing was on it.
But by the time thar
was thar was candy
on it. and evry one
danced for joy.
and that was that.

FIGURE 11 – 6
*Amy*
*Grade 2*

grade teacher involved in this child's newest story, "The Candy Tree."
The time is mid-November. As Amy's teacher receives this paper, (see
Figure 11 – 6) her actions demonstrate she is an "interactor" not a
"reactor."

1. The teacher reads Amy's *whole* paper through before commenting
   at all.
2. Initially, no words are circled for incorrect spelling, no capitals are
   put in their proper places.
3. Sensing that Amy is both anxious for approval and extremely proud
   of this piece, her teacher says, "It sounds like you have a great idea
   here, Amy. Your characters think this tree is bare, but lo-and-
   behold, it grows candy! I like your ending, too [teacher reads] "and
   everyone danced for joy." Now, you've done a lot of writing for today.
   Let's put your story away until tomorrow, then we'll look at it together and make sure it says just what you want it to say."

What has Amy's teacher shown us?

1.  She respects Amy enough to realize her ideas are more important than her incorrect spelling, poor sentence structure, lack of correct punctuation, and so on.
2.  She's kind enough to read Amy's whole story through in order to grasp what Amy is trying to say.
3.  Realizing that young children are emotionally involved with their work and that their writing represents an extension of themselves, she responds positively to "The Candy Tree" by saying, "It sounds like you have a great idea here."
4.  Knowing that it's hard to see problems with a paper just after drafting it, she asks Amy to put her story away for the day, but promises to work with her tomorrow.

Amy's teacher is interacting with, not reacting to, her composition.

The next day, as Amy reread her draft, she was asked to underline any areas that sounded fuzzy or unclear. Amy underlined: (1) "and it grew so fast you could barly see it" and (2) "But by the time thar was thar was candy on it."

What did Amy mean to say here? She explained to her teacher that the first sentence meant, "They were so amazed that it grew so fast, that they didn't even notice there was nothing on it." In the second underlined phrase, Amy explained, "I was trying to say that at first there was only a couple of pieces of candy. But each night some more candy grew on it."

Sensing that this expansion was quite difficult for Amy, her teacher printed these short explanations out for her. Then Amy was asked to return to her seat and work them into her rough draft. She added the sentence "But there was nothing on it."

The quality of the teacher's response demonstrated by this interchange goes far beyond the use of stickers and comments that focus only on a paper's mechanical points. Writing is thinking, and Amy is thinking her way into becoming a writer.

## Conclusion

The process of writing — composing — may well be the same for adults and children. Young children, to be sure, are limited by their still-developing handwriting skills in the amount and rate of writing they can produce. There are psychological differences as well, attention span and self-centeredness being prime ones. Still, the process by which everyone composes involves stages of *rehearsing, drafting,* and *revising.* Everyone alternates between *collecting, connecting, writing,* and *reading.*

Adults who write regularly and often are usually conscious of the process by which they write best, and they are realistic about what they must do in order to write well. They "fool around" with their ideas before they begin to write. They write rough drafts and recognize that these serve mainly to show *themselves* what they think about their topic. They write more drafts and seek responses from others to show them what effects their drafts have on readers. Then they write final drafts and make sure the spelling, grammar, and punctuation are presentable. Adults who write often get to be better and better writers through this process.

In order to teach children to write, it seems wise to encourage them to enjoy the same advantages that adult writers afford themselves when writing. We should allow them to explore their ideas before writing; to get their first ideas on paper without being hampered by concerns for mechanics; and to receive helpful criticism before the work is considered finished.

**References**

1. Donald Murray. "How Writing Finds Its Own Meaning" in T. R. Donovan and B. W. McClelland (eds.), *Teaching Composition: Theory Into Practice.* Champaign, Ill.: NCTE (in press).
2. Peter Elbow. *Writing Without Teachers.* New York: Oxford University Press, 1976.
3. Murray, "How Writing Finds Its Own Meaning," p. 5.
4. Ibid., p. 9.
5. Ibid., p. 10.
6. James Moffett. *Teaching the Universe of Discourse.* Boston: Houghton Mifflin, 1968.
7. Donald Graves. "An Examination of the Writing Processes of Seven Year Old Children," *Research in the Teaching of English* 9 (winter 1975): 227–241.
8. Ronald Cramer. *Children's Writing and Language Growth.* Columbus, Ohio: Merrill, 1978 (see especially Chapter Nine).

# Exercises for part three

1. The same topic may be written about in the *expressive, transactional,* or *poetic* voice. For each of the following topics, write the first two lines of a piece in each of the voices. For each topic, that is, you should write three different beginnings.
   a. a love affair
   b. a highway accident
   c. travel in outer space

2. The "vegetable" assignment in Chapter Eight was only partly successful in encouraging children to write pieces that had the form of stories. See if you can write three assignments according to the suggestions made in the end of that chapter to lead children into writing stories.

3. Write three assignments to lead children into transactional writing. It is helpful to decide in advance whether the writing should give directions, describe, argue a point, or accomplish some other purpose — and work the purpose into the assignment. Consider also the topic and the audience, making sure the former is one that is appropriate to the age group and background of the children you have in mind.

4. You can get a feel for Donald Murray's model of the writing process if you try to follow it yourself. We suggest these steps (adapted from Peter Elbow, *Writing Without Teachers* [New York: Oxford University Press, 1976]):
   a. Pick as your topic a person or place that has rich associations for you.

b.  "Brainstorm" a list of your thoughts about that person or place, jotting down a word or two for each thought on a piece of scratch paper.

c.  When you feel ready, write out your thoughts. Put them down as they occur to you, without stopping or correcting yourself, for ten minutes.

d.  Read what you have written and decide what it has to say. Underline the sentences that seem most true, most colorful, closest to your vision of the person or place.

e.  Write a new draft of the paper, using the sentences that you underlined and adding to them. Write this draft for ten minutes also, again without stopping or correcting yourself.

f.  Now write a final draft, adding on a beginning and an ending, if you do not already have them.

g.  Have a friend read your paper and tell you what it brings to mind.

h.  Repeat this activity three or four times on different occasions.

i.  After two days or more have passed, look at a paper you wrote using this activity. How does it seem to you now? Revise the paper further if you feel it will make it better.

# Epilogue:
## Playing with Literature and Language:
## Amy's Story

> Ma Goodness she's coming a-skippitty skoppetty
> > skippitty skoppetty
> > skippitty skoppetty
>
> Ma Goodness she's coming a-skippitty skoppetty
> All doon the hill.
>
>
> > Pop Corn he's a-coming a-hippitty hoppetty
> > hippitty hoppetty
> > hippitty hoppetty
>
> Pop Corn he's a-coming a-hippitty hoppetty
> All doon the hill.[1]

Children are language lovers and eight-year-old Amy is no exception. When she was five, Edna Preston's magical words, "skippitty-skoppetty" mesmerized her at every sitting. So did Winnie the Pooh's famous hum:

> Tra-la-la, tra-la-la, tra -la -la,
> Rum-tum-tiddle-um-tum.
> Tiddle-iddle, tiddle-iddle, tiddle-iddle,
> Rum-tum-tum-tiddle-um.[2]

And then there was John Ciardi's humorous poem, "Sit Up When You Sit Down," and Charlotte Zolotow's comforting words about William's need for a doll:

> "He needs it," she said
> "to hug
> and to cradle
> and to take to the park

209

> so that
> when he's a father
> like you,
> he'll know how to
> take care of his baby
> and feed him
> and love him
> and bring him
> the things he wants,
> like a doll
> so that he can
> practice being
> a father."[3]

These were some of Amy's favorites.

At first, literature's effect on children is very subtle — just moments in time, shared and treasured by parents and children alike. But soon, it seems, rhymes are imprinted on their lips.

> "Little pig, little pig, let me come in."
> "Not by the hair of my chinny-chin-chin."
> "Then I'll huff and I'll puff and I'll
>      blow your house in."[4]

Chanted over and over by little people, and Amy too, magical words like "Little pig, little pig" stick powerfully in their memories.

> A, B, C, tumble-down D,
> the cat's in the kitchen
> and can't catch me.[5]

. . . yet another rhyme remembered.

Slowly, as children grow older, the effects of literature become more profound. By the age of six Amy began creating her own poems, chants, and stories. Quite often they sounded familiar:

> Peanut butter, peanut butter
> Smooth as silk,
> You really taste good,
> with a glass of milk.

It didn't take much for Amy's parents and teachers to realize that something was becoming internalized within her: a sense of sound, a sense of rhythm, a sense of language, perhaps a sense of form. Fortunately, some of Amy's language play was recorded by her mother using a dictated language-experience format. Just a few days after the peanut butter rhyme, Amy coaxed her mother to record this paragraph:

> Last night it started snowing.
> When I woke up this morning the
> ground was covered with snow and
> ice. I feel happy that it is finally winter.

Is it just coincidence that Amy heard Charlotte Zolotow's story, *Hold My Hand,* a few days earlier?

> . . . The wind stops.          I look at you
> Everything is still            and suddenly the air
> There is only the cold         is full of snow.
> cold cold cold.                the snow flakes cling
> Oh hold my hand.               like bits of ice
>                                to our mittens.[6]

Later, that same month, Amy wanted this popular song recorded:

> I told the witch-doctor I was in love with you,
>     bum, bum, bum, bum.
> I told the witch-doctor I was in love with you,
>     bum, bum, bum, bum.
> And then the witch-doctor, he told me what to do.
> He said, "OO, EE, OO, AH, AH, TING, TANG, WALLA
>     WALLA, BING-BANG
>         OO, EE, OO, AH, AH, TING-TANG, WALLA-WALLA,
> BANG-BAND!"[7]

Amy had etched into her memory another string of cherished sounds: another string of words she wanted to capture for herself.

First grade brought many changes. By January Amy was writing alone — no more dictation, no more middlemen! At first her stories came on little bits of paper. Her mother remembers Amy tiptoeing downstairs in her pink pajamas, clutching her first hand-written "story" (Figure 1). Slowly she crept into the living room, slipped this note onto her mother's desk, and barely audibly, she whispered, "Here's a *real* story."

**FIGURE 1**
*Amy*
*6 yrs. 9 mos.*

As the year progressed, Amy's little descriptions turned into full blown accounts. Try and follow her development (see Figures 2 to 7). What seems to be changing?

Now (Figure 8) Amy is eight and in second grade. Recently her teacher shared many tall tales with her class, mostly Paul Bunyon episodes.

Amy is not an exceptional youngster. The only thing that may be exceptional is her warm relationship with the adults that surround her and her personal desire to make written language a part of her life. Since Amy's relationship with literature has been nurtured, and since love of language has been modeled by her teachers and parents, it's no wonder that Amy has become a writer.

Let children know you treasure language, and they'll treasure it also. Help them understand, as early as possible, that language is theirs

**FIGURE 2**
*Amy*
*6 yrs. 10 mos.*

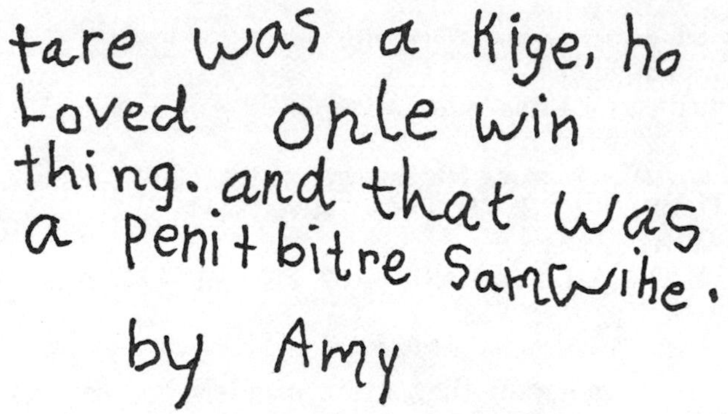

tare was a Kige, ho
Loved onle win
thing. and that was
a peni+bitre samwihe.

by Amy

**FIGURE 3**
*Amy*
*6 yrs. 10 mos.*

a Mouse was in
a house. the Mouse
was So happe.
he had a Little
chare. and a Little
tabil.

by Amy

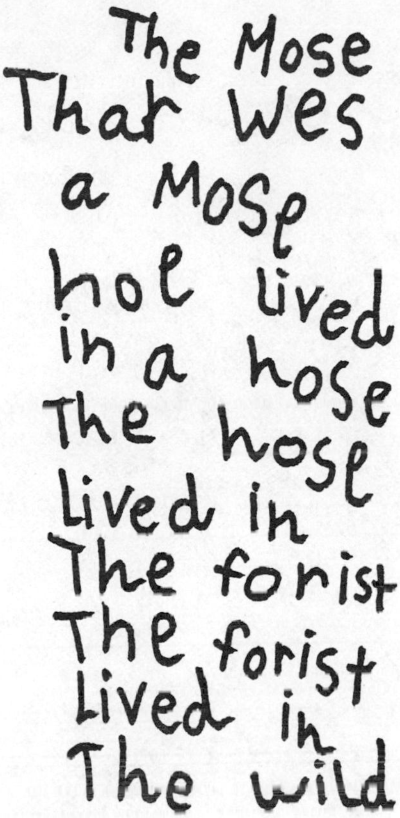

The Mose
That wes
a Mose
hol lived
in a hose
The hose
lived in
The forist
The forist
lived in
The wild

Thar was
a little gril
how onle liked
One Thing and
Thet was a flowr

FIGURE 4
Amy (left)
6 yrs. 11 mos.

FIGURE 5
Amy (right)
7 yrs. 0 mos.

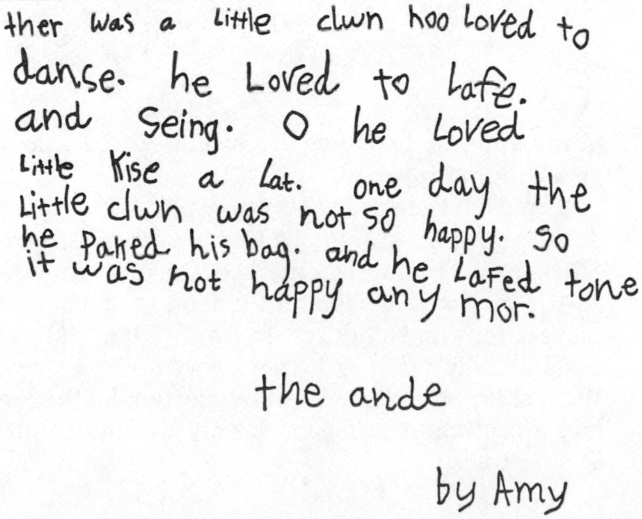

ther was a little clwn hoo loved to
danse. he Loved to Lafe.
and Seing. O he Loved
little Kise a Lat. one day the
Little clwn was not so happy. so
he Paked his bag. and he Lafed tone
it was not happy any mor.

the ande

by Amy

FIGURE 6
Amy
7 yrs. 1 mo.

**FIGURE 7**
*Amy*
*7 yrs. 6 mos.*

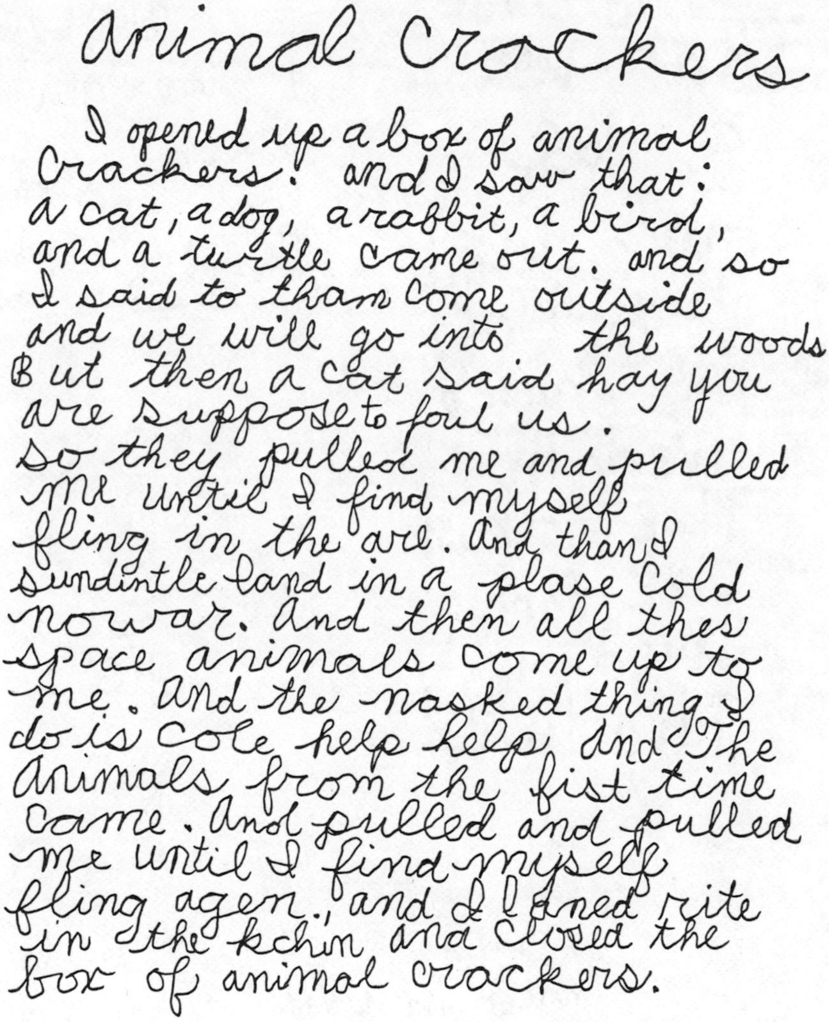

# animal crackers

I opened up a box of animal
crackers. and I saw that:
a cat, a dog, a rabbit, a bird,
and a turtle came out. and so
I said to tham come outside
and we will go into the woods.
But then a cat said hay you
are suppose to foul us.
so they pulled me and pulled
me until I find myself
fling in the are. And than I
sundintle land in a plase cold
nowar. And then all thes
space animals come up to
me. And the nasked thing I
do is cole help help, And The
animals from the fist time
came. And pulled and pulled
me until I find myself
fling agen. and I lned rite
in the kichin and closed the
box of animal crackers.

to manipulate, and they'll respond. There's no magical ingredient that
gets children to write.

We have shared with you aspects of Amy's growth as a writer. Her
development as a language aware youngster can be every child's accomplishment. The ingredients? Lots of literature, an outward and enthusiastic love of language on the part of teachers and parents, a profound
respect for what children say and what they want to record, and the
understanding that growth as a writer is a slow-moving process. Everything children write will not be spectacular, as Figure 9 shows. Be patient
and accepting; give feedback and love; and chuckle when you get "love
and best wishes."

# The Dancer That Could Srach her Leg

**FIGURE 8**
*Amy*
*7 yrs. 11 mos.*

Once a dancer went to her stoodeo, and she leeped ocross the the room. One of the other things she could do was was strach her leg. (Her name was mary) One day she strached her leg to the liberdy bell and mary rang it. The people thout there was going to be war with no warning. Mary was so scard for the people soon found out about this.

And that is how Mary almost mad war.

**FIGURE 9**
*Amy*
*7 yrs. 11 mos.*

Dear Granny and Grampa,
I Love you and miss you very much. It's cold here, the snow is to feet deep.

Love and best wishes,

Amy

**References**

1. Edna Mitchel Preston. *Pop Corn and Ma Goodness*. New York: Viking Press, 1969.
2. A. A. Milne. *Winnie-the-Pooh*. Racine, Wis.: Whitman Publishing Company, 1926.
3. Charlotte Zolotow. *William's Doll*. New York: Harper & Row, 1972.
4. Joseph Jacols, collector. "The Story of the Three Little Pigs," in Bryna Untermeyer and Louis Untermeyer, *Stories and Poems for the Very Young*. New York: Golden Press, 1973.
5. Sonia DeLaunay. *Alphabet*. New York: Crowell, 1970.
6. Charlotte Zolotow. *Hold My Hand*. New York: Harper & Row, 1972.
7. Sheb Wooly. *"The Witch Doctor Song."* BMI.

# Suggested Further Reading

Applebee, Arthur. *A Child's Concept of Story*. Chicago: University of Chicago Press, 1978. As reported in this research children's acquisition of story concepts appears to be a developmental process also.

Bissex, Glenda. *Gnys at Wrk: A Child Learns to Write & Read*. Cambridge: Harvard University Press, 1980. A detailed, longitudinal study of one child's development in writing and reading

Britton, James. *Language and Learning*. Harmondsworth, England: Penguin Books, 1970. This important work treats the development of the compositional voices in children from ages eleven to eighteen.

Chomsky, Carol. "Approaching Reading Through Invented Spelling," in Lauren Resnick and Phyllis Weaver (eds.) *Theory and Practice of Early Reading, vol. 2*. Hillsdale, N. J.: Erlbaum, 1979. Chomsky argues that invented spelling precedes beginning reading and that early writing is a natural introduction to reading.

Chomsky, Carol. "Write Now, Read Later." *Childhood Education* 47 (1971): 296 – 299. Chomsky presents a case for children's learning how to read by creating their own spellings. Examples are given of children using plastic letters and alphabet blocks to invent the words they want, even before they can write.

Clay, Marie. *What Did I Write?* Exeter, N. H.: Heinemann Educational Books, 1975. Clay outlines the concepts and principles that develop as children become perceptually aware of print. She explains how writing helps children to explore the significant details of written language.

Cramer, Ronald. *Children's Writing and Language Growth: An introduction to language arts*. Columbus, Ohio: Charles Merrill Co., 1978. The teaching of writing in the lower elementary grades is treated with especially good sections on teaching editing skills and spelling.

DeVilliers, P. A. and J. G. DeVilliers. *Early Language.* Cambridge: Harvard University Press, 1979. A short, lively introduction to the subject of children's language acquisition by two respected researchers in the field.

Elbow, Peter. *Writing Without Teachers.* New York: Oxford University Press, 1976. A thorough presentation of the techniques of free writing and peer editing, based on the author's experience teaching adults to write, but adaptable to elementary classrooms or activity groups.

Gelb, I. J. *Study of Writing.* Rev. ed. Chicago: University of Chicago Press, 1963. This classic work covers the history and evolution of writing from earliest times to the present.

Graves, Donald H. "Research Update: A New Look at Writing Research." *Language Arts,* 57 (1980): 913 – 919. This survey of research in writing provides an overview for the research that is still needed. Especially useful for teachers and parents is the reference list which includes the reports of the research done at the National Institute of Education project in New Hampshire. Articles by Graves, Calkins, and Sowers are cited.

Henderson, Edmund H. and James W. Beers (eds.). *Developmental and Cognitive Aspects of Learning to Spell.* Newark, Del.: International Reading Association, 1980. A dozen articles concerning children's developing concepts of words and spelling, as well as suggestions for suitable instruction.

Holdaway, Don. *The Foundations of Literacy.* New York: Ashton Scholastic, 1979. Practical suggestions for the teacher based on developmental studies of children's learning and classroom experience.

Moffett, James. *Teaching the Universe of Discourse.* Boston: Houghton Mifflin, 1968. A theoretical statement on the nature and varieties of language experience, related generally to teaching strategies.

Moffett, James and Betty Wagner. *Student Centered Language Arts & Reading, K – 13: A Handbook for Teachers.* 2d ed. Boston: Houghton Mifflin, 1976. This methods text gives examples of how one can implement a production-centered language arts curriculum. Contains many good ideas for teaching writing, as well as other language arts, from kindergarten to college.

Ogg, Oscar. *Twenty-Six Letters.* 3d rev. ed. New York: Crowell, 1971. A colorful and informative history of the alphabet and of printing.

Read, Charles. *Children's Categorization of Speech Sounds in English.* NCTE Research Report #17. Urbana, Ill.: NCTE, 1975. An extensive and detailed work on invented spelling that is the most authoritative account available.

Read, Charles. "Pre-School Children's Knowledge of English Phonology." *Harvard Educational Review* 41 (1971): 1 – 34. An early report on Read's important research into invented spelling.

Sealey, Leonard; Nancy Sealey; and Marcia Millmore. *Children's Writing: An approach for the primary grades.* Newark, Del.: International Reading Association, 1979. Ideas for structuring the writing program in the primary grades are drawn from the Learning Research and Development Center at the University of Pittsburgh.

Zutell, Jerry. "Some Psycholinguistic Perspectives on Children's Spelling." *Language Arts* 55 (1978): 844 – 850. A sound introductory article on invented spelling, with guidelines for teaching.

# Translations

| Figure | | |
|---|---|---|
| 5 – 1 | I got bit by mosquitoes and it hurt. | **Chapter 5** |
| 5 – 2 | I am going to Virginia and I have a headache. | |
| 5 – 3 | I live in Goliad, Texas. | |
| 5 – 4 | A man robbed shoes. The police found him. We saw the man at the store. The police got him. | |
| 5 – 5 | Friday I saw the Blue Angels. They are airplanes. They crossed each other and flew up into the clouds. | |
| 5 – 6 | I got Baby Alive and some dishes and a pogo stick. | |
| 5 – 7 | Baby monster is on the big monster. The supper is waiting for the boy. | |
| 5 – 8 | The parrot is always colorful. He likes to fly. He likes to chirp. He always likes to play. | |
| 5 – 9 | Jody. It is spring. | |
| 5 – 10 | The lady is drinking. | |
| 5 – 11 | Do you have a dog? No, I don't. Do you? No. But I wish I had one. Do you have a cat? Yes, I do have a cat but he ran away. All I have is a horse. I don't have a pet. My dad won't let me have a pet. The end. | |
| 5 – 12 | My fish is red. | |
| 5 – 14 | The girls went to the zoo. They saw a goat and an alligator. | |

*Figure*

| | |
|---|---|
| 5 – 15 | The family are drinking Hi-C. |
| 5 – 17 | This is spring. |
| 5 – 18 | My baby home to sleep. |
| 5 – 19 | Today is valentine for my mother. |

**Chapter 6**

6 – 1   She is picking her flowers. Yellow flowers by her flower house. She is wearing a blue dress. Her flower house is white.

6 – 2   Can I go play with Billy, Mom? I like to play with Billy. We are going now. Are you coming? I like to go to Granny's house. Dad is home Mom. I will be there in a minute.
Can I play with you?
Bill won't let me play, Mom.

6 – 3   At my house I have some daisies. They are flowers. They grow in the spring. I pick them in the spring. The rain makes the flowers grow and in the summer they all dry up and more flowers grow back and they have new leaves and I pick them again.

6 – 4   Can you see snow flakes. They are very pretty. They make me think of Jesus when he was little and Mary, his mother.

6 – 5   I have a duck. I(t) can drink water. She has a baby ducklings. They live in a barn. They are yellow. They can take a bath and the sun is out and we play a lot with them.

6 – 6   Once upon a time we bought a little kitten and you know how they are when they're little. They are little rascals. But this one loved to climb trees and scratch people. He was a mean rascal.

6 – 8   I like the rivers and I like candy. This is what I love, my cousins, I will write their names: Kim, Matt, Frankie. This is what I hate: to be. . .

6 – 9   When the swamp ghost comes out, all of the swamp monsters come out and then all of the witches come out.

6 – 10   We went to the park.
We went on a nature trail. They hid the eggs. I found 7 eggs. I found candy. We ate barbecue. We had fun. We played baseball.

6 – 11   I like school, especially when we have art.

6 – 12   I like to go to town with you, Darla. I like to go to town with you, too. Ask you Mom if you can go to town with me. Okay. Can you? Yes, I can. Where are we going? We are going to the grocery store.

6 – 13   On the holiday. I went to my grandma's house and we went to Mexico

*Figure*

    and I got a jewelry box and I hunted Easter eggs and I got eleven and my brother found three and my sister got eleven.

6 – 14    Once there was two dogs. He chewed on the sofa and anything he can get a hold of.

6 – 15    I love my daddy. My daddy is nice, nice, nice. He hugs me when I go to bed. I have dreams.

6 – 16    I have a friend. Her name is Pat. She has a red and blue dress. She and I play a lot. She has a pet, a pet frog. She plays with it. It is green. It has blue eyes. It had baby tadpoles. They can swim in the water.

6 – 17    I went to the park.
I swing on the swing.
I slide on the slide.
I pushed the merry-go-round and I rode my bike.
Then I sped on it at my house. Then I came to school.

6 – 18    These are names of animals that lived long ago. Tyrannosaurus Rex. Dinosaurs are long ago animals. They lived about 1000 years ago.

6 – 19    Do you like the sunshine? I like it because you can't play when it is cold. That is why I told you that's why I like it when it is hot.

7 – 9    He had a blue cloth. It turned into a bird.    **Chapter 7**

7 – 10    Can we go see the farm? Well, we might go later. O.K. When will we go, Mom? This afternoon. O.K. I will get ready now. No, it's not time yet. Oh, I will go play then. O.K. Can I go to Darla's house?

8 – 1    My dad has a beard and he is a Rabbi. He is nice too and he can't come home that much.    **Chapter 8**

8 – 2    My mom has brown eyes and a fat tummy, because she is having a baby.

8 – 3    My dog is loveable. She is black.

8 – 4    My parrot is always colorful. He likes to fly. He likes to chirp. He always likes to play.

8 – 5    I love the ABC's.
I love the 1,2,3.
But most of all, I love music.

8 – 6    First you get on your bicycle and put your left hand on one bar. Then put your left foot on one pedal. And your other foot on the other pedal. And then you put your butt on the seat and you know how to ride a bike.

*Figure*

8 – 7  I want to drive a car.
Dear Mom and Dad. Would you let me drive your car no–o–o! O.K. I want to. No–o. I'll go drive the car tonight. They are asleep. I'll go get the car.

8 – 8  I saw a bird in the sky, Tom. You did? Yes, I did. Where is it? It's gone now. Well, let's go home and get some bread and jam.

8 – 9  Saint Patrick's day is coming in two weeks. My teacher hasn't got a chance to put up the pictures for it. I like it because we get to eat goose and turkey, but the best part is you get to get fat. Boy, is this boring. St. Patrick's day is in two months, if you think that's not boring, tell me what is. No getting to eat turkey. No Pilgrims, no Indians, no anything. Like I say, if you don't think that's not boring, what is?

8 – 10  I wish I had high-heeled shoes, but my mother thinks I'm too young, but who cares? Because I like to wear them and they make people pretty and if you are small, they make you tall and I like the flip-flop ones. They just look pretty to me.

8 – 11  *The Planet Story*
The farthest planet away from the sun is Pluto. The nearest to the sun is Venus. And that's all on the 6 o'clock scene.

8 – 12  How to float on your back.
I lay on my tummy and stand still for a while and move very slow. And the water keeps me up.

8 – 13  You pretend that you are laying on a bed and you just lay back.

8 – 14  *My Dog*
He is big and he has brown eyes.

8 – 15  Dear Mother,
Why can't I play in the rain? When it rains there is nothing to do. When it rains I want to put my shorts and my short-sleeved shirt on and go outside and play in the rain. One time I played in the rain because Daddy said I could.

8 – 16  Dear Mom,
Why can't I jump on my bed? It's so, so fun, it doesn't make too much noise downstairs. Oh, please, let me jump on my bed. It's like a trampoline. I could learn how to do flips and other things. Please, please, please!

**Chapter 9**  9 – 1  *One Dog.*
Once there was a dog named Zip. He went to the zoo. And he looked at the fish, licking his lips then he saw a cat named Nip.
"What's your name?"

*Figure*

"My name is Nip. I came to look for you. And fish."
"Oh! They're over there."
"Oh, thank you. Oh, I love you."
"And I love you."
"We will be married by the pig."
And they kissed.
"Why are you, I mean, why did you want me?"
"Oh, I just wanted to sing for you."
"And I wanted to sing for you, too."

9 – 2    I like a cucumber, because I am a cucumber. Do you know why I am a cucumber and we do not. Know why you are a cucumber.

9 – 3    A carrot grows and grows out of the ground, then it comes out of the seed. Then I am taken to the store.

9 – 4    I am a tomato. I like tomatoes. They are my favorite kind of vegetable. I dream about my favorite vegetable.

9 – 7    The story about a carrot. Carrots are good for people, don't you think? I eat carrots for snacks. They are good. I went swimming. When I got out, I ate some carrots. They were good carrots I eat carrots every day.

9 – 9    Me carrot. It started off me being a little bitty seed. Then a girl named Julie bought me. She buried me and I grew and grew and grew, then I was a carrot. Then she picked me. But now tonight, they're going to eat me and I am so, so sad. So goodby, farewell.

0 – 10   I had a pickle. It ran and one day four roaches came and saw it. They started to run. The pickle saw them coming at him. He ran too. They were catching up with him. Then he jumped up and tricked them. He was safe. The end.

9 – 11   My goodness! Someone opened my package and I fell out. Splash! Where am I? I must be in a sewer. The next day the little seed couldn't move. Something had attached it to the water. "I look orange-like," he said. "I am a carrot!" he shouted. One week later someone found the carrot. So he got a stick and cut the roots, washed it, and ate it, gulp!

9 – 12   *The Adventure of the Cabbage Head*
Once upon a time there was a cabbage head. He wanted a house of his own. So he set off the next morning and he's far off in the woods. He ran into a garden. A carrot was in the garden. I asked the carrot where I was. He would not talk, so I went on. I met a lettuce and an ear of corn.

9 – 13   *I Am a Carrot*
Hello, my name is carrot and I'm going to tell you a story. Once there was a boy and he planted me. And let me grow and until I got big. And got me out and he ate me up.

9 – 14    *Peas, Like Me*

First peas start out like little tiny seeds and we get put in all kinds of packages and sent to all kinds of stores. I went to Walkers' with my friends. A week after I was sleeping and somebody picked up the bag. I knew someone was going to buy us and I spread the words. When she splash some of us. I was the first one to be planted. They fed us and gave us some water. They picked me. That night they ate me and my family.

9 – 15    *The Adventure of a Carrot*

One day I was at the store and some of the people at the store needed some carrots. And then somebody stopped at the carrots and they picked me up and then we went home. And that person that had gotten me, they chopped me up and put me in a pot of hot, hot water and they put me in a plate and gave it to their children and the children ate me.

9 – 16    *I Am a Carrot*

I am a carrot. I live in the icebox and when I get eaten I call for help and I yell.

9 – 17    The carrots went to the flower and the farmer saw him. He ran to the front and he got back.

9 – 18    I eat carrots. They are good for your eyes. If I was a carrot, I would fly like super carrot.

**Chapter 10**    10 – 1    Dear Tooth Fairy,

I had a tooth come out and I lost it. So they say you are magic, so you can get it, please. This one has silver in it.

                                    Thank you
                                      Lot of teeth

10 – 2    Pins. I have lots of pins here they are! Health Team All-stars Kingswood camp, A. A. Novice, Colorado Hill, Brownies, for E.R.A., Caring for the future of your families, Willoway, You got to have art, Snoopy, Volunteers Make a Difference, and ribbons! Zionism, Doggie, one with stones, Old Fashion Girl. I like my pins.

10 – 3    Art is fun. You can learn a lot of things from it. And most of all you have to have a lot of practice. And I like to make things in Art and one day in art we made pâpier maché. In school the art teacher is Mrs. Gill. She is very nice. I like it because I am very creative and. That is why I like to do Art. And I'm a very, very, very good Artist. And I love making things with paper. And I like making things from pâpier maché, but, most of all I like making faces of people, cartoons, comics.

10 – 4    *Building Models*

It's like a jigsaw puzzle at first and now it is so simple I could finish it in half an hour. Mattering what kind it is, I could finish a snap-together model in 10 minutes and I could finish a hard glue-together in a half an hour and let it dry and put it on my shelf and show it to my friends. I have in models 1 glue-together and 7 snap-togethers and after I get time I paint them. I have 12 cars, 1 helicopter, and 5 airplanes and the ones that are tightly together I play with and have fun with my brother and I always win. I never lose.

10 – 5     *Hockey*
I know how to play forward and defense and goalie. I know how to shoot the puck. I know how to play right wing and left wing. I know how to play left defense and right defense. Hockey is very, very, very fun. I usually play defense.

10 – 7     *Space*
The sun was made by gases and dust forming a big cloud. One day the cloud started to burn and the dust and gases got tighter and turned into a ball of fire. This is what the sun is today. In about 5,000,000,000 years it will run out of gas to burn. Then it will burn up Earth and Mars and then it will get white and very, small. A teaspoon of it would weigh about a ton. Then it would turn into a hole. The sun is a medium size star.

10 – 8     *Superman*
Superman can see through anything, because he has an X-ray vision and he is the strongest in the world and he can fly and he is faster than a speeding bullet and he is able to leap tall buildings.

10 – 9     *Baby*
They make in their pants and cry all the time. They sleep in a crib and they're up all night and sleep in the day. They cry if they don't have food. When they want it they scream in my ears, but there is something funny. Because when my mom picks him up he stops and sometimes when my mom puts him down he screams. He only knows two words. He stays up until midnight. But sometimes he's just fine.

10 – 11     First thing you do is pedal. Then you balance yourself so you won't fall off your bike then you steer, so you won't run into something. And that's all you have to know.

10 – 12     *Describe about a bike*
You got to keep your balance and pedal and keep the wheel straight and turn going around a turn.

10 – 16     Dear Debbie,
One day Debbie, Pow! Right in the kisser. O.K. Why is it always we have to play baby. We never ride bikes.

11 – 4     It is fun to play with other toys. But I like my doll the most, because I pretend I am in Fantasy Land. I pretend that every bedroom in my house is an apartment. Me and my doll go to other people's apartment. Me and my doll are very good friends.     **Chapter 11**

*Figure*

---

**Epilogue**

1    I am a star. I am Rosie.

2    There was a king who loved only one thing. And that was a peanut butter sandwich.

by Amy

3    A mouse was in a house. The mouse was so happy. He had a little chair. And a little table.

by Amy

4    *The Mouse*
There was a mouse who lived in a house. The house lived in the forest. The forest lived in the wild.

5    There was a little girl who only liked one thing and that was a flower.

6    There was a little clown who loved to dance. He loved to laugh. Oh, he loved little kids a lot. One day the little clown was not so happy. So he packed his bag and he left town. It was not happy anymore.

# Index

Affrication of consonant clusters 77
Alphabet, origin of 14
Alphabetic principle 14
Alphabetic writing 15
Argumentative writing
 assignment for 181
 audience's effect on 185
 approaches to 180, 184–185
 defined 188
 demands on writer of 180–181
 and transactional voice 141
Assignments for writing
 interpretation of 169–170, 180
 elements of 148, 150, 170
 and setting topics 192
Atmosphere for writing 191, 193
Audience
 in argumentative writing 180, 183
 in expository writing 179–180
 influence on composing 177–178, 180
 in teaching writing 193
 in writing assignments 148, 170

Britton, James 131, 134, 135
Brown, Roger 5

Caxton, William 86
Children's literature 209–215
Chinese writing 11
Choral reading 113
Ciardi, John 209
Classifying in perception 20–21

Clay, Marie 27, 29, 30, 35, 38, 41, 47, 48,
 49, 114
Composition
 defined 130
 elements of 131
 forces at work in 187, 188–190
 forms of 144
 literature and 209–215
 process of 180–191
 stages of 187
 teaching of 191–204
Conceptual learning 111–112
Consonant digraphs 64–65
 invented spelling of 67–68
Consonants
 digraph 64, 67–68
 initial 61–63
 nasal 69–70
 production of 65–67
 representational 63–64
Copying, letter formation and 47–49
Correct spelling, stage of 108
Cramer, Ronald 202

Descriptive writing 140–141
Development of spelling ability (see Stages
 of spelling development)
Dialogue
 in poetic writing 152
 in transactional writing 183, 184
Dictated experience stories 114
Digraphs (see Consonant digraphs)
Directed Listening-Thinking Activity 165

Directionality
  as feature of writing 43
  of letters 37, 38, 39
Discovery in learning to write 1–2
Distinctive features
  in perception 21
  in writing 21–25
Drafting
  as composing stage 187
  teaching of 196–199
Drawing 161–163, 165–166

Early phonemic spelling 103, 105
  teaching for stage of 113–116
Editing workshops 202
Egyptian scribes 12
English spelling, history of 84–87
English writing system 14–15
Errors in spelling 9
Expository writing 168–180
  assignments for 170, 180
  children's attempts at 171–180
  and transactional voice 138–139
Expressive voice 131–134
  and argumentative writing 183
  and expository writing 169, 175–176
  and stories 152, 153, 157

Features of writing 22–25
Ferreiro, Emilia 32, 44–46
Flexibility principle 34–36, 43, 47
Formulas in language learning 6
Free writing 187
French language 86, 108
Functions of composition (see Purposes for
  writing)
Functions of language 7–9

Generalizations in spelling 108
Generating, letter formation and 47, 48,
  49
Gibson, Eleanor 20, 22, 24, 26
Generative principle 29–30, 41, 43
Gentry, Richard 109
Gothic manuscript 93, 94
Grading and spelling 115–116
Grammatical features
  order of learning 5
  spelling of 85
Graphic principles (see Principles of
  writing)
Graves, Donald 118, 195
Great vowel shift 87
Greek language 14, 108

Halliday, Michael 7–8
Hieroglyphs 12

Ideographic writing 11, 15
Imitation in language learning 3–5
Initial consonants 61–63
Innateness hypothesis 2, 6
Invented spelling 57–123 (see also
  Spelling)
Inventories
  in exposition 175, 176
  in stories 153
Inventory principle 49

Japanese writing 13
Johnson, Dr. Samuel 86

Language-experience approach 114, 117,
  119
Language learning 3–10
  biological limits on 9
  compared to writing 9–10
  direct teaching and 5, 10
  imitation and 3, 4, 5
Lap method 113
Latin language 85, 86, 108
Lavine, Linda 22, 23, 26
Laxness as vowel feature 74
Leads, multiple 196
Letter formation
  copying and 47, 48, 49
  generating and 47, 48, 49
  tracing and 47
Letter-name spelling 60–82, 103, 106
  instruction for stage of 116–118
Letter-name strategy 61
Letter-to-sound relationships 57–59, 108
Linearity feature 24, 25
Linear mock writing 29
Linear principles 36–37
Literature and composition 209–215
Logos and sign concept 33
Long vowels, spelling of 70–71

Manner of articulation 65–67
Marking of vowels 71–87
Marking systems in spelling 85, 88–93
Martin, Bill, Jr. 114
Materials for writing 52–53
Mechanics of writing 200
Memory, role of in spelling 120
Middle English 86, 87
Modeling and early writing 50–51

Moffett, James 113
Monologue 152
Morpheme conservation rules 98–101
Morphemes 98
Multiplicity feature 25, 41
Murray, Donald 186

Names in language learning 6–7
Names in learning to write 46–47, 49, 114
Nasal consonants 69–70
Nonpictoriality feature 23–25, 41

Old English 85, 87, 108
Oral language in writing rehearsal
    193–194

Page arrangement principles 36–40
Parents' role
    in children's literacy 209–215
    in early graphics 50, 51, 52–54
    in spelling 112, 113, 115, 116
Perceptual learning theory 19–21
    applied to written language 21–25
Phonemes 57, 61
Phonemic segmentation 79–80
    in early phonemic spelling 114
    in letter-name spelling 116–117
    in teaching for 115
Phonetic principle 12
Phonological rules 95–98
Pictures 31
Place of articulation 65, 66, 67
Plots 158, 159
Poetic voice 133, 148
    defined 134
    examples of 142–144
Prephonemic spelling 103, 104, 105
    instruction for stage of 112–113
Preston, Edna 209
Principles of writing 27–42
    directionality 37, 38, 39, 43
    flexibility 34, 35, 36, 43, 47
    generativity 29–30, 41, 43
    page arrangement 36–40
    recurrence 28–29, 41, 43
    sign concept 31–32, 41, 43–46
Pronunciation changes and spelling 85,
    95–98
Purposes for writing
    in assignments 148, 167, 170
    in exposition 148, 152, 175, 178

Questioning techniques in composing
    199–200

Reading and transitional spelling 108
Rebus writing 12
Recurring principle 28–29, 41, 43
Rehearsing in writing 187, 190
    forces at work in 195
    oral language in 193–194
    teaching of 192–196
    topic in 194–195
Representational consonants 63–64
Response to children's writing 192
    by peers 202
    by teachers 202–204
Revising 187–188, 191, 199–204
Risk taking 115–116
Rules
    in learning to talk 3, 4, 5, 6, 9
    in writing and spelling 9, 68, 87, 88

Scribal traditions 85, 93–95
Scribbles 18, 19
Scribbling (see Principles of writing)
Shaw, George Bernard 59
Short vowels, spelling of 71–73
Sign concept 31–32, 41, 43–46
Sowers, Susan 153
Spaces between words 40–41
Speech sounds 65–67
Spelling 57–123
    conceptual learning in 111–112
    of consonant clusters 77
    of consonants 61–70
    English, history of 85–87
    errors in 9
    grading and 115–116
    morpheme conservation and 98–101
    parents' role in 112, 113, 115, 116
    pronunciation changes and 85, 95–98
    role of memory in 120
    scribal traditions and 85, 95–98
    of syllabic sonorants 76–77
    of vowels 70–73
    (see also Stages of spelling development)
Spelling dictionary 118
Stages of spelling development
    assessment and 109–111
    correct stage 108
    early phonemic stage 103, 105, 113–116
    letter-name stage 60–82, 103, 106,
        116–118
    prephonemic stage 103, 104, 105,
        112–113
    transitional stage 78, 84, 103, 107, 108,
        118–120
Stauffer, Russell 165
Stimulus for writing 193
Stories
    assignments for 148, 163, 165

grammar of (*see* structure of)
psychological aspects of 160–163, 166
sequence in 146
structure of 143, 146, 157–160, 165
Syllabic sonorants 76–77
Syllabic writing 13, 15

Teaching
  of composition 191–204
  of early phonemic spellers 113–116
  of graphic principles 50–54
  of language 5, 10
  of letter-name spellers 116–118
  of prephonemic spellers 112–113
  and spelling development 109, 111
  of transitional spellers 118–120
Tenseness as vowel feature 74
Topic
  in argumentative writing 180, 183
  in assignments generally 148, 170
  in expository writing 171, 178
  limiting of 176, 195
  in story writing 148, 150
  and writing rehearsal 194–195
Tracing and letter formation 47
Transactional voice 131
  as argumentation 141
  defined 134
  as description 140–141
  as exposition 138–139
  patterns of organization in 168
  types of 138–141
Transitional voice 137, 138
  between expressive and poetic 153
  between expressive and transactional
    169
Transitional spelling 78, 84, 103, 107, 108
  instruction for stage of 118–120
Twins, language of 6

Variety feature 24, 25, 41
Voicing in speech production 66, 67
Vowels
  historical changes in 87
  laxness as feature of 74
  marking length of 71, 87
  pairing of 75
  production of 73–75
  spelling of 70–73
  tenseness as feature of 74

Word, concept of 80–81, 106
  in early phonemic spelling 114
  in letter-name spelling 116
  in prephonemic spelling 104
  teaching for 113–114
Word banks 117
Word sorting 119
Writer's block 199
Writing
  alphabetic 15
  Chinese 11
  defined 19
  hieroglyphic 12
  ideographic 11, 15
  Japanese 13
  materials for 52–53
  stimulus for 193
  syllabic 13, 15
  systems of 10–15
  (*see also* Argumentative writing;
    Composition; Expository writing;
    Features of writing; Principles of
    writing; Purposes for writing; Stories)

Zolotow, Charlotte 209